AF326697

How to Attract Women 5-in-1

The Complete Guide to Grab Her Attention, Spark Chemistry, Read Her Signals, Make Her Want You, and Start a Real Relationship

TABLE OF CONTENTS

OVERALL INTRODUCTION: THE SCIENCE AND ART OF MODERN ATTRACTION

You stand at the edge of a room. You see her. She laughs at something her friend says, and for a split second, she looks your way. Your heart rate spikes. Your palms sweat. You want to walk over there. You want to say something that makes her stop, look at you, and smile. You want to connect. But you hesitate. The moment passes. She turns away. The opportunity vanishes.

This scenario plays out thousands of times every weekend in cities all over the world. It happens in coffee shops, libraries, and office break rooms. Men see women they want to meet, but they stay rooted to the spot. Or, worse, they approach and say the wrong thing, forcing a polite but firm rejection.

You bought this book because you want to change that dynamic. You are tired of guessing. You are done with "waiting for the right moment" that never comes. You want a system. You want to know what works, why it works, and how to execute it without feeling fake or manipulative.

This collection of five books is that system. It is not a list of magic pickup lines. It is not a guide to tricking women into liking you. It is a comprehensive manual on how to align your natural behavior with the biological and psychological triggers that govern human attraction.

We often think of love and attraction as mysterious forces. We call it "chemistry" or "fate." But science tells a different story. Attraction is not magic. It is a biological process. It is a series of signals, assessments, and chemical reactions that have evolved over millions of years to ensure the survival of our species. When you understand the machinery behind the emotion, you stop relying on luck. You start creating your own opportunities.

The Conflict Between Biology and Modern Society

We live in a strange time. We possess the same brains and bodies as our ancestors who hunted on the savannah, yet we live in a world of dating apps, social media, and shifting gender roles. This creates friction. Your instincts tell you one thing, but society tells you another.

Evolutionary psychologists have studied human mating strategies for decades. They found that certain traits are universally attractive because they signaled survival value to our ancestors. Traits like physical health, social dominance, resource acquisition, and emotional stability were not just "nice to have." They were essential. A woman who chose a mate without these traits risked her own survival and the survival of her offspring.

David Buss, a professor of psychology at the University of Texas at Austin, has conducted extensive research on human mating strategies. His work shows that while cultural norms change, the fundamental desires remain remarkably consistent across the globe. Women prioritize status, resources, and commitment cues. Men prioritize cues of youth and fertility. This is not sexism; it is biology. It is the hardware we are all running.

However, the modern world complicates this. We no longer fight saber-toothed tigers. "Status" does not mean being the strongest hunter; it might mean leading a team at work or having a large social circle. "Resources" doesn't just mean meat; it means financial stability and ambition.

The problem is that many men have lost touch with how to signal these traits effectively. They confuse arrogance with confidence. They confuse money with value. They try to buy affection instead of earning it through character. Or, they swing too far the other way. They become passive, overly agreeable, and terrified of offending anyone. They suppress their masculinity to appear "nice," only to find that "nice" does not spark desire.

This book bridges that gap. It takes the raw data of evolutionary psychology and applies it to the modern social landscape. You will learn how to trigger those ancient attraction switches while remaining a modern, respectful, and sophisticated man.

Why Most Advice Fails

You have likely read other books or watched videos on this subject. You might have seen "pickup artists" who treat women like puzzles to solve. They teach you to use canned lines and psychological tricks. This might work for a night, but it rarely leads to a fulfilling connection. It builds a house on sand. Eventually, the real you comes out, and if the foundation is fake, the relationship collapses.

On the other side, you have the "just be yourself" advice. This is well-meaning but useless. If "being yourself" means sitting on your couch, not grooming, and being afraid to speak to strangers, then "being yourself" is the problem. You need to be your *best* self. You need to be the version of you that is capable of attracting the partner you want.

This collection focuses on **Value**. High-value men attract high-value women. Value is not just about your bank account or your height. It is about your behavior. It is about how you carry yourself, how you speak, and how you handle conflict.

When you possess high value, you do not need to manipulate. You do not need to beg. You simply present yourself, and women respond. They respond because they are biologically programmed to seek out men who display competence, confidence, and reliability.

We have structured this collection into five distinct books. Each represents a phase in the lifecycle of a relationship, from the first glance to the long-term commitment. You cannot skip steps. You cannot start a relationship (Book 5) if you have not sparked chemistry (Book 2). You cannot make her want you (Book 4) if you cannot read her signals (Book 3).

Book 1: Grab Her Attention This is where it starts. Before you speak a word, you communicate. Studies suggest that a vast majority of communication is nonverbal. We judge people within seconds of seeing them. Book 1 focuses on these first few seconds. We look at the work of researchers like Albert Mehrabian, who highlighted the dominance of nonverbal cues. We discuss posture, style, and grooming. But we go deeper. We talk about the "energy" you project. Are you apologetic for taking up space? Or do you move with purpose? You will learn to fix your external presentation so that when you do approach, you are already halfway to success.

Book 2: Spark Chemistry Once you have her attention, you must keep it. This is where many men fail. They run out of things to say. They ask boring interview questions: "What do you do?" "Where are you from?" Book 2 teaches you how to move from logic to emotion. Attraction is not a logical decision. She does not look at your resume and decide to like you. She feels it in her gut. We use principles from social dynamics to teach you how to banter, how to use humor, and how to create tension. We discuss the concept of "push and pull," a technique that creates a safe but exciting emotional rollercoaster. You will learn to listen—really listen—so that she feels understood, not just heard.

Book 3: Read Her Signals Dating is a feedback loop. You act, she reacts. If you cannot read her reaction, you are driving blind. Book 3 is your manual for decoding female behavior. Women often communicate indirectly. This is not to be difficult; it is often a safety mechanism and a social filter. You need to learn the difference between a polite smile and a flirtatious one. We look at the research on micro-expressions and body language. You will learn to spot the "green lights" that tell you to move forward and the "red lights" that tell you to back off. This skill alone will save you from embarrassment and wasted time.

Book 4: Make Her Want You Attraction is great, but desire is deeper. How do you go from being a "fun guy" to being the man she can't stop thinking about? Book 4 focuses on emotional investment. We discuss the principle of scarcity. Humans value what is rare. If you are always available, always eager, and always seeking approval, your value drops. We teach you how to set boundaries. We teach you how to demonstrate passion for your own life. When she sees that you have a mission outside of her, she becomes more intrigued. You become a prize to be won, not a fan to be managed.

Book 5: Start a Real Relationship The final stage is the transition from dating to partnership. This is where the game stops and the real work begins. Many men get the girl but lose her because they stop trying. Or they fail to define the relationship and it drifts into ambiguity. Book 5 provides the roadmap for this transition. We discuss how to align values, how to handle the inevitable conflicts, and how to keep the spark alive when the novelty wears off. We look at the psychology of long-term attachment and how to build a bond that strengthens over time.

The Role of Confidence and Competence

Throughout all five books, one theme repeats: Confidence. But we must define this term clearly. Confidence is not loud. It is not aggressive. True confidence is the quiet knowledge that you can handle what happens next.

If you approach a woman and she rejects you, a confident man accepts it and moves on. He does not crumble. His self-worth is not tied to her validation. This type of non-neediness is incredibly attractive. It signals emotional stability.

Competence is the other side of the coin. You need to be good at being a man. This means taking responsibility. It means making decisions. In the dating phase, this is as simple as picking the restaurant. "I know a great Italian place, let's go there at 7," is attractive. "I don't know, what do you want to do?" is not. The first shows leadership; the second places the burden of decision on her.

Women deal with decision fatigue just like you do. When a man steps up and leads—respectfully and competently—it allows her to relax into her feminine energy. It allows her to enjoy the experience rather than managing it. This dynamic is central to sparking chemistry.

The Scientific Backbone

We will rely on data. For instance, we will look at the *Mere Exposure Effect*, studied by Robert Zajonc, which explains how familiarity breeds comfort—but we will also look at how over-exposure kills desire. We will look at the *Ben Franklin Effect*, which suggests that doing favors for someone makes you like them more. We will flip this: getting a woman to invest in you (by doing small things for you) increases her attraction to you.

We will discuss the *pratfall effect*, which shows that small mistakes can actually make competent people more likable. You don't need to be perfect. In fact, perfection is intimidating. Being human, with small flaws owned confidently, is charismatic.

We will also address the biology of hormones. Testosterone and cortisol play huge roles in how you act. If you are stressed (high cortisol) and low energy (low testosterone), you signal low status. We will give you practical tips on how to regulate your state before you even leave the house.

How to Use This Book

Do not just read this book. Study it. Apply it.

Read one chapter, then go out and test the concept. If you read the chapter on eye contact, spend the next day focusing on your eye contact with everyone you meet. The barista, your boss, the bus driver. Get comfortable holding a gaze until it feels natural.

If you read the chapter on voice tonality, record yourself speaking. Do you sound squeaky and unsure? Or do you speak from your chest with downward inflection? Practice until the new behavior becomes a habit.

This is a process of calibration. You will make mistakes. You might try to be "assertive" and come off as rude. That is part of learning. You adjust. You try again. The goal is to internalize these principles so you don't have to think about them.

Think of learning to drive. At first, you have to think about the pedals, the steering, the mirrors, and the road signs all at once. It feels overwhelming. But with practice, it becomes automatic. You drive home without thinking about it.

Social skills are the same. Right now, you might feel awkward trying to "read signals" while also trying to "be funny" and "stand up straight." It feels like too much. But stick with it. Soon, you will walk into a room, spot the signals, adjust your posture, and open a conversation on autopilot. That is when dating becomes fun.

A Note on Ethics

We must address the morality of "attraction strategies." Some people argue that using strategies is manipulative. They say you should just let things happen naturally.

This is a naive view. We all use strategies. Wearing a nice shirt is a strategy. Brushing your teeth is a strategy. Trying to be funny is a strategy. You are already trying to present your best self. This book just helps you do it effectively.

The distinction lies in your intent. If your intent is to lie, deceive, or harm women, put this book down. We do not support predatory behavior. If your intent is to connect, to bring value to a woman's life, and to find a partner to share experiences with, then these tools are ethical. You are simply learning the language of attraction so you can communicate your value clearly.

Women *want* to meet great men. They *want* to feel that spark. They *want* to be swept off their feet. By learning how to provide that experience, you are not taking something from them. You are giving them something they desire. You are ending the awkwardness and confusion that plagues modern dating.

Your Commitment

This transformation requires work. You cannot change your results without changing your actions. You might have to face some uncomfortable truths about yourself. Maybe you have been lazy with your appearance. Maybe you have been boring in conversation. Maybe you have been too nice because you are afraid of conflict.

Facing these truths is painful, but it is necessary. Growth only happens outside your comfort zone.

Commit to the process. Commit to the exercises. Do not look for shortcuts. The man you want to be—the man who attracts the women you want—is waiting for you to build him.

Let us begin.

BOOK ONE
GRAB HER ATTENTION

CHAPTER 1

INTRODUCTION: WHY FIRST IMPRESSIONS ARE BIOLOGICAL, NOT ACCIDENTAL

You have likely heard that "getting your foot in the door" is the hardest part of any endeavor. In the world of social dynamics, this is a literal truth. Before a woman can appreciate your humor, your career achievements, or your kind heart, she must first notice you. She must decide, in a fraction of a second, that you are someone worth her time and energy.

Book 1 is about mastering that opening moment. We call this phase "Grabbing Her Attention," but it is not about being the loudest person in the room. It is not about performing antics or wearing neon colors to be seen. In fact, those behaviors often signal low status and a desperate need for validation—the exact opposite of what we want to achieve.

Real attention is earned through **presence**.

When a high-value man enters a room, he doesn't have to shout to be noticed. There is a weight to his movement. There is a stillness in his gaze. He occupies his space with a quiet authority that suggests he belongs exactly where he is. This is the "signal" we are going to help you broadcast.

The Biological Reality of the Filter

To understand why attention is the first hurdle, we have to look at the cognitive load of the modern woman. In any given social environment—a bar, a coffee shop, or a professional networking event—a woman is processing a staggering amount of data. She is assessing the safety of the room, the social hierarchy of her peers, and the intent of every man who makes eye contact.

Because the human brain cannot focus on everything at once, it utilizes a "gatekeeper" known as the Reticular Activating System (RAS).

This is a bundle of nerves at our brainstem that filters out "noise" and only allows "important" information through to the conscious mind. If you are standing in a crowd and someone whispers your name, you hear it. That is your RAS at work. It decided that your name was more important than the background music or the clinking of glasses.

In the context of attraction, a woman's RAS is tuned to specific biological markers. If you do not display these markers, you are "noise." You are filtered out before she even realizes you are there. You become part of the background, like the chair she is sitting on or the wallpaper behind her.

This is the "Problem of Invisibility." Modern life has trained many men to be small. We spend our days hunched over desks and looking down at smartphones. We are taught to be polite, to stay out of the way, and to avoid making waves. While these are useful traits for a corporate office or a quiet library, they are disastrous for attraction.

If you blend into the wallpaper, you never give attraction a chance to start. You become "the guy over there" instead of "the man I want to meet."

The Evolutionary Logic of the "Alpha" Signal

Evolutionary biology tells us that females in almost every species are the "selectors." They are the ones who filter through potential mates to find the best possible candidate. This is known as Parental Investment Theory, proposed by Robert Trivers in 1972. Because the biological cost of reproduction is higher for females, they must be more selective.

To be selected, you must first be seen. But you must be seen as a "contender," not a "pretender."

In the animal kingdom, this is often done through displays of physical health or social dominance. Think of a peacock's feathers or a silverback gorilla's chest-beating. In humans, the displays are more subtle but no less potent. We signal value through our "vibe"—a combination of our physical health, our ease in the environment, and our perceived status.

When a woman's RAS identifies a man displaying high-value signals, it triggers a small release of dopamine. This is the "spark." It is an involuntary physiological response. She is now curious. She has been "interrupted" from her internal thoughts and is now focused on you.

Why the "First Five Seconds" Rule is Non-Negotiable

We will rely heavily on the concept of **Thin-Slicing**, which we touched on in the overall introduction. Research by psychologists like Dr. Nalini Ambady has shown that we make incredibly accurate judgments about people's status, warmth, and competence based on "thin slices" of their behavior—sometimes lasting less than five seconds.

In these first five seconds, you aren't being judged on your character. You are being judged on three primary factors:

1. **The V-Taper:** This is the ratio of your shoulders to your waist. Biologically, this is a proxy for testosterone levels and physical health. Even if you aren't a bodybuilder, the way your clothes fit can either highlight or hide this ratio.

2. **Symmetry and Grooming:** Symmetry is a universal indicator of genetic health. Grooming—the neatness of your hair, the cleanliness of your skin—signals that you have the resources and the discipline to maintain yourself.

3. **Non-Reactive State:** This is perhaps the most important. How much are you affected by the chaos around you? A man who is darting his eyes around, looking for approval, or constantly checking his phone appears "low-status." He looks like he is looking for permission to exist. A man who moves with a steady, unhurried pace appears to be the master of his environment.

The Myth of "The Loudest Man"

A common mistake men make when trying to "grab attention" is thinking they need to be the life of the party. They think they need to tell the loudest jokes, wear the flashiest clothes, or be the center of every conversation.

This is a misunderstanding of social value.

In social hierarchy, the person who works hardest for the attention of others is usually the one with the least power. This is called "chasing." If you are chasing attention, you are signaling that you do not believe you inherently deserve it.

High-value attention is "magnetic," not "electric." It pulls people toward you; it doesn't shock them into looking at you. Think of the difference between a neon sign and a lighthouse. The neon sign is desperate; the lighthouse is a fixed point of strength.

What This Book Will Solve

Many men want to skip to the "talking" part. They want the perfect opening line. But if your physical and visual signals are sending a "low-value" message, no line in the world will save you. You will be fighting an uphill battle from the first word.

When you master the art of grabbing attention correctly, the "talking" part becomes infinitely easier. You aren't a stranger trying to break in; you are a person of interest who has been invited in by her curiosity.

In this book, we are going to rebuild your "Broadcast Signal."

- **We will fix your style.** We will move away from "boyish" clothes and toward a "masculine uniform" that commands respect.

- **We will fix your posture.** We will address the "tech-neck" and slumped shoulders that signal defeat and replace them with a stance that signals victory.

- **We will fix your movement.** You will learn to move through a room like a man who owns it, using "slow-motion" secrets that trigger a woman's interest.

- **We will utilize Social Proof.** You will learn how to use the people around you—your friends, the staff at a venue, and even other women—to "vet" you before you even speak.

The Psychology of Being "Vetted"

One of the most powerful ways to grab a woman's attention is through **Pre-Selection.** This is a biological phenomenon where a woman finds a man more attractive if she sees that other women already find him attractive.

In a study published in the journal *Evolutionary Psychology*, researchers found that women rated a man as significantly more desirable when he was shown surrounded by women who were smiling at him, compared to when he was alone or with men.

Why? Because it reduces her risk. If other women have already "vetted" you and found you safe and interesting, she can skip the "threat assessment" phase and move straight to "attraction." We will teach you how to build this "aura" of being a man who is already liked and respected.

A Note on Internal State

While Book 1 focuses heavily on external factors—what you wear, how you stand, where you walk—we must acknowledge that these are mirrors of your internal state.

If you feel like a fraud, it will show in your eyes. If you are terrified of rejection, it will show in the tension in your jaw. This book is about more than just "acting" confident. It is about adopting the habits of a confident man until those habits become your reality.

Aristotle once said, "We are what we repeatedly do." By repeating the behaviors of a high-value man—by dressing well, standing tall, and moving with purpose—you eventually become that man. Your brain catches up to your body.

How to Approach This Section

Do not look at these chapters as "tips." Look at them as an overhaul. You might feel uncomfortable changing your style or standing "too straight" at first. That is your old, "invisible" self trying to stay in the comfort zone.

Push through it. The man you want to be—the man who walks into a room and turns heads—is waiting on the other side of that discomfort.

You are about to stop being a spectator in your own social life. You are about to become the protagonist.

CHAPTER 2

FIX YOUR EXTERNAL PRESENTATION AND STYLE

The Silent Language of the Exterior

There is a common modern fallacy that "what's on the inside is all that matters." While this is a beautiful sentiment for a graduation speech or a children's book, it is a dangerous misunderstanding of human biology and social hierarchy. In the cold, hard reality of human interaction, your external presentation is the primary data point people use to categorize you.

Before you speak a single word, your clothes, your grooming, and your physical "packaging" have already told a story. They have broadcasted your social status, your level of self-discipline, your attention to detail, and your awareness of social norms. If your "wrapper" is sloppy, the world—and specifically high-value women—will assume the "gift" inside is sloppy as well.

Style is not about vanity. It is about **communication**. It is about mastering the non-verbal signals that allow you to bypass a woman's initial "threat and low-value filter." When you fix your external presentation, you aren't changing who you are; you are finally allowing who you are to be seen without the interference of a bad wardrobe.

The Science of Enclothed Cognition

To understand why style matters, we must first understand how it affects *you*. In 2012, researchers Hajo Adam and Adam Galinsky from Northwestern University coined the term **"Enclothed Cognition."** Their research demonstrated that clothes possess a symbolic meaning and that wearing specific garments triggers psychological processes in the wearer.

In one of their most famous experiments, participants were asked to wear a white lab coat. One group was told it was a doctor's coat, while the other was told it was a painter's smock. The group that believed they were wearing a doctor's coat performed significantly better on tasks requiring sustained attention and accuracy. The "symbolism" of the coat physically altered their brain's performance.

When you wear a well-tailored suit, a crisp shirt, or high-quality leather boots, you are not just "looking good." You are signaling to your own brain that you are a man of importance. This shift in internal state is palpable. It changes the way you hold your head, the resonance of your voice, and your willingness to take social risks. If you dress like a man who is invisible, you will act like a man who is invisible. If you dress like a leader, your biology will eventually follow suit.

The Biological Imperative: Signaling Health and Status

From an evolutionary perspective, clothing serves as a proxy for the biological markers we no longer display openly. In the ancestral past, a man's value was determined by his physical prowess and his access to resources. Today, we use "luxury markers" and "grooming standards" to signal those same traits.

1. The V-Taper and Physical Dominance

The "V-taper"—broad shoulders tapering down to a narrow waist—is the most potent visual signal of high testosterone and physical fitness in the male body. This is why a well-fitted blazer is the most powerful tool in a man's wardrobe. The padding in the shoulders and the nipped-in waist of a jacket are designed to artificially enhance this V-taper. It is a biological "hack" that signals strength and dominance to a woman's lizard brain, even if you haven't spent the last six months in the gym.

2. Resource Acquisition and Social Intelligence

Women are biologically wired to look for "providers"—men who can navigate social structures to acquire resources. In the modern world, "resources" are signaled by the quality of your materials. Natural fibers like wool, leather, and cotton suggest a man who has the means to choose quality over the "disposable" nature of fast fashion.

Furthermore, your ability to "calibrate" your style to your environment signals high social intelligence. A man who wears a tuxedo to a beach party or a hoodie to a high-end gala is signaling that he is socially "blind." He doesn't understand the unwritten rules of the tribe. High-value women are attracted to men who can lead in any environment, and that starts with understanding how to dress for those environments.

Pillar 1: The Rule of Fit

If you take nothing else from this chapter, remember this: **Fit is everything.** The most expensive Italian suit will look like a costume if it is two sizes too large. Most men are terrified of "tight" clothes, so they buy garments that drown them in fabric. This excess fabric creates a silhouette of weakness. It makes you look shorter, heavier, and less certain of yourself.

- **The Shoulders:** The seam of your shirt or jacket should sit precisely on the edge of your shoulder bone. If it hangs an inch over, the garment is too big. This is the "anchor" of your entire look.

- **The Sleeve Length:** Your jacket sleeve should end just above your wrist bone, allowing about half an inch of shirt cuff to show. This "small detail" signals that the clothes were made for *you*, not just picked off a clearance rack.

- **The Trousers:** You want a "slight break" or "no break" at the bottom of your pants. This means the fabric barely touches the top of your shoe. "Puddling" fabric around your ankles makes you look like a child wearing his father's clothes.

- **The Taper:** Your clothes should follow the natural lines of your body. Your pants should get narrower as they reach the ankle. Your shirts should not "billow" at the waist. If they do, take them to a tailor.

A tailor is the most underrated tool in the masculine arsenal. For $20, a tailor can take a $50 shirt and make it look like it cost $500. It is the ultimate "status hack."

Pillar 2: Grooming and The "Discipline Markers"

Grooming is the baseline of social respect. It signals that you have the discipline to maintain your own "equipment." If a man cannot be bothered to trim his beard or clean his fingernails, why would a woman trust him with the complexities of a relationship or a family?

The Hair and Face

Your face is the first thing she will look at.

- **The Haircut:** Do not go to a "budget" salon. Find a high-end barber who understands face shapes. A good haircut can fix a weak jawline or a high forehead. It is an investment in your facial symmetry.

- **The Beard:** If you have facial hair, it must look intentional. This means clean lines on the cheeks and a defined neckline (usually one finger-breadth above the Adam's apple). An untrimmed beard signals "laziness," while a groomed beard signals "style."

- **The Skin:** You don't need a ten-step Korean skincare routine, but you do need a cleanser and a moisturizer. Clear, hydrated skin is a universal signal of health and vitality.

The Hands and Nails

This is a "hidden" filter. Women notice hands. Dirty, bitten, or jagged nails are an instant "turn-off" because they suggest high anxiety (biting) or poor hygiene (dirt). Keep them short, clean, and smooth. It sounds trivial; it is actually vital.

The Scent (The Olfactory Anchor)

Scent is the only sense with a direct line to the limbic system—the part of the brain that handles memory and emotion. A man who smells good is memorable.

- **The Rule of Subtlety:** Scent should be a "discovery," not an "announcement." She should only smell your cologne when she enters your personal space (within two feet).
- **Quality over Quantity:** One bottle of $150 cologne is better than ten bottles of cheap body spray. Look for "Eau de Parfum" which has a higher oil concentration and lasts longer.

Pillar 3: The "10% Rule" and Calibration

One of the biggest fears men have is "overdressing." They don't want to look like they are "trying too hard." This fear leads to a "race to the bottom" where everyone is wearing the same generic t-shirt and jeans.

To grab her attention, you must stand out, but you must do so within the bounds of social reality. This is the **10% Rule**.

Look at the environment you are going into. If the average man is wearing a t-shirt and cargo shorts, you wear a well-fitted t-shirt, dark denim, and clean boots. You are 10% better. If the average man is wearing a button-down shirt, you wear a button-down with a casual blazer or a high-end watch.

You are signaling that you are the "Alpha" of that specific environment. You are part of the group, but you are clearly the highest-ranking member of it.

The "High-Value Uniform"

If you are overwhelmed by style, stop trying to be "fashionable" and start being "classic." Fashion is fleeting; style is permanent. A high-value man doesn't need a thousand outfits. He needs a "uniform"—a collection of high-quality pieces that work together effortlessly.

The Essentials:

1. **Dark Indigo Denim:** No holes, no "distressing," no baggy fit. These can be dressed up with a blazer or down with a t-shirt.

2. **The White Button-Down:** Crisp, tailored, and clean. It is the most versatile item a man can own.

3. **A Tailored Navy Blazer:** It works for dates, meetings, and dinners. It instantly improves your silhouette.

4. **Brown Leather Boots or Brogues:** Shoes are the most important investment. Women use shoes as a proxy for your financial stability and your attention to detail.

5. **The Classic Watch:** An analog watch signals that you value time. It is the only "jewelry" every man should wear.

Action Steps: The Style Overhaul

1. The "Mirror Audit" Put on your favorite outfit. Stand in front of a full-length mirror.

- Is there excess fabric under your arms?

- Do your pants "puddle" at your shoes?

- Do you look like a man who is "taking up space," or a man hiding in his clothes? Be ruthless. If it doesn't fit, it goes to the tailor or the donation bin.

2. The Grooming Reset Book an appointment with the best barber in your city. Ask for a "style consultation." Spend the extra $40. Buy a high-quality facial moisturizer and a bottle of reputable cologne (e.g., Bleu de Chanel or Terre d'Hermès).

3. The Shoe Upgrade If you are wearing gym sneakers in non-gym settings, stop. Go out and buy one pair of high-quality brown leather boots (like Chelsea boots or Chukkas). Wear them for a week and notice the difference in how people—especially service staff and women—interact with you.

Conclusion

Your external presentation is the "signal" you send out to the world. If that signal is weak, distorted, or sloppy, the world will treat you accordingly. By fixing your style and grooming, you aren't being "fake." You are simply removing the noise so your true value can be seen.

When you look like a man of status, you begin to feel like a man of status. And when you feel like a man of status, you act with a confidence that is naturally magnetic. You have fixed the "wrapper." Now, in the next chapter, we will fix the way that wrapper moves through space.

CHAPTER 3
CORRECT YOUR POSTURE TO SIGNAL STRENGTH

The Silent Broadcast of the Spine

If style is the "wrapper" of the gift, then posture is the **structural integrity** of the gift itself.

Imagine walking into a room and seeing two men. One is dressed in a $5,000 bespoke suit but is hunched over his phone, shoulders rolled forward, neck protruding like a turtle, and eyes darting nervously. The other is wearing a simple, well-fitted white t-shirt and jeans, but he stands with his chest open, his head held high, and a stillness in his limbs that suggests total comfort in his environment.

Who do you notice first? Who do you respect more?

Evolutionarily, the answer is always the second man. Before we developed complex language, we communicated through the geometry of our bodies. High-status individuals in almost every primate species occupy more space. They are "expansive." Low-status individuals make themselves smaller to avoid conflict and signal submission. They are "contractive."

When you slouch, you aren't just "relaxing." You are broadcasting a biological signal of defeat, low testosterone, and high anxiety. You are telling every woman in the room that you are "prey" rather than a "protector." To grab her attention, you must first fix the frame through which she sees you.

The Evolutionary Logic of Expansion

To understand why posture is so deeply tied to attraction, we have to look back at our ancestors. For millions of years, the primary indicator of a male's value to a tribe was his ability to defend and provide. Physical robustness wasn't just about muscle mass; it was about the **presence** of strength.

In the animal kingdom, from lobsters to chimpanzees, the hierarchy is physically manifested. A dominant male chimp stands taller, fluffs his hair to appear larger, and moves with a deliberate, unhurried pace. A submissive male shrinks, rounds his back, and avoids direct eye contact. This isn't a choice; it is a neurological and hormonal manifestation of his place in the world.

When a woman scans a room today, her "lizard brain" is performing a status audit. She is looking for the "Apex" signal. A collapsed posture suggests a man who is burdened by the world—someone who is defeated by stress or lacks the physical vitality to hold himself upright. Conversely, an open, upright posture signals that you are not only healthy but that you are comfortable enough in your environment to expose your "vitals" (your neck, chest, and stomach).

The Hormonal Engine: The "Winner Effect"

Posture is not merely a physical habit; it is a chemical regulator. Your spine is essentially the antenna for your endocrine system.

In the previous chapters, we discussed the "High Testosterone, Low Cortisol" profile of high-value men. Your posture is the primary throttle for these hormones. When you stand in an expansive, upright position— shoulders back, chin level, feet shoulder-width apart—your brain receives a signal through a process called proprioception. It interprets your physical expansion as a sign of dominance.

Research into the **"Winner Effect"** shows that animals (including humans) that occupy dominant postures experience a surge in testosterone. This surge makes them more likely to win the next encounter. Conversely, those who adopt a submissive, "defeated" posture experience a spike in cortisol, which increases anxiety and makes them more likely to lose again.

A study conducted by Dr. John Coates, a former Wall Street trader turned neuroscientist, found that traders with higher morning testosterone levels made more profit, and those profits further boosted their testosterone, creating a "virtuous cycle." This cycle starts with how you carry yourself. If you walk into a social environment with a "defeated" posture, you are chemically priming yourself for a social loss. By consciously correcting your frame, you are forcing your brain to produce the chemicals of a winner.

The Modern Epidemic: "Tech-Neck" and the Shrinking Man

We are currently living through a crisis of masculine presence. Our modern environment is designed to make us "small."

- **The Desk:** We spend 8–10 hours a day hunched over keyboards, causing our pectoral muscles to shorten and our upper back muscles to weaken.
- **The Smartphone:** We spend hours looking down, creating "Tech-Neck"—a forward head posture that adds up to 60 pounds of pressure on the cervical spine.
- **The Chair:** Sitting for long periods deactivates the glutes and tightens the hip flexors, leading to an "Anterior Pelvic Tilt" (where the butt sticks out and the gut hangs forward).

This physical collapse is a disaster for attraction. A forward-leaning head suggests a lack of presence; rolled shoulders suggest a lack of protection; a collapsed core suggests a lack of vitality.

When you see a man with "Tech-Neck," you don't see a leader. You see a worker. You see someone who is subservient to his devices and his environment. To stand out, you must physically rebel against these modern habits.

To correct your posture, you must think of your body as a series of stacked blocks. If one block is out of alignment, the entire structure is compromised.

1. The Foundation: Feet and Hips

Attraction starts at the floor. Most men stand with their feet too close together, which makes them look easily toppled—physically and metaphorically.

- **The Stance:** Keep your feet shoulder-width apart. Point your toes slightly outward. This creates a "base of power."

- **The Weight:** Distribute your weight evenly across both feet. Avoid "shifting" from side to side, which signals restlessness and a desire to leave the situation.

- **The Hips:** Engage your glutes slightly. This pulls your pelvis into a neutral position, flattening your stomach and making you appear taller.

2. The Engine Room: The Core and Chest

This is where masculine "presence" is generated.

- **The Sternum:** Imagine there is a string attached to the center of your chest, pulling it slightly upward and forward. You aren't "puffing" your chest out like a cartoon character; you are simply opening your heart to the room.

- **The Shoulders:** Do not "pull" your shoulders back with tension. Instead, imagine "dropping" your shoulder blades into your back pockets. This opens the collarbones and removes the "hunch" without making you look stiff.

3. The Command Center: The Head and Neck

The position of your head dictates how people perceive your intelligence and authority.

- **The Chin:** Keep your chin parallel to the ground. If it's too high, you look arrogant and "nose-up." If it's too low, you look submissive or depressed.

- **The Crown:** Imagine a string pulling the crown of your head toward the ceiling. This elongates the neck and creates a "regal" silhouette.

Proxemics: The Psychology of Space

In the 1960s, anthropologist Edward T. Hall coined the term **Proxemics** to describe the study of how humans use space. There are four distinct zones of space: Intimate, Personal, Social, and Public.

A man of high value understands how to occupy his own space and respect the boundaries of others. However, the most common mistake "invisible" men make is not occupying *enough* space.

When you sit at a table, do you pull your elbows in tight? Do you cross your legs and hunch over your drink? This is "turtle" behavior. You are trying to take up as little room as possible so as not to offend anyone.

A high-value man leans back. He spreads his arms across the back of the booth. He uses "expansive" gestures. This isn't about being a jerk or invading someone else's personal space; it is about signaling that you are comfortable enough to own the space you are in. When a woman sees a man who is comfortable taking up space, she subconsciously associates him with safety and abundance.

The Social Mechanics of Movement: The "Slow-Motion" Secret

Posture is static, but **movement** is dynamic. Once you have fixed your frame, you must learn how to move that frame through a room.

High-value individuals move slower than low-value individuals.

Think of a king versus a servant. The servant moves quickly, darting around to fulfill requests, checking over his shoulder, and reacting to every sound. The king moves with intentionality. He knows that the world waits for him. He is the "stationary point" around which the room revolves.

- **The Walk:** When you walk, move from your hips, not your knees. Keep your strides long and rhythmic. Allow your arms to swing naturally by your sides—do not put them in your pockets, which is a classic "hiding" gesture.

- **The Turn:** When someone calls your name or taps your shoulder, do not "snap" your head toward them. Turn your entire torso slowly. This signals that you are not easily startled and that you are the one in control of the interaction.

- **The "Stillness":** When you are standing still, *actually* stand still. Avoid fidgeting with your watch, your phone, or your drink. Stillness is a primary indicator of a calm nervous system.

The "Gaze" and the Neck

The way you move your neck is a primary indicator of your level of anxiety. Nervous men have "darting" eyes and "jerky" neck movements. They are constantly scanning for threats or for approval.

High-value men have a "predatory" stillness. Their eyes move first, followed slowly by the head. This suggests that you are the observer, not the observed. It suggests that you are analyzing the environment from a position of strength.

When you make eye contact with a woman across a room, do not look away quickly if she catches you. This is a "submission" signal. Instead, hold the gaze for a heartbeat, give a slow, subtle nod or a slight smirk, and *then* look away slowly. You have just transformed a "glance" into an "interaction."

The Feedback Loop: How She Sees Your Spine

A woman's attraction is often a response to the "vibe" of safety and strength a man provides. When you stand tall, you are physically signaling that you are a "protector."

From a distance, a woman's peripheral vision picks up your silhouette. This is part of the "thin-slicing" we discussed in Chapter 1. If that silhouette is expansive and upright, her brain tags you as a "potential mate of interest." By the time you are close enough to speak, the "heavy lifting" of attraction is already done.

If you are slouched, she has to "work" to find you attractive. You are asking her to look past your physical weakness to find your "inner soul." A high-value man never asks a woman to do the work for him. He makes it easy for her to be attracted by providing a clear, high-status signal from the start.

The Vagus Nerve and Emotional Regulation

There is a deeper, more neurological reason why posture matters. The vagus nerve is the longest nerve of the autonomic nervous system, running from the brainstem down to the abdomen. It is the primary driver of the "rest and digest" (parasympathetic) system.

When you slouch and compress your chest, you are physically inhibiting the vagus nerve and shallowing your breath. This triggers the "fight or flight" (sympathetic) system. You become more anxious, your heart rate increases, and your social intuition (your ability to "read the room") decreases.

When you stand tall and breathe deeply into your belly, you activate the vagus nerve. This sends a signal to your brain that you are safe. This "safe" state allows you to be more charming, more humorous, and more present. Posture, therefore, is the physical gateway to your best social self.

Practical Exercises: Rebuilding the Frame

You cannot fix 20 years of slouching in 20 minutes. Posture is a result of muscle memory. To change it, you must retrain your posterior chain.

1. The Wall Drill (The "Reset")

Stand with your heels, glutes, upper back, and the back of your head touching a flat wall. Your chin should be tucked slightly.

- Hold this for 2–5 minutes every morning.
- While in this position, breathe deeply into your stomach.
- This "resets" your brain's internal map of what "straight" feels like. Most men feel like they are leaning backward when they first do this; that is how skewed your "normal" has become.

2. The "Silver Thread" Visualization

Throughout the day, imagine there is a silver thread attached to the crown of your head, pulling you gently toward the sky. This visualization helps you maintain "active" posture without looking stiff or forced.

3. The Doorway Stretch

Place your forearms on either side of a door frame and lean forward to stretch your chest muscles. Tight pecs pull your shoulders forward into a "hunch." Stretching them allows your shoulders to rest naturally in an open position.

4. The "Phone Rule"

Never look down at your phone. Bring the phone up to eye level. This prevents the "C-curve" in your spine and keeps your head in alignment with your shoulders. More importantly, it keeps you looking "up" at the world, making you appear more approachable and engaged.

5. Glute Activation

If you sit all day, your glutes are likely "asleep." Your glutes are the anchor of your posture. Do three sets of 15 bodyweight squats or glute bridges every morning. A strong base makes for a strong spine.

Integration: Posture in Different Contexts

Posture must be calibrated, just like style.

- **In a High-Energy Club:** Your posture should be extremely expansive. You need to be a "fixed point" in a sea of movement. Lean against a pillar or sit with your legs wide to signal dominance.

- **On a First Date:** Your posture should be "open" but "leaning in" slightly to show interest. Avoid crossing your arms, which creates a physical barrier between you and her.

- **In a Professional Meeting:** Your posture should signal "Alert Authority." Sit at the edge of your chair, back straight, hands on the table.

Conclusion

Your posture is the foundation of your presence. It is the silent language that speaks before you do, telling the world whether you are a man of status or a man of submission.

By correcting your alignment, you are doing more than just "standing straight." You are reclaiming your masculine space. You are hacking your hormones to increase confidence. And you are signaling to every woman you meet that you are a man who is comfortable in his own skin—and therefore, a man worth getting to know.

You have now fixed the "wrapper" (Style) and the "structure" (Posture). You are no longer invisible. You are a man of presence. In the final chapter of Book 1, we will explore how to use the environment and the people around you to "vet" that value through **Social Proof.**

CHAPTER 4

PROJECT CONFIDENCE BEFORE YOU SPEAK

The Silent Dialogue: The Air Between Us is Never Empty

Most men live under the illusion that an interaction begins when they open their mouths. They spend hours rehearsing "lines," memorizing "openers," and worrying about what they will say five minutes into a conversation. They treat social interaction like a theatrical play where the script is everything.

In reality, by the time you speak your first word, you have already been talking to her for several minutes. You have been broadcasting a continuous, high-fidelity stream of data through the tension in your jaw, the frequency of your blinks, the stillness of your hands, and the specific "weight" of your gaze.

This is the phase of **Pre-Communication**. It is the bridge between the "Hardware" (your style and posture) and the "Software" (your conversation). This chapter is about the **Bio-Signal**—the energetic frequency you broadcast to every nervous system in the room. To grab a woman's attention, you must project a "Silent Confidence" that suggests you are the most grounded, centered, and socially secure person in the environment.

The Neuroscience of Presence: Mirror Neurons and the Simulation Theory

To understand why your silent energy is so powerful, we must look at a breakthrough in neuroscience: **Mirror Neurons**. Discovered in the 1990s by Giacomo Rizzolatti and his team at the University of Parma, these are brain cells that fire both when an individual performs an action and when that individual observes someone else performing that same action.

Mirror neurons allow for what psychologists call "Internal State Simulation." When a woman looks at you, her brain is literally mapping your physical state onto her own. If you are projecting "Micro-Stressors"—shrugging your shoulders toward your ears, darting your eyes nervously, or clenching your fists—her mirror neurons fire as if *she* were the one feeling anxious. This creates a visceral sense of discomfort in her. She won't consciously know why she wants to look away; she will simply feel a "bad vibe."

Conversely, if you are genuinely relaxed, your movements are slow and deliberate, and your breathing is deep, her mirror neurons will simulate *your* calm. You become a "Social Anchor." In a world filled with high-energy, anxious, and reactive people, the man who provides a "Safe Harbor" of calm through his own physiology becomes instantly magnetic. You are not just "projecting" confidence; you are inviting her nervous system to enter a state of ease.

The Eye Contact Spectrum: Mastering the High-Value Gaze

The eyes are the most direct window into the amygdala—the brain's emotional processing center. In a single heartbeat, eye contact can communicate dominance, submission, desire, or fear. To project confidence before you speak, you must move away from "reactive" eye contact and master the "High-Value Gaze."

1. The Submissive Glance (The Submission Signal)

This is the most common mistake made by men who feel "inferior" in a social setting. You look at a woman, she catches your eye, and you immediately look down at the floor or jerk your head away to the side.

- **The Biology:** Looking down is a universal primate signal for "I am not a threat; I acknowledge your superiority."
- **The Result:** It tells her that you are intimidated by her beauty or the social environment. You have failed the "first test" of confidence before a word was spoken.

2. The Aggressive Stare (The "Creep" Signal)

This is the "predatory" gaze. It is wide-eyed, unblinking, and lacks warmth.

- **The Biology:** This gaze triggers the "fight or flight" response. It signals that you are laser-focused on "taking" value rather than "exchanging" it.
- **The Result:** It triggers her danger response. It shows a lack of social calibration.

3. The High-Value Gaze (The Gaze of Intent)

This is the "sweet spot." It is characterized by three distinct physical markers:

- **The Slow Blink:** Anxious people blink rapidly (sometimes up to 50 times per minute) to keep their eyes lubricated during a "threat scan." High-value men blink slowly and infrequently. This signals a low-cortisol, high-testosterone state.
- **The "Heavy" Lids:** Relax the muscles around your eyes. This is the "soft gaze." It suggests you are comfortable enough in the room to not be hyper-vigilant. It conveys a sense of quiet amusement.
- **The "One-Second Hold":** When you make eye contact, do not be the first to look away. Hold the gaze for exactly one second longer than is socially "required." Give a subtle, slow nod—not a "please like me" nod, but an "I acknowledge you" nod. Then, look away *slowly* to the side, never down.

Micro-Expressions and the Leakage of Truth

Psychologist Paul Ekman, the world's leading expert on facial expressions, spent decades cataloging the 43 muscles in the human face. He discovered that the face is capable of over 10,000 expressions, many of which are **Micro-Expressions**—involuntary flashes of emotion that last only 1/15th to 1/25th of a second.

Even if you have the "perfect" style and "perfect" posture, if you are "faking" confidence, your face will "leak" your true internal state. For example, a "Pan-Am" or "fake" smile only uses the muscles around the mouth. A genuine "Duchenne" smile involves the *orbicularis oculi* muscles, which pull the skin around the eyes, creating "crow's feet."

To project confidence, you must achieve **Internal Alignment**. You cannot simply "act" confident; you must prime your mind. If you walk into a room thinking, *"I hope these people like me,"* your face will leak "Neediness." If you walk in thinking, *"I'm here to see who is worth my time,"* your face will leak "Selectivity." Selectivity is one of the most attractive traits a man can possess because it implies he has high standards and options.

The Power of Stillness: Reactance vs. Inertia

In any high-energy social environment—a busy bar, a corporate gala, or a crowded cafe—stillness is the ultimate status symbol.

Low-status individuals are hyper-reactive. They are constantly adjusting their clothing, touching their necks (a "pacifying" gesture used to calm the vagus nerve), checking their phones, or shifting their weight. This is "Physical Leakage." It tells the world that their nervous system is overwhelmed by the environment.

High-status individuals possess **"Social Inertia."** They move only when they have a reason to move.

- **Keep your hands still and visible:** Hiding your hands suggests you are hiding a weapon (evolutionarily) or hiding your anxiety (modernly). Keep them relaxed at your sides or on a table.

- **The Slow Turn:** When someone calls your name or you hear a loud noise, do not "snap" your head toward it. Turn your head slowly, or better yet, turn your entire torso. This signals that you are the "Source" of your own movement, not a "Reacter" to outside stimuli.

- **Diaphragmatic Breathing:** Most men breathe high in their chests when they are nervous. This looks like a "heaving" motion that signals panic. Breathe into your stomach. A still, calm chest is the hallmark of a man who is in total control of his physiology.

The "Selective" Smirk: Using Non-Verbal Wit

A full, eager grin as you walk into a room is often interpreted as "Auditioning." It says, *"I am friendly and I hope you approve of me!"* A high-value man uses the **Selective Smirk**. This is a slight, often asymmetrical upturn of one corner of the mouth, accompanied by relaxed eyes. It is the expression of a man who has a "secret"—someone who is observing the room and finding the social "dance" mildly amusing.

This smirk is a powerful curiosity trigger. When a woman sees a man who looks genuinely amused but is not "trying" to be funny, her brain asks: *"What does he know that I don't?"* It creates an "Inquiry Gap" that she will feel compelled to close.

Emotional Contagion: Becoming the Social Anchor

Humans are biologically wired for **Emotional Contagion**. In any group, the emotions of the most "certain" or "dominant" person will eventually spread to the others.

If you are projecting a "heavy," calm, and grounded energy, people will begin to synchronize their breathing and heart rates with yours. You become a "Social Anchor." People—especially women—will naturally gravitate toward you because being in your "aura" makes them feel better.

This is what people mean when they talk about "vibe." It isn't magic; it is the result of one person having a more stable and certain internal state than the people around them. Before you say a word, your goal is to be the most "certain" person in the room regarding your right to be there.

Proxemics and the Ownership of Space

How you "claim" space is a silent broadcast of your rank. This is the study of **Proxemics**.

When a low-status man sits in a public space, he "contracts." He keeps his elbows in, his knees together, and his head down. He is trying to take up as little "resource space" as possible to avoid offending the "alpha" of the tribe.

A high-value man "expands."

- **The Lean:** When standing at a bar, lean one elbow on the counter. This shows you are comfortable enough to "attach" to the environment.

- **The Triangle Stance:** Stand with your feet slightly wider than your shoulders. This makes you physically harder to move and projects a "solid" base.

- **The "Vitals" Exposure:** Do not cross your arms over your chest. This is a defensive posture that protects your heart and lungs. By keeping your chest and stomach "open," you are signaling that you do not perceive any threats in the room. This is a massive "Safe/Dominant" signal.

The "Gaze" and the Pre-Approach

Before you ever walk over to a woman, you can "test the waters" with your silent broadcast. This is the **Pre-Approach Look.**

1. **The Sweep:** Look around the room slowly. When your eyes pass over her, do not stop. Keep moving. This signals that you are not "hunting."

2. **The Re-Connect:** A few minutes later, "accidentally" catch her eye again. This time, hold it for the "one-second hold." Give the "Selective Smirk."

3. **The Disengage:** Look away slowly to the side.

If she maintains eye contact, smiles, or even looks away and then looks back, you have "cleared" the silent dialogue. You are no longer a stranger; you are a "Person of Interest." The "ice" is already cracked before you even start walking.

The secret to projecting confidence before you speak lies in your **Internal Frame**. Most men walk into a room with a "Stranger Frame," thinking: *"I don't know these people, I hope I don't mess up."*

A high-value man uses the **"Assume Rapport" Frame**. He walks into a room as if everyone inside is already an old friend he hasn't seen in a while.

- This frame automatically relaxes the muscles in your face.
- It gives you a warm, "knowing" look in your eyes.
- It makes your movements fluid and natural.

When you "Assume Rapport," you stop "performing" and start "existing." Existence is far more attractive than performance.

Action Plan: Developing the "Silent Engine"

To master these silent signals, you must practice them in low-stakes environments until they become your "default" setting.

1. The "Stillness" Drill Next time you are in a coffee shop or waiting for a meeting, set a timer on your watch for 5 minutes. Your goal is to remain perfectly still. Do not check your phone. Do not touch your hair. Do not shift your feet. Focus on deep, belly breathing. Notice the "panic" your brain feels when it can't "fidget" away its energy. Mastering this stillness is the foundation of presence.

2. The "Slow-Motion" Day For one entire day, commit to moving 20% slower than your usual pace. Walk slower. Turn your head slower. Reach for your coffee cup slower. Notice how people begin to "wait" for you. Notice how your own internal anxiety levels drop as you refuse to be "rushed" by the world.

3. The "Last to Look Away" Challenge In every interaction today—with the cashier, your boss, or a stranger on the street—be the last person to break eye contact. Do it with a friendly, relaxed face. You will be amazed at how much "power" you feel simply by owning the visual space.

4. The "Mirror" Audit Stand in front of a mirror and practice your "Selective Smirk." If it looks forced, relax your face completely and think of something genuinely funny or ironic. Notice how your eyes change. That is the look you want to bring into the lounge.

Conclusion

Confidence is not a loud shout; it is a "heavy" silence. When you fix your internal state and master the silent dialogue of eye contact, stillness, and space, you become a man who is noticed before he is heard.

You are no longer "auditioning" for attention. You are broadcasting a signal of such high value and groundedness that attention is naturally drawn to you. You have prepared the hardware, the structure, and the engine. Now, in the next chapter, we will look at how to use your **Environment** to provide the ultimate validation: **Social Proof.**

USE YOUR ENVIRONMENT TO CREATE SOCIAL PROOF

The Herd Instinct: Why We Look to Others

If the previous chapters have been about building your internal signal—your style, your posture, and your silent presence—this chapter is about the **amplification** of that signal. In the complex world of human social dynamics, you are never judged in a vacuum. You are judged by the company you keep and the way the environment reacts to you.

This is the principle of **Social Proof**. At its core, social proof is a psychological shortcut. Humans are "herd animals." For 99% of our evolutionary history, being ostracized from the group meant certain death. Consequently, our brains evolved to constantly scan the environment to see who is valued by the tribe and who is being ignored.

When you walk into a room, a woman's brain is performing an automated "status audit." She isn't just looking at your watch or your shoes; she is looking to see if the world treats you like a man of importance. If you are standing alone, staring at your phone, you are an "unverified" entity. If you are laughing with the staff, introduced by friends, or surrounded by high-energy people, you have been "vetted." Social proof does the heavy lifting of attraction for you, bypassing her logical defenses and speaking directly to her biological instinct for a high-value mate.

The Science of Mate Choice Copying

To master social proof, we must understand its biological origin: **Mate Choice Copying**. This is a phenomenon observed across the animal kingdom, from guppies and birds to primates and humans. It occurs when a female's preference for a male increases after she observes other females interacting with or choosing him.

In humans, this is often called **Pre-selection**. A study published in the *Journal of Experimental Social Psychology* found that women rated a man as significantly more attractive when he was surrounded by other women than when he was alone or with other men. This isn't just "jealousy." It is an efficiency strategy. Evaluation is "expensive" in terms of time and risk. If other women have already spent time with you and found you safe, charming, and high-value, a new woman can "copy" that assessment without having to do the investigative work herself.

By leveraging your environment to create social proof, you are providing "evidence" of your value. You are showing, rather than telling, that you are a man of status.

The Three Tiers of Social Proof

Social proof is not a monolith. It exists in three distinct layers, each providing a different type of validation. To "Grab Her Attention" effectively, you should aim to trigger at least two of these tiers in any given environment.

Tier 1: Environmental Social Proof (The Regular Effect)

This is your relationship with the "physics" of the room. It involves the staff, the layout, and the "vibe" of the venue.

- **The "Home Court Advantage"**: When the doorman nods to you, the bartender knows your name, or the owner stops by to shake your hand, you are signaling that you are an "Insider."

- **The Value of Being a Regular:** High-value men are not "transients" in their environments; they are stakeholders. Being a "regular" at a high-end establishment suggests you have the resources to frequent it and the social skills to be liked by those who work there.

Tier 2: Peer Social Proof (The Tribe Effect)

This is the validation provided by your immediate social circle.

- **The Halo Effect:** If you are surrounded by fit, well-dressed, and successful men, their value "rubs off" on you.
- **The Hub Position:** Social proof is highest when you are the "leader" of your group—the one making the decisions, leadings the toasts, or telling the story that has everyone else leaning in.

Tier 3: Female Social Proof (The Pre-selection Effect)

This is the most potent form of attraction.

- **The "Safe" Signal:** The presence of women in your life tells a new woman that you are not a "creep" or a threat.
- **The Competition Trigger:** It subtly signals that your time and attention are in demand.

The "Host" Mentality: Becoming the Center of the Room

Most men enter a lounge or a bar with a "Consumer" mentality. They are there to *consume* drinks, *consume* music, and *consume* the attention of women. This is a low-status position. You are a "guest" in someone else's world.

To maximize social proof, you must adopt the **"Host" Mentality**. A host is the provider of value. He is the one who ensures everyone is having a good time. Even if you don't own the venue, you can act with the "spirit of a host."

How to Execute the Host Mentality:

1. **The "Entrance Warm-Up":** Don't walk in and go straight to a corner. Spend the first 10 minutes talking to "low-stakes" people—the doorman, the coat check, the groups near the door.
2. **The Connector:** If you see someone standing alone, bring them into your group for a moment. Introduce your friends to people you just met.

3. **The Energy Source:** Be the person who is laughing the loudest (genuinely) and moving with the most purpose.

When a woman sees a man who is "hosting" the room, she sees a man who is in control of his reality. She sees a leader. This makes you the most interesting person in the environment before you ever speak to her.

The Bartender Strategy: Manufacturing Status

In any social venue, the bartender is the "high priest" of status. They control the flow of resources (drinks) and the "vibe" of the bar. If the bartender likes you, the room knows it.

The Tactical Approach:

- **Tip Heavily on the First Round:** This isn't just about being generous; it's about "buying" a moment of their time and attention in a busy environment.

- **Learn the Name:** Use it throughout the night. "Thanks, Mark, I appreciate it."

- **Be the "Low-Maintenance" Customer:** High-value men don't complain about the wait; they are patient and polite. This contrasts sharply with the "low-status" men who are demanding and rude to service staff.

The Result: Later in the night, when you are standing at the bar next to a woman you want to meet, the bartender will likely greet you with a smile and ask, "The usual, [Your Name]?" This is a massive "Status Injection." It proves you are a "known" entity with "Insider" access.

The "Social Anchor" and the Power of the Group

Your social circle is your "marketing team." If you go out with three guys who are all staring at their phones or looking "hungry" for women, you are drowning in low-value signals.

Building the High-Value Group:

- **The 50/50 Rule:** Try to ensure your group is an even mix of men and women. A "stag" group of four men looks like a "hunting party," which triggers defensive responses in women. A mixed group looks like a "social party," which invites participation.

- **The "Laughter" Metric:** High-value groups are the ones having the most fun. When people are laughing, they release endorphins. If your group is the source of the laughter, everyone in the room wants to "catch" that energy.

The Digital Extension of Social Proof

In 2026, the "environment" is no longer just the physical room; it is the digital space that surrounds you. Before a woman commits to a long conversation or a date, she will often perform a "Digital Audit."

- **The Tagged Photo Strategy:** Your social proof is higher in photos you didn't take. Being tagged in photos of you at events, with friends, or doing interesting activities is 10x more powerful than a selfie. It proves that *others* find you worth documenting.
- **The "Lifestyle" Broadcast:** Your social media should look like a curated "Best Of" reel of your life. It shouldn't be about "showing off"; it should be about "documenting a life well-lived."

If your physical social proof is high (you are the "hub" of the room) and your digital social proof is high (you have an active, connected life), you become "vibrationally irresistible."

The "Pioneer" vs. The "Follower"

In the "Grab Her Attention" phase, social proof allows you to be a **Pioneer**. Most men wait for a woman to be alone or for "the perfect moment" to approach. A man with high social proof creates the moment.

Because he has the support of the environment, his approach doesn't feel like an "intrusion." It feels like he is "allowing" her into his already-great world. This shift in frame is the difference between "begging" for attention and "granting" it.

Action Steps: Engineering Your Social Proof

1. The "Staff Audit" (This Week) Pick three venues (a coffee shop, a gym, and a lounge). Commit to becoming a "Known Regular" in all three. Learn the names of three staff members in each. Your goal is to be the person they are happy to see walk through the door.

2. The "Pre-Approach" Warm-Up Next time you go out, set a "Social Quota." You must talk to five people you are *not* attracted to before you talk to one person you *are* attracted to. This builds your "momentum" and creates a visual history of you being social in the room.

3. The "Group Pivot" If you are out with friends, be the one who suggests the next move. "Hey guys, let's move to the other side of the bar." "Let's go grab a table." Being the "Director" of the group's movement signals high status to everyone watching.

4. The "Photo Hack" Next time you are out with friends, don't take a selfie. Hand your phone to someone else and ask them to "capture the vibe." Get photos of you in the middle of a conversation or laughing. Use these to build your digital "Social Resume."

Conclusion

Social proof is the "Wind in Your Sails." Without it, you are rowing against the current of her natural skepticism. With it, you are being carried toward attraction by the collective agreement of the room.

By leveraging the staff, your peers, and the presence of other women, you are proving your value without saying a word. You are no longer just a man in a room; you are a man of the room.

You have now mastered the foundation: Style, Posture, Presence, and Social Proof. You have successfully "Grabbed Her Attention." Now, it is time to do something with that attention. In the final chapters of Book 1, we will learn how to **Initiate the First Interaction** and bridge the gap between "Looking" and "Talking."

CHAPTER 6

INITIATE THE FIRST INTERACTION WITHOUT HESITATION

The Great Divide: From Observer to Actor

You have optimized your style. Your posture is a broadcast of strength. Your silent presence has already begun to ripple through the room, and the environment is validating you through social proof. You have "Grabbed Her Attention." She has seen you, her "lizard brain" has given you a preliminary green light, and the "Inquiry Gap" is wide open.

But now comes the moment that separates the **High-Value Man** from the **Spectator**: The Initiation.

In the world of social dynamics, there is a "Threshold of Action." On one side of this threshold is the world of "What If"—a place where men wait for the "perfect moment," rehearse lines in their heads until they become stale, and eventually watch as the opportunity walks out the door. On the other side is the world of "What Is"—a place where men move with intentionality, accept social risk as a cost of doing business, and lead the interaction.

To grab her attention is a passive victory. To **initiate** is an active one. This chapter is about the mechanics of the approach: why we hesitate, the biological cost of that hesitation, and the tactical framework for crossing the room without losing your momentum.

The Biology of the "Amygdala Hijack"

Before we discuss *how* to approach, we must address why your heart is currently pounding against your ribs. "Approach Anxiety" is not a character flaw; it is an evolutionary survival mechanism.

For our ancestors, approaching a stranger—especially a high-value female who might be protected by other high-value males—was a high-stakes gamble. A social mistake could lead to physical confrontation or, worse, exile from the tribe. Exile was a death sentence. Consequently, your brain developed a "Better Safe Than Sorry" protocol.

When you see a woman you want to meet, your amygdala—the brain's alarm system—fires. It sends a signal to your hypothalamus, which triggers a flood of adrenaline and cortisol. Your pupils dilate, your heart rate spikes, and your "logical" prefrontal cortex begins to shut down. This is the **Amygdala Hijack**. Your brain is literally treating a beautiful woman like a saber-toothed tiger.

High-value men do not "lack" this fear; they simply have a different relationship with it. They understand that the "fear" is just a chemical signal that something important is happening. They use the adrenaline as fuel for movement rather than a reason for paralysis.

The 3-Second Rule: The Death of Hesitation

The most effective tool for overcoming the Amygdala Hijack is the **3-Second Rule**.

The rule is simple: Once you see someone you want to meet, you have exactly three seconds to begin your movement toward them.

Why three seconds?

1. **Hormonal Shift:** Within the first three seconds, your body is in a proactive "action" state. If you wait longer, your brain begins to produce cortisol (the stress hormone). You move from "Opportunity Seeking" to "Threat Assessing."

2. **Social Perception:** If you look at a woman for ten seconds before moving, you look like a "hunter" or a "stalker." If you see her and move immediately, the interaction feels spontaneous, natural, and confident.

3. **The Overthinking Trap:** Your brain is a "justification machine." If you give it more than three seconds, it will find ten "logical" reasons why you shouldn't approach: *"She looks busy," "She's with friends," "I'm not in the right mood."*

When you move within three seconds, you bypass the "Justification Machine." You are signaling to her—and to yourself—that you are a man of action who trusts his instincts.

The Social Physics of the Approach

How you move through the space is just as important as the speed at which you move. A high-value approach is characterized by **Social Fluidity.**

1. The Angle of Approach

Never approach a woman from directly behind or directly in front ("head-on").

- **The "Head-On" Approach** feels like a confrontation. It triggers a defensive "fight or flight" response.

- **The "Behind" Approach** is startling and creepy.

- **The "45-Degree" Approach:** Approach from the side/front. This allows her to see you coming in her peripheral vision, giving her brain time to "vet" you before you arrive, but it doesn't block her path. It is the most non-threatening and socially calibrated angle.

2. The "Point of Entry"

Don't aim for her face; aim for the "air" about two feet in front of her. This shows you are not "invading" her space, but rather "entering" her environment. Your first words should happen while you are still slightly moving or just as you arrive, creating a sense of "passing through" rather than "stopping to hunt."

3. The "Torso Turn"

When you arrive, your feet should be pointed slightly away from her, while your torso is turned toward her. This is a "non-committal" posture. It signals: *"I'm here to say something, but I'm not desperate to stay."* It lowers the pressure of the interaction for both of you.

The "No-Line" Opener: The Art of Observation

The biggest fear men have is "not knowing what to say." They look for "magic lines" or "canned routines." But high-value attraction is based on **Presence**, not **Performance.** The most effective openers are **Low-Stakes Observational Openers.** You aren't trying to be "the most interesting man in the world" in the first five seconds. You are simply acknowledging a shared reality.

The Situation-Opinion-Question (SOQ) Framework

To create an effortless opener, use the SOQ framework:

Component	Description	Example
Situation	An observation about the environment or her.	"This music is significantly louder than it was ten minutes ago."
Opinion	Your brief, non-reactive take on it.	"I'm starting to feel like I'm in a 90s action movie."
Question	An invitation for her to participate.	"Are you a fan of the chaos, or are you just tolerating it for the drinks?"

Why this works:

It's "organic." It doesn't feel like a "line" you practiced in the mirror. It feels like a thought that just occurred to you, which suggests you are a man who is "present" in the moment.

The "Pawn Move": Micro-Interactions

If the idea of a full approach still feels overwhelming, use **"Pawn Moves."** In chess, pawn moves are small, low-risk advances that set up the board for the "power pieces."

Examples of Pawn Moves:

- **The "Comment to the Air":** While standing near her at the bar, make a comment to the bartender or the air about the venue. If she responds or smiles, the "ice" is already broken.

- **The "Prop Interaction":** "That looks like a very serious drink. Is it as dangerous as it looks?"

- **The "Shared Struggle":** If the line is long or the music is too loud, a simple roll of the eyes and a "Can you believe this?" to the person next to you is an approach.

Pawn moves build **Social Momentum.** Once you have had three or four "pawn move" interactions with various people in the room, the "big approach" feels like a natural extension of your night rather than a terrifying leap into the dark.

The "Exit Strategy": The Gift of the Out

One of the primary reasons women are "guarded" during an initial interaction is the fear that they will be "stuck" talking to a guy they aren't interested in for the next hour.

A high-value man removes this fear by providing an **Implicit or Explicit Exit Strategy.**

- **The Explicit Out:** "I have to get back to my friends in a second, but I had to ask..."

- **The Implicit Out:** Body language that is "leaning away."

When you tell a woman (either through words or movement) that you aren't going to "cling" to her, her defenses drop. She feels safe to engage with you because she knows she can leave the interaction whenever she wants. Paradoxically, the more you show you are willing to leave, the more she will want you to stay. This is the **Law of Scarcity** in action.

Handling the "Social Check": The Resilient Response

When you initiate, a high-value woman will often give you a "Social Check" (sometimes called a "test"). She wants to see if your confidence is real or just a mask.

Example: You: "I love the energy of this place, but the lighting makes everyone look like they're in a heist movie."

Her: "Is that the best line you could come up with?"

The Low-Status Response: Getting defensive, apologizing, or trying to "explain" yourself. ("Oh, I didn't mean it was a line, I just thought...")

The High-Status Response: Amused Non-Reactivity.

"Actually, I have a much better one, but you haven't earned it yet." (With a smirk).

A high-value man is **Psychologically Resilient.** He is not shaken by a woman's challenge. In fact, he enjoys it. He sees her challenge as a sign that she is a woman of status herself, and he welcomes the "sparring."

The Psychology of Rejection: The "Data Point" Mindset

The fear of initiation is ultimately the fear of rejection. We interpret a "No" as an indictment of our entire being.

Reframing Rejection:

High-value men do not see rejection as a "loss." They see it as a "Data Point."

- A "No" simply means she isn't in the mood, she has a partner, she's having a bad day, or you aren't her type. None of these have anything to do with your fundamental worth as a man.

- In fact, the only "failure" is **Hesitation.** If you approach and get rejected, you have "won" because you have trained your nervous system to handle social risk. You have "leveled up" your courage.

  "The man who approaches ten people and gets rejected nine times has ten times more 'social data' and ten times more 'courage' than the man who sits in the corner and approaches zero."

How you handle a rejection is a massive broadcast of your status to the rest of the room.

If a woman says, "I'm not interested" or "I'm waiting for someone," and you slink away with your head down, your social proof in the room plummets. Everyone saw you "lose."

If, however, you smile, say "Fair enough, have a great night," and walk back to your friends (or to the bar) with the *exact same posture and energy* you had before the approach, your status actually **increases.** You have shown that your internal state is not dependent on her approval. You have shown that you are "The Source" of your own value.

The Tactical Drill: The "10-Person Warm-Up"

To eliminate hesitation, you must "desensitize" your amygdala. You do this through volume.

The Exercise:

Tonight, or next time you are out, your goal is not to "get a number" or "find a date." Your goal is to have 10 micro-interactions with 10 different people.

1. Ask a guy what kind of beer he's drinking.
2. Tell the bartender you like the playlist.
3. Ask a group if they know where the best late-night food is.
4. Tell a woman you like her shoes and keep walking.
5. ... and so on.

By the time you get to the 11th person—the woman you are actually interested in—your "Initiation Muscle" is warm. The fear is gone. You are in a "Social Flow State."

The "Decisive Walk": The Physicality of Intent

Finally, your walk must match your intent.

- **The "Meandering" Walk:** Looking left and right, stopping, starting. This looks like someone who is "searching" or "predatory."

- **The "Decisive" Walk:** You have a destination. Even if your destination is her, you walk with a steady, rhythmic pace. Your shoulders are "quiet." Your head is still.

When she sees you walking toward her with this level of physical certainty, she is already "prepared" for a high-quality interaction. You are telegraphing that you are a man who knows what he wants and isn't afraid to go after it.

Conclusion: The Threshold is Crossed

Initiating the interaction is the final "stress test" of everything we have covered in Book 1. It requires the Style to be seen, the Posture to be respected, the Presence to be felt, and the Social Proof to be trusted.

When you move without hesitation, you are making a claim on your reality. You are saying, *"I am a man of value, and I have something to contribute to this environment."* Most men will spend their entire lives waiting for permission to speak. A high-value man gives himself permission.

You have now "Grabbed Her Attention" and "Initiated the Interaction." You have crossed the most difficult bridge in the world of attraction. You are now "In the Conversation."

But the conversation is a new landscape with its own set of rules. In **Book 2: Break the Ice**, we will explore how to transition from the "Opener" into "Rapport," how to use humor and "cold reading" to build interest, and how to ensure that the attention you've grabbed turns into a genuine, lasting connection.

CHAPTER 7

CONCLUSION: THE FOUNDATION OF ATTRACTION

The Architecture of the Unseen

We have traveled a considerable distance together. We started this journey in the microscopic world of neurocircuitry, examining the amygdala and the limbic system. We moved through the wardrobe, the gym, and the mirror, adjusting the physical casing of the man. We stepped into the social arena, dissecting the invisible lines of status, energy, and validation that crisscross every room you enter.

Throughout Book 1, our focus has been singularly fixed on the **"Pre-Vocal"** phase of attraction. We have treated the first ten minutes of your night not as a random social casualty, but as a high-stakes engineering project.

The thesis of this book is simple yet profound, and it bears repeating one final time: **Attraction is not a choice; it is a biological response to a specific set of signals.**

If you have truly integrated the lessons from Chapters 1 through 6, you are no longer the same man who started this book. You have moved from being an accidental participant in your social life to being a deliberate architect. You have learned that before you say "Hello," your clothes, your spine, your eyes, and your peers have already told a story about you. The question is no longer *if* you will grab her attention, but what you will do with the magnetic pull you have created.

This conclusion is not just a summary; it is a synthesis. It is about how to lock these separate skills into a unified "identity" that functions automatically, allowing you to move through the world with the ease of a man who knows his own worth.

The "Force Multiplier" Effect: Synthesizing the Pillars

To solidify this foundation, we must look at how these individual pillars interact. In systems engineering, there is a concept known as a "Force Multiplier"—a factor that dramatically increases the effectiveness of an item or group.

Your Style, Posture, Presence, and Social Proof are not additive ($1 + 1 + 1 + 1 = 4$). They are multiplicative ($2 \times 2 \times 2 \times 2 = 16$). When these elements align, they create a "Halo Effect" so powerful that it does the heavy lifting of attraction for you.

Let's review the "Stack" one last time to understand how they feed into one another.

1. The Biological Mandate (The "Why")

We began by stripping away the romance and looking at the biology. You now understand that a woman's "Snap Judgment" is an evolutionary safeguard. Her brain is scanning for fitness, health, and status in 100 ms.

- **The Shift:** You have stopped fighting the system. You no longer view "being judged" as an insult or a shallowness; you view it as a language you are now fluent in. You understand that "Attraction" is simply the brain's way of saying, *"This organism has high survival value."*

2. The Aesthetic Signal (The "Wrapper")

Your style is no longer just "clothing." It is your **Visual Resume**. By fixing your presentation, you have removed the friction of "The Creep Filter."

- **The Synergy:** When you dress well, you trigger a psychological phenomenon called **Enclothed Cognition**. You don't just look better to her; you *think* differently about yourself. You stand taller (Pillar 3) because your clothes demand it. You feel more entitled to be in the room (Pillar 4) because you look like you own it.

3. The Structural Frame (The "Skeleton")

Your posture is the "skeleton" of your confidence. By correcting your alignment—the retracted scapula, the neutral pelvis, the elongated neck—you have moved from a "defensive" biological posture to an "expansive" one.

- **The Feedback Loop:** Remember the study on "Power Posing." By physically taking up space, you are manually lowering your cortisol and raising your testosterone. This chemical shift makes it easier to maintain the "High-Value Gaze" (Pillar 4) and easier to take risks (Pillar 6). Your body is literally hacking your brain.

4. The Energetic Broadcast (The "Signal")

You have mastered the **Silent Dialogue**. Through the use of mirror neurons and the "High-Value Gaze," you are projecting a low-cortisol, high-testosterone energy.

- **The Vibe:** You have learned that stillness is power. While other men are fidgeting, checking their phones, and looking for validation, you are the "Eye of the Storm." This stillness allows the Social Proof (Pillar 5) to settle around you. You look like the prize because you are not frantically "selling" yourself.

5. The Environmental Validation (The "Proof")

You have transformed your surroundings into a **Social Proof Machine**. By becoming the "Host" of your environment and leveraging the validation of the staff and your peers, you have lowered the "cost of entry" for a woman to interact with you.

- **The Trust Factor:** Because you look the part (Style) and act the part (Presence), the environment treats you like a VIP (Social Proof). This creates a "virtuous cycle." She sees the bartender smile at you, which validates her initial biological assessment that you are a high-status male.

6. The Decisive Movement (The "Spark")

Finally, you have learned to cross the **Threshold of Action**. By utilizing the 3-Second Rule and the SOQ Framework, you have bridged the gap between being a "High-Value Silhouette" and a "High-Value Individual."

- **The Reality Check:** All the preparation in the world is useless without the spark of ignition. You have learned that hesitation is the only true failure, and that movement is the antidote to anxiety.

The "Uncanny Valley" of Self-Improvement

As you begin to implement these changes, you may experience a strange psychological phenomenon. In robotics, the "Uncanny Valley" refers to a robot that looks *almost* human but is slightly off, causing unease. In self-improvement, this refers to the period where your new behaviors feel "mechanical," "forced," or "fake" to *you*.

You might feel like you are "wearing a costume" when you put on a blazer instead of a hoodie. You might feel like you are "performing" when you force yourself to hold eye contact for that extra second. You might feel like an imposter when you walk into a high-end lounge and act like you own it.

This is not a sign that you are failing. It is a sign that you are growing.

This feeling is called **Cognitive Dissonance**. Your "Old Self" (the one who slouched, dressed poorly, and hesitated) is fighting for survival. It is trying to drag you back to the "comfort zone" of mediocrity.

The High-Value Secret: Authenticity is not a fixed point in the past; it is a trajectory toward the future.

- If you are acting like a man of higher value than you currently feel, you are not being "fake." You are **practicing** the man you are becoming.

- A pilot in a flight simulator is not "faking" flying; he is training his nervous system so that when the real flight happens, he is ready.

- You are currently in the simulator. Eventually, the "performance" becomes the "personality." The retracted shoulders will no longer feel like an effort; they will feel like home. The eye contact will no longer feel aggressive; it will feel natural.

Do not retreat when you hit the Uncanny Valley. Push through it. The discomfort is merely the sensation of your old identity dying and your new one being born.

The Law of Abundance vs. The Law of Scarcity

The most significant shift this foundation provides is not physical; it is mental. It is the move from a **Scarcity Mindset** to an **Abundance Mindset.** This is the "Master Key" of attraction.

The Scarcity Mindset (The "Beggar")

A man in scarcity "needs" the attention of a woman to feel validated. He approaches her because he is "hungry."

- **The Signal:** This hunger is visible in his micro-expressions. It is in the way he leans in too close. It is in the way he laughs too hard at her jokes. It is in the desperation of his eyes.

- **The Reaction:** Women are biologically wired to detect neediness. Neediness signals a lack of options. If you *need* her, it implies that other women do not want you. This triggers her "Mate Choice Copying" mechanism in reverse: *"If no one else wants him, why should I?"*

The Abundance Mindset (The "King")

A man in abundance "wants" to share his high-value reality with others, but he does not *need* them to validate it. He approaches because he is curious, not because he is starving.

- **The Signal:** He projects a "light" energy. He is willing to walk away (The Exit Strategy). He is willing to challenge her (The Social Check). His value is already secured by his style, his posture, and his social circle.

- **The Reaction:** Paradoxically, the moment you stop "needing" her attention is the moment you become the most attractive recipient of it. She feels no pressure from you. She senses that you are a challenge—a man who has options.

Book 1 has given you the tools to **manufacture abundance.** Even if you don't have a phone full of dates yet, you can have the *posture* of a man who does. You can have the *style* of a man who does. You can have the *social proof* of a man who does.

When you know you look good, stand strong, and are liked by the room, your "need" for her approval vanishes. You become **Outcome Independent**. Whether she says "Yes" or "No," your night is still great. That level of emotional stability is the ultimate aphrodisiac.

The Concept of "The Filter"

Another crucial paradigm shift you must embrace as we conclude this book is the idea of **The Filter.**

Most men view rejection as a judgment of their worth. They think, *"She didn't like me; therefore, I am not good enough."*

The High-Value Man views his entire presentation—his style, his gaze, his opener—as a **Filter.**

- You are projecting a specific frequency of "High Value."
- If a woman is insecure, intimidated by confidence, or looking for a pushover to manipulate, she will be *repelled* by your signal. **This is a good thing.** Your confidence filtered out a bad match.
- If a woman is confident, high-status, and looking for an equal, she will be *attracted* to your signal.

By building this foundation, you have stopped trying to "please everyone." You have started "qualifying the right ones." You are no longer a beggar with a cup; you are a gatekeeper with a velvet rope. You decide who gets access to your energy.

The Transition: From "Visual Signal" to "Conversational Leader"

You have built a magnificent facade. The lights are on, the music is playing, and the door is open. She has noticed you. She has smiled. You have walked over and initiated the first few words.

But a foundation is not a house.

A high-value first impression gets you into the "Inquiry" phase, but it does not guarantee a relationship, a date, or even a ten-minute conversation. You have earned her **Attention**, but you have not yet earned her **Interest** or her **Investment**.

The "Grab Her Attention" phase is about **biology**. The next phase is about **psychology**.

Now that you have her attention, you must know how to **hold it**. You must move from being a "Visual Signal" to being a "Conversational Leader." Many men fail here. They look like James Bond, but the moment they open their mouths, they speak like a nervous accountant. They run out of things to say. They ask boring interview questions ("So, what do you do?"). They let the tension die.

This is where the journey continues.

The Roadmap Ahead: Book 2

As we close the cover on Book 1, take a moment to reflect on your "Social Engine." Is it tuned? Are the signals clear? If you still feel a "clunkiness" in your style or a "slouch" in your spine, return to those chapters. This foundation must be solid before you attempt the advanced conversational maneuvers in the books to follow.

In **Book 2: Break the Ice**, we will leave the realm of the silent and enter the realm of the verbal. We will dive deep into the first sixty seconds of interaction—the most critical minute of the "game."

Here is a glimpse of what lies on the other side of the threshold:

- **The Hook:** How to turn a simple opener into a compelling conversation loop that makes her want to chase *you*.

- **Cold Reading:** The art of "guessing" her personality rather than asking boring questions. This technique (used by psychics and mentalists) creates instant intimacy and intrigue.

- **Playful Tension:** How to use humor, teasing, and the "push-pull" dynamic to ensure the interaction doesn't stall in "The Friend Zone." We will teach you how to be "Safe" enough to trust, but "Dangerous" enough to desire.

- **Active Listening:** The high-status way to make her feel like the only person in the room, triggering a dopamine loop in her brain that she associates with you.

- **Storytelling:** How to answer questions in a way that demonstrates value without bragging.

The Challenge: The Man in the Arena

There is a famous speech by Theodore Roosevelt known as "The Man in the Arena." It is the guiding philosophy of this book series.

> *"It is not the critic who counts; not the man who points out how the strong man stumbles, or where the doer of deeds could have done them better. The credit belongs to the man who is actually in the arena, whose face is marred by dust and sweat and blood; who strives valiantly..."*

By reading this book and implementing these steps, you are entering the arena. You are stepping out of the shadows of the internet, out of the safety of your gaming chair, and out of the comfort of your excuses. You are no longer a critic sitting in the stands, wondering why "luck" hasn't brought you the women you desire.

You are the man in the center of the room. You are taking responsibility for your broadcast, your presence, and your actions. You are accepting the risk of rejection in exchange for the glory of connection.

This path is not easy. It requires discipline to go to the gym when you are tired. It requires effort to iron your shirt when you are in a rush. It requires courage to look a stranger in the eye when your heart is racing.

But the reward is a life lived on your own terms. The reward is looking in the mirror and respecting the man staring back at you. The reward is realizing that you are not at the mercy of the world, but a creator of your own destiny.

You have fixed your foundation. You have poured the concrete. You have let it set. Now, pick up your tools. Let's build the house.

CHAPTER 8

REFLECTION QUESTIONS

The Difference Between Knowledge and Wisdom

We have arrived at the end of Book 1. You have consumed thousands of words on evolutionary psychology, fashion, biomechanics, neuroscience, and social dynamics. You have intellectually agreed with the concepts of the "High-Value Gaze," the "3-Second Rule," and the "Host Mentality."

But there is a vast, dangerous canyon between **Intellectual Assent** and **Behavioral Competence**.

Most men read self-improvement books as a form of "mental masturbation." Reading about approaching women releases a small hit of dopamine that tricks the brain into feeling like it has *actually* approached a woman. It is the illusion of progress. You can read every book on swimming ever written, understand the fluid dynamics of water, and memorize the mechanics of the butterfly stroke, but if you jump into the deep end without practice, you will still drown.

Chapter 8 is not about new information. It is about **Integration**. It is about taking the external data from the previous seven chapters and hard-coding it into your internal operating system.

This chapter is designed as a **Workshop**. It requires you to be honest, brutal, and analytical about your current state. We are going to perform a "Forensic Audit" of your romantic and social life. We will break down every pillar we have discussed, diagnose your current level of competence, and prescribe specific "Micro-Drills" to bridge the gap.

If you skip this chapter, you are merely a tourist in the world of high value. If you do the work, you become a resident.

Part 1: The Biological & Mindset Audit (Reviewing Chapter 1)

Everything begins with the "Internal Frame." If you are still harboring resentment toward the way attraction works, or if you are still operating under the "Just Be Yourself" fallacy, your foundation is cracked.

The Diagnostic Questions:

1. **The "Shallow" Trap:**
    - *Question:* When you see a woman reject a man because he is poorly dressed or awkward, what is your immediate emotional reaction? Do you think, *"She's shallow/mean,"* or do you think, *"Her biology is filtering for high-status signals"*?
    - *The High-Value Reality:* If you still feel resentment, you are in a "Victim Mindset." You are arguing with gravity. A high-value man accepts the rules of the game so he can win it.

2. **The "Creep" Fear:**
    - *Question:* On a scale of 1-10, how terrified are you of being perceived as "creepy"?
    - *Analysis:* A score of 7 or higher means you are **Self-Censoring**. You are prioritizing *her* potential mild discomfort over *your* potential happiness. "Creepiness" is not about attraction; it is about a lack of calibration. If

you follow the rules of Book 1 (Space, Social Proof, calibrated eye contact), it is mathematically impossible to be a creep.

3. **The Selection Mindset:**
   - *Question:* When you walk into a room, are you thinking, *"I hope I see someone I like,"* or *"I hope someone here likes me"*?
   - *The Shift:* This is the difference between the Buyer and the Seller. The Seller is anxious; the Buyer is relaxed. You must audit your thoughts every time you cross a threshold.

The Prescription:

For the next 7 days, keep a "Thought Log." Every time you feel social anxiety, write down the specific thought associated with it. You will likely find 90% of them are "Mind Reading" errors (e.g., "Everyone is looking at me," "She thinks I'm ugly"). Challenge these thoughts with the data from Chapter 1.

Part 2: The Visual Audit (Reviewing Chapter 2)

Your "Packaging" is the gatekeeper. You cannot demonstrate your personality if your appearance gets you rejected in the first 0.1 seconds.

The Closet Purge Protocol:

Go to your closet right now. We are going to perform the "Binary Test" on every item you own.

1. The Fit Test:

Put on your favorite shirt and look in the mirror.

- Is there excess fabric ballooning around the waist? (The "Muffin Top" effect).
- Is the shoulder seam sliding down your bicep?
- *Verdict:* If the answer is yes, it goes in the "Tailor" pile or the "Trash" pile. No exceptions. A $50 shirt that fits perfectly looks better than a $500 shirt that fits poorly.

2. The Shoe Audit:

Look at the shoes you wear when you go out.

- Are they running shoes? (Unless you are running, the answer should be no).
- Are they square-toed dress shoes? (These belong in 2004).
- Are they scuffed, dirty, or worn down at the heel?
- *Verdict*: Women look at shoes second (after the face). Your shoes tell her if you take care of details. If your shoes are sloppy, she assumes your life is sloppy. Buy one pair of high-quality leather boots (Chelsea or Chukka) or clean white minimalist sneakers.

3. The Grooming Check:

- *The Beard*: Is it shaped, or is it neck-beard territory? A "scruffy" look requires *more* maintenance than a clean-shaven look to ensure it looks intentional, not lazy.
- *The Nails*: Look at your hands. Are they clean? If you are going to touch a woman (on the small of the back, holding her hand), your hands must be pristine.

The Micro-Drill:

"The Uniform Strategy." Do not rely on inspiration. Create one "Go-To Outfit" that is bulletproof. Dark jeans (tailored), a charcoal t-shirt or crisp button-down (tailored), and your best boots. Wear this outfit 3 times this week in different social settings. Notice how your posture changes when you know you look optimal.

Part 3: The Structural Audit (Reviewing Chapter 3)

You can be wearing a $5,000 suit, but if you are slumped over like a question mark, you signal "Low Status" and "Low Energy."

The Mirror Test:

Stand in front of a full-length mirror naturally. Close your eyes, shake your body out, and settle into your "default" stance. Open your eyes.

1. **The Ear-Shoulder Line:**
   - Is your earlobe directly above the center of your shoulder? Or is your head jutting forward (Tech Neck)?
   - *Correction*: Imagine a string pulling the crown of your head toward the ceiling. Tuck your chin slightly.

2. **The Hand Position:**
    - o Where are your hands? Are the backs of your hands facing forward (Internal Rotation/Gorilla posture)? Or are your thumbs facing forward (Neutral/Open posture)?
    - o *Correction:* Squeeze your shoulder blades together, then release them halfway. This opens the chest and rotates the arms externally.
3. **The Pelvic Tilt:**
    - o Is your lower back arched excessively (Anterior Pelvic Tilt)? This makes your gut stick out and signals weakness.
    - o *Correction:* Engage your glutes slightly and pull your belly button toward your spine (about 20% effort).

The "Vulnerability" Factor:

Ask yourself: Why do I slouch?

Psychologically, slouching is a defensive maneuver. It protects the vital organs (heart, throat, solar plexus). Standing up straight exposes these targets. It requires Courage. Are you brave enough to take up space?

The Micro-Drill:

"The Doorway Trigger." For the next week, every time you walk through a doorway, you must physically reset your posture. Shoulders back, head up, chest open. Use the environment as your reminder. If you walk through 20 doorways a day, that is 20 reps of high-status posture.

Part 4: The Energetic Audit (Reviewing Chapter 4)

This is the hardest metric to quantify, but the most felt. It is the "Vibe."

The Anxiety Leakage Check:

Think back to your last social interaction. What were your hands doing?

- Were you tapping your foot?
- Were you peeling the label off your beer bottle?
- Were you checking your phone every 3 minutes?
- *Diagnosis:* These are "Pacifying Behaviors." They are biological attempts to discharge excess cortisol. They scream to the room:

"I am uncomfortable here."

The Eye Contact Challenge:

Be honest. When you walk down the street and see an attractive woman walking toward you:

1. Do you look down at your phone?

2. Do you look away the moment she looks at you?

3. Do you hold her gaze until she passes?

If you answered 1 or 2, you are signaling **Submission**. You are telling her, before you even speak, that you do not believe you are in her league.

The "Heavy Gaze" Visualization:

Most men have a "grasping" gaze. Their eyes dart around looking for validation. You need to develop a "giving" gaze. Imagine your eyes are physical hands. When you look at someone, you are not "taking" a look; you are "resting" your gaze on them. It has weight. It is calm.

The Micro-Drill:

"The Sidewalk 5." Next time you are walking in a public place, you must make eye contact with 5 strangers. You do not need to smile (though you can). You simply need to lock eyes and wait for them to break contact first. Do not be aggressive; be calm. Just see them. Prove to your amygdala that you will not die if you hold a gaze.

Part 5: The Social Audit (Reviewing Chapter 5)

You are the average of the five people you spend the most time with—and in a bar, you are judged by the three people standing next to you.

The Wingman Review:

Look at the friends you go out with.

- **The Saboteur:** Does he get jealous when you talk to women?

- **The Anchor:** Is he poorly dressed, loud, or obnoxious?

- **The Wallflower:** Does he stand in the corner looking terrified, forcing you to babysit him?

- *Hard Truth:* You cannot project high value if you are surrounded by low value. You do not need to "dump" your friends, but you may need to curate who you go "out" with.

The "Host" vs. "Guest" Audit:

When you enter a venue, what is your default behavior?

- *Guest Mode:* Find a corner, protect your drink, watch the room, wait for something to happen.
- *Host Mode:* Greet the bouncer, tip the bartender immediately, high-five a random group, turn your body toward the room.

The Micro-Drill:

"The Mayor Campaign." Go to a coffee shop you frequent. Your goal is to learn the names of two employees. Not just "Hey," but "I'm [Name], by the way. I'm in here all the time, I figured I should actually introduce myself." Next time you walk in, they will say "Hey [Name]!" This is instant, verifiable social proof for anyone watching.

Part 6: The Action Audit (Reviewing Chapter 6)

This is the final barrier. The "Threshold of Action."

The Hesitation Log:

Think of the last time you wanted to approach a woman but didn't. What was the exact excuse your brain gave you?

- "She looks busy."
- "I don't want to interrupt."
- "I'll do it after I get a drink."
- "She's out of my league."

Recognize that **Logic is a liar.** Your brain invents the logic *after* the fear has already triggered. You are not being "respectful"; you are being "fearful."

The "3-Second" Analysis:

Do you honestly adhere to the 3-second rule? Or do you hover?

Hovering is the number one cause of "creepy" vibes. When you hover, you are watching her without her consent. When you approach, you are engaging her. Engagement is respectable; surveillance is not.

The Rejection Reframing:

How many times have you been rejected in the last month?

- *0 times:* This is a failure. It means you haven't tried.
- *1-5 times:* Good. You are in the arena.
- *10+ times:* Excellent. You are gathering data.

The Micro-Drill:

"The Low-Stakes Opener." You need to break the seal. Go to a grocery store. Ask an old lady which pasta sauce she recommends. Ask a guy in line if he's tried the new energy drink. Do not flirt. Just initiate. Train your brain that "Talking to Strangers = Safe."

Part 7: The "Graduation" Challenge

You cannot proceed to Book 2: *Break the Ice* until you have passed the Book 1 Field Test. This is a cumulative exam. It combines Style, Posture, Presence, Social Proof, and Action.

The Mission:

You are going to go to a social venue (bar, lounge, gallery opening, or even a busy cafe) alone or with one trusted wingman. You will stay for 90 minutes.

The Checklist:

1. **Preparation (The Armor):**
   - Wear your "Uniform" (from Part 2). Grooming must be 10/10.
   - Do a 2-minute "Power Pose" in the bathroom before entering to spike testosterone.

2. **The Entrance (The Broadcast):**
   - Walk in. Pause for 2 seconds at the door. Scan the room slowly (High-Value Gaze).
   - Walk to the bar. Do not look at your phone.

3. **Social Proof (The Setup):**
   - Interact with the staff. Learn the bartender's name.
   - Make a "Pawn Move" comment to a guy or a mixed group near you. *"Is the whiskey sour here actually sour, or is it just sugar water?"*

4. **The High-Value Audit (The Check):**
    - Set a timer for 30 minutes. During this time, you are **The Statue.** You cannot fidget. You cannot check your phone. You must sip your drink slowly. You must lean back. Observe the room. Let the tension of doing "nothing" wash over you.

5. **The Initiation (The Climax):**
    - Identify a woman you find attractive.
    - Apply the **3-Second Rule.** Count 3, 2, 1, GO.
    - Walk over with the "Decisive Walk" (Chapter 6).
    - Deliver a Situation-Opinion-Question opener. *"I have to get a second opinion. Is this DJ a genius, or is he just pressing play on a Spotify playlist?"*
    - **The Goal:** The goal is *not* to get her number. The goal is to deliver the line, look her in the eye, and **stay in the pocket** for at least 60 seconds.

Pass/Fail Criteria:

- If you approach and she rejects you? **PASS.** (You took action).
- If you approach and it goes well? **PASS.**
- If you stand there for 90 minutes, look cool, but never approach? **FAIL.** (You are just a well-dressed statue).

Part 8: The Psychological "Valley of Death"

As you prepare to move to Book 2, I need to warn you about a specific psychological trap.

You are going to have nights where you do everything right—you look great, you feel great, you approach with confidence—and you still get blown out. You will encounter women who are rude. You will encounter women who simply don't "see" you.

In those moments, your brain will scream: *"This doesn't work! I should go back to being the Nice Guy/The Invisible Man. It was safer there."*

This is the **Valley of Death.** It is the place where 90% of men quit.

They quit because they crave **linear progress.** They want $Input = Output$. They think *Nice Shoes + Good Posture = Date.*

Human dynamics are **non-linear**. You are dealing with another human being who has her own trauma, her own bad days, her own preferences, and her own amygdala.

The Stoic Anchor:

You must decouple your Self-Worth from the Outcome.

- **Book 1 is about YOU.** It is about things you control 100%. You control your shirt. You control your spine. You control your feet moving across the floor.

- **Book 2 is about US.** It is about the interaction. You can influence it, but you cannot control it.

If you base your confidence on whether she smiles back, you are her slave. If you base your confidence on the fact that you had the guts to approach her, you are her equal.

Part 9: Journaling Prompts for Integration

Before you close this book, take 20 minutes to write out the answers to these three deep-dive questions. This utilizes "The Generation Effect"—information is better remembered if it is generated from your own mind rather than simply read.

Prompt 1: The "Why"

- "Why am I doing this? Is it to get revenge on an ex? Is it to prove I'm 'enough'? Or is it because I genuinely want to connect with high-quality women and share my life?"

- (Note: Anger and validation are powerful fuels, but they burn dirty. Connection and abundance burn clean.)

Prompt 2: The "Old Story"

- "What is the story I have told myself about my social value for the last 5 years? (e.g., 'I'm the funny fat friend,' 'I'm the quiet smart guy'). What evidence do I have that this story is no longer true?"

Prompt 3: The "Future Self"

- "Describe the man I want to be in one year. How does he stand? How does he handle a rude comment? How does he wake up in the morning? What is he tolerating today that he will not tolerate then?"

Conclusion: The End of the Beginning

Congratulations. You have completed the foundation.

You are no longer "unconscious" of the signals you are sending. You know that when you slouch, you are shouting "victim." You know that when you fidget, you are shouting "anxiety." You know that when you hesitate, you are shouting "fear."

You have taken control of the broadcast.

But the broadcast is just the signal. Now, we must focus on the **Transmission.**

In **Book 2: Break the Ice**, we are going to get tactical. We are going to zoom in on the verbal chess match of the first interaction.

- We will learn how to **"Cold Read"** so you never have to ask boring interview questions again.

- We will learn the art of **"Push-Pull"** to create emotional spikes that keep her addicted to the conversation.

- We will learn how to handle **"Tests"**—those sharp, cutting remarks women make to see if you will crumble.

- We will learn how to **"Bridge"** from a casual chat to a meaningful connection.

You have the Look. You have the Vibe. You have the Guts.

Now, you need the Words.

Take a breath. Stand up straight. Reset your shoulders.

Turn the page. The real game begins now.

BOOK TWO
SPARK CHEMISTRY

CHAPTER 1

INTRODUCTION: MOVING BEYOND LOGIC TO EMOTION

The Invisible Transition

You have mastered the "Silent Dialogue." You have optimized your aesthetic, corrected your posture, and successfully navigated the 3-second rule to initiate an interaction. In Book 1, we built the hardware. We ensured the machine was sleek, powerful, and attractive to the eye. But now, as you stand in front of her and the first few seconds of silence begin to tick away, you are entering a different domain.

Welcome to **Book 2: Spark Chemistry**.

If Book 1 was about **Attention**, Book 2 is about **Retention and Resonance**. This is where most men—even the well-dressed and high-status ones—fail. They understand how to "get her to look," but they have no idea how to "get her to feel."

The most common mistake men make at this stage is staying in the realm of **Logic**. They treat a conversation like a job interview or a data exchange. They ask about her career, her hometown, and her commute. They seek facts, thinking that facts lead to familiarity, and familiarity leads to attraction.

They are wrong.

Attraction is not a logical conclusion; it is a chemical event. It is an emotional "spike." To spark chemistry, you must move beyond the "What" of her life and dive into the "Why" and the "How." You must stop talking to her brain and start talking to her nervous system. This chapter is the bridge between the man who is *seen* and the man who is *felt*.

The Neurobiology of Chemistry

Before we discuss tactics, we must understand the "Chemistry" we are trying to spark. When people say, "We had great chemistry," they aren't talking about a shared interest in 19th-century literature. They are describing a synchronized release of specific neurotransmitters.

1. The Dopamine Spike (The "Hook")

Dopamine is the neurotransmitter of anticipation and novelty. When you use humor, "Cold Reading," or "Push-Pull" (which we will cover in later chapters), you are triggering dopamine. You are making the interaction unpredictable. If she knows exactly what you are going to say next, her dopamine levels flatline. Chemistry requires the "Element of Surprise."

2. The Norepinephrine Rush (The "Tension")

This is the chemical cousin of adrenaline. It causes the racing heart, the sweaty palms, and the "butterflies." It is triggered by social risk, lingering eye contact, and playful challenge. Without norepinephrine, a conversation is just "nice." With it, it becomes "electric."

3. The Oxytocin Bond (The "Comfort")

Once the spikes of dopamine and norepinephrine have done their job, oxytocin—the "cuddle hormone"—begins to flow. This is triggered by vulnerability, active listening, and shared stories. It transforms "Excitement" into "Trust."

The Chemistry Equation:

$$\text{Chemistry} = (\text{Dopamine} \times \text{Norepinephrine}) + \text{Oxytocin}$$

If you have only excitement (Dopamine/Norepinephrine), you are a "fling" or a "player." If you have only trust (Oxytocin), you are the "best friend." To be the **High-Value Man**, you must master the art of balancing both.

The Death of the "Interview Mode"

The primary enemy of chemistry is **Logical Rapport.** Most men are terrified of silence, so they fill it with "Interview Questions":

- *"What do you do for work?"*

- *"Where are you from?"*

- *"How long have you lived here?"*

While these questions are socially "safe," they are emotionally "dead." They require her to use her prefrontal cortex—the logical, analytical part of the brain. When she is in "Logic Mode," she is not in "Attraction Mode." She is processing data, not feeling a connection.

The High-Value Shift: We do not ask for facts; we ask for Motivations.

Instead of "What do you do?", you ask, "What's the most exciting thing you've worked on this week?" Instead of "Where are you from?", you ask, "What's the one thing from your hometown that you actually miss?"

By shifting the question slightly, you force her to search her memory for a **Feeling** rather than a **Fact**. When she finds that feeling, she associates the warmth of that memory with *you.*

The "Safe vs. Dangerous" Paradox

To spark chemistry, a man must embody a specific paradox: he must be **Safe** enough to trust, but **Dangerous** enough to desire.

- **Too Safe:** If you are too agreeable, too polite, and never disagree or challenge her, you are "Safe." You are predictable. Predictability is the death of Dopamine. She feels no "spike" with you because there is no risk.

- **Too Dangerous:** If you are aggressive, disrespectful, or overly sexual too quickly, you trigger her "Threat Assessment." Her amygdala fires, and she looks for an exit.

The Sweet Spot: The High-Value Man is a "Controlled Flame." He is warm and inviting (Safe), but he has an edge (Dangerous). He challenges her opinions, he uses "mischievous" humor, and he isn't afraid to let a silence linger just a second too long to see if she can handle the tension.

The Power of Emotional Leading

In Book 1, we talked about "Social Leading"—taking her to a different part of the room or introducing her to people. In Book 2, we focus on **Emotional Leading**.

Women are generally more attuned to the "Emotional Climate" of an interaction. If you are nervous, she will feel nervous. If you are bored, she will feel bored. However, if you are **Amused**, she will eventually become amused.

The "Amused Mastery" Mindset:

You must enter the interaction with the assumption that this is going to be fun. You are not "seeking" a result; you are "enjoying" a process. When you operate from a place of internal amusement, you become a "gravity well" for her emotions. She will naturally "match" your energy.

If you want her to feel chemistry, *you* must feel the chemistry first. You must be present enough to enjoy the way the light hits her eyes or the clever way she phrased a sentence. Your enjoyment is the "permission" she needs to enjoy herself.

The Concept of "The Bubble"

When chemistry is sparked, the rest of the world begins to fade away. This is called "The Bubble."

In the beginning of an approach, you are two strangers in a crowded room. There is noise, there are people walking by, and there is social pressure. Your goal in these first few minutes is to use your **Presence** and **Tonality** (which we will cover in Chapter 5) to create a private world for the two of you.

How to build The Bubble:

1. **Lower the Volume:** As the conversation deepens, speak slightly quieter. This forces her to lean in, physically closing the gap.

2. **Narrow the Focus:** Stop looking around the room. Give her 100% of your "presence" (not necessarily 100% eye contact, but 100% of your attention).

3. **Use "We" Language:** Start using "We" and "Us" as if you are already a team. *"We should probably get out of the way before we get trampled,"* or *"I feel like we are the only two people here who aren't taking this way too seriously."*

"The Bubble" is where the oxytocin starts to flow. It signals that this interaction is unique and separate from the "background noise" of the night.

Emotional Spiking: The Heartbeat of Chemistry

A conversation without "spikes" is a flatline. A flatline means death.

To spark chemistry, you must move the conversation through different "altitudes" of emotion. You shouldn't be "Funny Guy" for 20 minutes straight, nor should you be "Serious Philosopher" for 20 minutes. You must move between them.

The Four Altitudes of Conversation:

1. **Playful/Banter (Dopamine):** Teasing, jokes, challenges.

2. **Observational (Intelligence):** Commenting on the environment, "Cold Reading" her vibe.

3. **Deep/Vulnerable (Oxytocin):** Sharing a real motivation, a struggle, or a passion.

4. **Sexual/Tension (Norepinephrine):** Lingering eye contact, physical proximity, lowered voice.

The "Spark" happens in the **Transitions**. When you move from a joke (Altitude 1) to a sincere observation (Altitude 3) in a single sentence, it creates an "Emotional Whiplash" that is incredibly engaging. It shows you have "Range."

> "A man with range is a man with mystery. If she can't put you in a box, she has to keep paying attention to find out who you really are."

Authenticity vs. Performance

As we move through Book 2, you will learn many "techniques." But there is a vital distinction you must maintain: **Technique is a tool; Authenticity is the hand that holds it.**

If you use a "Cold Read" or a "Push-Pull" line just because you read it in a book, it will feel "thin." She will sense the "performance," and it will trigger her "manipulation alarm."

To avoid this, every technique must be grounded in **Reality**.

- Don't "tease" her about something you don't actually find funny.
- Don't "share a story" that isn't true.
- Don't "lead" to a place you don't actually want to go.

The High-Value Man uses techniques to **reveal** his personality, not to **hide** his lack of one. The techniques are the "magnifying glass" that allows her to see your best traits more clearly.

The "Why" Behind the "Chemistry"

Why are we doing this? Is it just to "get the girl"?

No. The ability to spark chemistry is the ability to **Impact Others.** When you learn to move beyond logic to emotion, you become more effective in every area of your life. You become a better leader, a better friend, and a better negotiator. You are learning the language of the human heart.

Most people live lives of "quiet desperation," having surface-level conversations that mean nothing. When you walk into a woman's life and, within ten minutes, make her feel excitement, tension, and trust, you are giving her a **gift**. You are giving her a "High-Value Experience."

Chemistry is the antidote to the mundane. It is the proof that two people can collide in a random universe and create something that wasn't there before.

Preparation for the Journey

In the following chapters, we will break down the mechanics of this emotional alchemy.

- **In Chapter 2**, we will learn how to use **Observation and Humor** to break the ice without looking like a clown.

- **In Chapter 3**, we will master **Active Listening**, showing you how to hear what she *isn't* saying.

- **In Chapter 4**, we will craft your **Character Stories**, the verbal "hooks" that reveal your value.

- **In Chapter 5**, we will explore the "Instrument of Attraction": your **Voice**.

- **In Chapter 6**, we will master the advanced art of **Push and Pull**, the ultimate tool for creating sexual tension.

You have the foundation. You are standing in the arena. She is looking at you, waiting to see if you are just another "nice guy" or if you are the man who is going to change the temperature of her night.

It's time to move beyond the logical and enter the emotional. Let's begin.

CHAPTER 2

BREAK THE ICE WITH OBSERVATION AND HUMOR

The Anatomy of the "Cold Opening"

In Book 1, we covered the physical act of the approach: the 3-second rule, the walk, and the presence. You are now standing in her space. The "broadcast" of your style and posture has cleared the initial path of resistance. But now, the silence must be broken.

Most men fail here because they rely on a **"Canned Opener"**—a pre-scripted line they found on an internet forum. The problem with canned openers is that they are "detached" from reality. A woman can feel when you've said the same thing to five other people that night. It lacks the "Electric Now."

To spark chemistry, your first words must prove that you are **present**. You must show her that you are not just a man looking for *any* woman, but a man who has noticed *this* specific woman. This is the difference between a "Standard Approach" and a "High-Value Interaction." This chapter focuses on the twin engines of social ignition: **Observation** and **Humor**.

The Power of the Observation (The "Cold Read")

The most effective way to break the ice is not to ask a question, but to make a **statement**. Questions require the other person to do cognitive work; statements allow them to simply react. Specifically, we use **Observational Statements**—often called "Cold Reads."

A Cold Read is an educated guess about her personality, her mood, or her history based on a physical or behavioral detail.

Why Observations Beat Questions

When you ask, *"What do you do for a living?"*, you are a stranger seeking data. This triggers the "Interview Mode," which is the death of attraction. When you say, *"You have the energy of someone who is either a high-powered attorney or a professional troublemaker,"*, you are an observer offering an insight.

Even if your observation is wrong, it doesn't matter. If you guess she's a lawyer and she's actually a nurse, she will laugh and say, *"No! Why did you think that?"* The conversation is now off to the races. You are talking about **vibes** and **perceptions** rather than dry facts.

The Three Levels of Observation

1. **Level 1: The External (The "Wrapper")**

   o *Focus:* Her clothing, jewelry, or choice of drink.

   o *Strategy:* Look for the "Outlier"—the one thing she chose specifically to express herself.

   o *Example:* "That ring looks like it has a story. It's either a family heirloom or you stole it from a museum in Paris. I'm hoping for the museum story."

2. **Level 2: The Behavioral (The "Movement")**

   o *Focus:* How she is interacting with the room or her friends.

   o *Strategy:* Note the "Vibe" she is projecting.

   o *Example:* "I noticed you're the only person in this room who is actually listening to the music while everyone else is shouting. You're either a musician or you're currently plotting your escape."

3. **Level 3: The Internal (The "Vibe")**
    - *Focus*: Her energy or "aura."
    - *Strategy*: Make a "Polarizing" guess about her personality.
    - *Example*: "You look like the kind of person who is incredibly responsible at work but secretly the most impulsive person in your friend group once you've had exactly one cocktail."

The Mechanics of High-Value Humor

Humor is the "Social Lubricant" that lowers her defenses. However, "High-Value Humor" is not about being a clown. It is not about "performing" for her. It is about **Amused Mastery.**

1. The "Self-Amusement" Principle

The secret to being funny is not "telling jokes." It is being **amused by the situation.** If you say something and *you* think it's funny, your brain releases dopamine. Because of mirror neurons, she will feel that dopamine.

- **Low-Value:** Telling a joke and looking at her to see if she laughs (Seeking Validation).
- **High-Value:** Making a dry observation and smiling to yourself because you find it hilarious (Outcome Independence).

2. The Art of the "Cocky-Funny" Tease

This is a specific type of humor that combines confidence with playfulness. It signals that you are not intimidated by her beauty.

- *The Misinterpretation:* Take something she does and playfully claim she is hitting on you.
- *Example:* She accidentally brushes your arm. You: "Whoa, slow down. You have to at least buy me a drink before you start getting physical. I'm a respectable man."

3. Situational Irony

High-value humor often comes from pointing out the absurdity of the environment.

- *Example*: "I love how everyone in this bar is pretending they aren't checking their reflections in the TV screens every five seconds. We're all so vain, it's refreshing."

Deep-Dive: The "Edge" of Humor

To spark chemistry, your humor must have "Edge." If your humor is too "nice," it's just friendly. If it's too "sharp," it's mean. The "Edge" is found in the **High-Value Tease.**

A tease targets something she is clearly proud of or something superficial. You never tease her about something she might be genuinely insecure about (like her weight or a physical flaw).

- **The "Nerd" Tease:** "Wait, you actually like [Niche Topic]? I was starting to think you were cool. Now I see I'm talking to a total geek. This is going to be a long night."
- **The "Troublemaker" Tease:** "You have that 'good girl' look, but I can see the mischief in your eyes. I bet you were the kid who started the food fights in school."

The Golden Rule of Teasing: Always deliver a tease with a **"Selective Smirk."** Your body language must signal: *"I'm playing."* If you are stone-faced, she will think you're an asshole. If you're grinning like an idiot, the tease loses its power.

The "False Time Constraint" (FTC)

When you break the ice, her biggest fear is that you will never leave. She worries that if she talks to you, she's "stuck" for the rest of the night. A High-Value Man removes this pressure by using a **False Time Constraint**. This is a verbal signal that you are leaving soon.

- *"I can only stay for a minute because my friends are at the bar, but I had to ask..."*
- *"I'm actually just heading out, but I noticed..."*

The Psychology: By signaling that your time is limited, you become more valuable (Scarcity). She relaxes because the "threat" of a boring, hour-long conversation is gone. This allows her to fully engage in the "now."

Once the ice is broken and she is laughing or reacting to your observation, you must **bridge** to a deeper flow. You cannot stay in "Joke Mode" forever. The bridge is built by **Validating and Expanding.**

If you made a cold read about her being a "professional troublemaker" and she laughs and says, *"Actually, I'm a kindergarten teacher,"* you don't just say, *"Oh, cool."*

You Expand: *"A kindergarten teacher? So I was right! You spend all day managing chaos. That requires a specific kind of 'General' mindset. Do you run your personal life like a classroom too, or is your house a disaster zone to compensate?"*

Now you are talking about her **personality**, her **lifestyle**, and her **inner world**. You have successfully moved from a stranger with a line to a man having a real, high-value conversation.

Advanced Observational Skills: Cold Reading Patterns

To make your observations hit with surgical precision, you should look for specific **archetypes**. Most people fall into certain social "scripts." Identifying these scripts allows you to "read her mind."

Archetype A: The Over-Achiever

- **Visual Cues:** Impeccable grooming, sharp clothing, slightly rigid posture, expensive watch or subtle designer logos.
- **The Observation:** "You look like the kind of person who has her entire life planned out on a color-coded spreadsheet, but you secretly wish someone would just come along and ruin your schedule for a night."

Archetype B: The Free Spirit

- **Visual Cues:** Bohemian jewelry, relaxed posture, expressive hand gestures, perhaps a unique tattoo or colorful hair.
- **The Observation:** "You have the energy of someone who would quit her job tomorrow if someone offered you a one-way ticket to a country you've never heard of. You're probably the person in your group who everyone goes to when they want to do something impulsive."

Archetype C: The "Protective" Friend

- **Visual Cues:** Facing the room (scanning for threats), arms crossed, checking the time, protective stance over her friends' bags.
- **The Observation:** "I noticed you're the 'Mom' of the group tonight. You're making sure everyone stays safe and hydrated. Who takes care of you when you're the one trying to have a good time?"

Developing the "Social Spidey-Sense"

Observation is a muscle. Most men walk through life with "tunnel vision," focused only on their own anxiety or their own phone. To build chemistry, you must develop "peripheral awareness."

The "Room Scan" Exercise: When you enter a venue, don't look for a woman to talk to. Instead, look for three "Stories."

1. Look at a couple: Who is the dominant one?
2. Look at a group of guys: Who is the leader?
3. Look at a group of women: Who is the one that wants to leave?

By training your brain to see these dynamics, you gain a massive advantage. When you finally do approach, your observation will be based on social reality, not just a guess. This creates a sense of **Social Intuition** that women find incredibly attractive.

The "Humor Threshold" and Calibrated Playfulness

Humor is a tool of **Calibration**. You must gauge her "Humor Threshold." Some women love sharp, biting banter; others are more sensitive and prefer light, goofy humor.

How to Test the Threshold:

1. **The Light Poke:** Start with a very mild tease. *"I like your outfit, it's very 'I'm ready for a safari in the middle of a lounge.'"*
2. **The Response Check:** Does she laugh? Does she tease back? Or does she look confused/offended?
3. **The Calibration:**
   - If she laughs: Increase the "Edge."

o   If she is quiet: Pivot to "Active Listening" (Chapter 3) to build more comfort first.

High-Value Humor is never a monologue. It is a game of **Verbal Tennis**. If you are doing all the talking and all the joking, you aren't building chemistry; you're doing a stand-up routine. The goal of the icebreaker is to get *her* to play the game.

The "Golden Ratio" of Observation and Humor

A perfect icebreaker follows the **30/70 Rule**:

- **30% Humor:** To signal high status and lack of neediness.
- **70% Observation:** To signal presence, intelligence, and genuine interest.

If you are 100% humor, you are a clown. If you are 100% observation, you are a detective. The "Spark" happens in the friction between the two.

The Psychology of Misinterpretation

One of the most powerful ways to use humor is the "Intentional Misinterpretation." This is where you take a standard, polite comment she makes and interpret it as a sexual or romantic advance.

- **She says:** "I really like your jacket."
- **You say:** "Hey, eyes up here. I'm more than just a piece of clothing. My heart is up here. You're moving a little fast for me."
- **The Result:** This creates **Role Reversal**. In the traditional dating script, the man is the pursuer and the woman is the pursued. By "accusing" her of pursuing you, you break the script. This is highly stimulating for her brain because it is novel and challenging.

The Exercises: Developing Your Observational Muscle

To master this, you must train your brain to see what others miss.

1. The "Three Details" Drill: Next time you are in public (a park, a mall, a gym), pick a stranger. Find three things about them that aren't obvious at first glance.

- *Detail 1*: They are wearing a watch on their right hand (Left-handed? Rebellious?).
- *Detail 2*: They have "frown lines" but a "smiling mouth" (Hard worker who loves life?).
- *Detail 3*: Their shoes are pristine but their jeans are ripped (Prioritizes accessories?).

2. The "Assumption" Challenge: For one day, stop asking questions. Replace every question with a statement.

- Instead of: *"Are you having a good day?"*
- Say: *"You look like you've had a remarkably productive morning and you're finally letting yourself relax."*
- Instead of: *"Where do you go to school?"*
- Say: *"You have the vibe of someone who studies something incredibly creative, like architecture or design."*

Watch how people open up when you stop "interviewing" them and start "perceiving" them.

CHAPTER 3

LISTEN ACTIVELY TO BUILD TRUST

The Silent Superpower

In the previous chapters, we focused on the "Spark"—the initial ignition of interest through appearance, presence, observation, and humor. But if humor is the spark that starts the fire, **Active Listening** is the hearth that keeps it burning safely and sustainably.

There is a common misconception in the world of social dynamics that the most "high-value" man in the room is the one talking the most. We see the trope in movies: the fast-talking charmer who has a witty retort for everything. But in reality, a man who talks incessantly is often perceived as anxious, needy, or self-absorbed. He is "broadcasting" because he is terrified of what might happen in the silence.

The true High-Value Man understands that **Listening is an Act of Leadership.** When you listen deeply, you are doing something that 99%

of people fail to do: you are giving someone your most precious resource—your undivided attention. In a world of digital distractions and "main character syndrome," being truly heard is a rare and intoxicating experience. If you can master the art of active listening, you don't just "build rapport"—you create a psychological sanctuary where a woman feels safe enough to drop her guard and reveal her true self. This is where trust is born, and without trust, chemistry is just a fleeting physical reaction.

The Neurobiology of Being Heard

Before we dive into the "how," we must understand the "why." What happens in a woman's brain when she realizes you are actually listening to her?

1. The Oxytocin Release

When humans engage in deep, empathetic communication, the hypothalamus releases oxytocin, often called the "bonding hormone." Oxytocin lowers cortisol (stress) and increases feelings of safety and attachment. By listening actively, you are literally changing her brain chemistry to make her feel more relaxed and connected to you.

2. Social Validation and the Reward Center

Talking about oneself triggers the same reward centers in the brain as food or money. According to Harvard neuroscientists, "self-disclosure" is inherently rewarding. When you facilitate this through active listening, you become the "provider" of that reward. She associates the pleasure of being understood with your presence.

3. The Vagus Nerve and Co-Regulation

Through a process called "physiological co-regulation," your calm, attentive listening helps regulate her nervous system. If she is telling a story about a stressful day at work, and you maintain a steady, grounded presence, her Vagus nerve (the "brakes" of the nervous system) signals her body to calm down. You become her "anchor" in the social storm.

Level 1 vs. Level 2 Listening: The "Wait-to-Talk" Trap

Most men operate at **Level 1: Internal Listening.** At this level, you aren't actually listening to her; you are listening to your own inner monologue *about* what she is saying. You are thinking:

- *"What should I say next so I look smart?"*

- *"Oh, I have a story that's way cooler than this one."*

- *"Is she into me yet?"*

When you are in Level 1, you miss the subtle cues—the micro-expressions, the shifts in tonality, and the emotional "hooks." You are a "Competitive Listener," waiting for a gap in the conversation so you can take the microphone back.

Level 2: Focused/Active Listening is where the High-Value Man lives. At this level, your "spotlight" is entirely on her. You aren't worried about your next line because you know that the "next line" will be hidden in whatever she says next. You are listening for the **Emotion behind the Fact.**

The Mechanics of Active Listening

Active listening is a full-body sport. It requires the integration of your physical presence, your verbal "back-channeling," and your ability to mirror.

1. Non-Verbal Attunement

Your body must confirm what your ears are doing. If you are looking at your phone or scanning the room while she speaks, you are signaling that she is secondary to the environment.

- **The "Frontal Alignment"**: Aim your torso directly at her. This signals that she has your full defensive and offensive attention.

- **The "Attentive Lean"**: A slight (not aggressive) lean forward shows interest.

- **The "Micro-Nod"**: Small, periodic nods signal that you are following her logic. It's a "green light" for her to keep going.

2. Verbal Back-Channeling

These are the small verbal cues that prove you are "in the pocket" with her.

- "Mm-hmm."
- "Right."
- "That makes sense."
- "I can see that."

These aren't interruptions; they are "fuel" for her narrative. They tell her the line is still open.

3. Tactical Empathy and Reflective Listening

This is the most powerful tool in the listener's arsenal. Instead of just hearing the words, you reflect the *feeling* back to her.

- **The "Mirror":** Repeat back the last 1–3 words of what she said as a question.
  - *She:* "I just felt so overwhelmed by the deadline."
  - *You:* "Overwhelmed by the deadline?"
  - *Effect:* She will automatically elaborate, going deeper into the emotion.
- **The "Label":** Give her emotion a name.
  - *You:* "It sounds like you felt really undervalued in that situation."
  - *Effect:* If you are right, she feels an instant "click" of being understood. If you are wrong, she will correct you, giving you even more accurate data. Both outcomes build trust.

The "Deep Dive" Technique: Finding the Emotional Hook

Every sentence a woman speaks contains two things: a **Fact** and a **Feeling.** * **Fact:** "I moved here from Chicago three years ago."

- **Feeling:** (Hidden) Courage, loneliness, excitement, or a desire for change.

The "Nice Guy" or the "Interview Mode Guy" follows the Fact. He asks, *"How do you like the weather here compared to Chicago?"* The High-Value Man follows the **Feeling.** He asks, *"What was the 'tipping point' that made you decide to leave everything behind and start over here?"*

By targeting the "tipping point," you are asking about her **motivations, values, and emotions.** You are inviting her to tell a story about who she is, not just where she has been.

The "Fixer" Mindset: A Deadly Error

One of the greatest obstacles men face in active listening is the biological urge to "solve the problem." If a woman shares a struggle—a difficult boss, a family issue, or a personal doubt—the male brain typically shifts into "Engineer Mode." You want to provide a 5-step solution to make the problem go away.

Stop.

In the early stages of building chemistry, she isn't looking for a consultant; she is looking for a **Witness.** When you offer a solution too early, you inadvertently signal that her emotions are "problems to be handled" rather than "experiences to be shared." It shuts down the vulnerability loop.

- **Instead of:** "You should just tell your boss that you won't work weekends."
- **Try:** "That sounds incredibly draining. How are you managing to keep your sanity through all that?"

By staying in the emotion, you allow her to process it. Once the emotional "pressure valve" has been released through your listening, she will often find her own solution—and she will love you for giving her the space to find it.

Vulnerability Loops: The Architecture of Trust

Trust is not a one-way street. Active listening is the "receiving" end, but to build a true connection, you must engage in **Vulnerability Loops.**

A Vulnerability Loop works like this:

1. **Person A** (You) shares a small, genuine vulnerability (a minor doubt, a passion, or a humanizing mistake).
2. **Person B** (Her) receives that vulnerability and acknowledges it.
3. **Person B** responds with a vulnerability of her own.
4. **Person A** acknowledges it.

As a High-Value Man, you often have to **signal safety first.** By being the first to show a crack in your "perfect" armor, you give her permission to be human.

- *Example:* "I'll be honest, when I first moved into this industry, I spent the first six months feeling like a total imposter. I was terrified someone would find out I had no idea what I was doing."

This isn't "complaining" or being "weak." It is **Strategic Vulnerability.** It shows that you are secure enough in your value that you don't need to hide your humanity.

The Power of the 4-Second Pause

Silence is a tool of leadership. Most men are terrified of a lull in conversation, so they "chase" her with words. They step on the end of her sentences because they are so eager to keep the "energy" up.

The High-Value Man uses the **4-Second Pause.** When she finishes a sentence, don't speak immediately. Look at her for 2–4 seconds.

- **What it signals to her:** "I am actually processing what you just said. I'm not just waiting for my turn to talk."

- **The Result:** Most people feel a slight "tension" in silence and will fill it by sharing more. Often, the most important part of her story—the "deep" part—comes out *after* she thinks she's finished, simply because you gave her the silence to keep going.

The "Selective Memory" Effect

High-value listening requires you to be a "Curator of Details." If she mentions in passing that she loves a specific obscure 90s band, or that her sister is graduating next week, **store that data.**

Bringing up a "minor" detail later in the conversation—or, even better, in a follow-up text—is the ultimate proof of value. It proves that you weren't just "nodding along" to be polite; you were actually **present.**

- *"By the way, did your sister end up graduating yesterday? How did the family dinner go?"*

This one sentence is worth more than ten "compliments." A compliment is about her appearance (which she didn't choose); remembering a detail is about her life (which she did).

Exercises: Training Your Listening Ear

Active listening is a muscle that must be trained. Use these "Social Drills" to increase your competence.

1. The "Last Three Words" Drill

In your next five conversations (with friends, coworkers, or strangers), practice the "Mirroring" technique. Wait for them to finish a sentence, and repeat the last 1–3 words back as a question.

- *Goal:* See how much more information they give you without you having to "lead" the conversation.

2. The "Emotion Labeling" Drill

Watch a documentary or an interview. After a person speaks, pause the video and try to "label" their emotion.

- *"It sounds like they feel... betrayed."*
- *"It sounds like they feel... cautiously optimistic."*
- *Goal:* Develop your "Emotional Vocabulary" so you can use it in real-time interactions.

3. The "No Solution" Challenge

Spend an entire dinner with a friend or family member where you are **forbidden** from offering any advice or solutions. Your only allowed responses are reflective questions and empathetic labels.

- *Goal:* Experience the power of "witnessing" someone's experience rather than "fixing" it.

Summary: The Listener as the Leader

To build trust, you must move from the "outer circle" (Appearance, Humor) to the "inner circle" (Values, Emotions). Active listening is the only way to get there.

When you listen, you are not being passive. You are being a "Social Alchemist." You are taking the raw data of her life and reflecting it back to her in a way that makes her feel seen, understood, and valued.

In a world full of men who are shouting for attention, be the man who is powerful enough to be quiet. Be the man who doesn't just "hear" her, but who **understands** her. That is the man who sparks chemistry that lasts.

CHAPTER 4

SHARE STORIES THAT REVEAL CHARACTER

The Narrative Mirror

In the first three chapters of *Spark Chemistry*, we focused on the initial spark and the art of listening. You have learned how to enter a room, break the ice with a calibrated observation, and build a foundation of trust by listening to her "inner world." But a conversation cannot survive on listening alone. If you only listen, you eventually become a therapist or a journalist. To create true chemistry, you must eventually step into the light and reveal who **you** are.

However, most men struggle with this transition. They fall into one of two traps:

1. **The Resume Trap:** They list their accomplishments, their job title, and the model of car they drive, hoping these "facts" will prove their value. This is boring and reeks of a need for validation.

2. **The Mystery Trap:** They remain so stoic and guarded that the woman has nothing to "latch onto." Without data points about your character, she cannot form an emotional attachment.

The High-Value Man uses a third path: **The Character Story.** A Character Story is not a list of events. It is a narrative "mirror" that allows her to see your values, your resilience, and your worldview without you having to state them explicitly. You don't tell her you are adventurous; you tell her about the time you got lost in a monsoon in Vietnam and had to navigate back to civilization using only the stars and a broken compass. You don't tell her you are compassionate; you tell her about the difficult decision you made to walk away from a high-paying job to take care of a family member.

In this chapter, we will deconstruct the architecture of storytelling and learn how to build a "Story Bank" that reveals your character and sparks deep, emotional chemistry.

The Neurobiology of the Story

Why does storytelling work? Why do we pay $20 to sit in a dark theater and watch a movie about people who don't exist? It is because the human brain is literally "wired for story."

1. Neural Coupling

When you tell a story, a phenomenon called "Neural Coupling" occurs. Using fMRI scans, researchers have found that the brain activity of the listener begins to mirror the brain activity of the speaker. If you describe a tense moment, her heart rate increases. If you describe a moment of joy, her reward centers light up. You are literally "syncing" your nervous systems.

2. The Chemical Cocktail: Cortisol and Oxytocin

A good story follows a specific chemical arc.

- **The Hook (Cortisol):** The beginning of a story should introduce a conflict or a question. This releases cortisol, which sharpens her attention. She wants to know: *What happens next?*

- **The Resolution (Oxytocin):** As the story concludes with a lesson or a moment of connection, the brain releases oxytocin. This creates a "bonding" effect between the listener and the storyteller.

3. Meaning-Making vs. Fact-Sharing

The brain processes stories in the **Limbic System** (the seat of emotion) rather than the **Prefrontal Cortex** (the seat of logic). Facts are easily forgotten; stories are felt. By sharing stories, you move from being a "person with attributes" to a "person with meaning."

The Anatomy of a High-Value Story

A story in a social setting should not be a twenty-minute monologue. It should be a "Micro-Story"—a 60 to 90-second burst of narrative that packs an emotional punch. Every high-value story must contain four specific elements:

1. The Hook (The "Why" I'm Telling This)

Never start a story out of nowhere. Use a bridge from something she said.

- *Example:* "That reminds me of the most absurd flight I ever took..." or "I wasn't always this calm. I actually used to be the most anxious person I knew until one specific Saturday in June..."

2. The Conflict (The "Low Point")

A story without a struggle is just a brag. To reveal character, you must show a moment where you were challenged, or even where you failed. This is the **Humanizing Element.** It makes you relatable.

- *Example:* "I was standing on the stage in front of 500 people, and I realized I had completely forgotten the entire second half of my presentation. The silence felt like it lasted a decade."

3. The Pivot (The Character Reveal)

This is the most important part. How did you react to the conflict? Did you give up? Did you find a creative solution? Did you laugh at yourself? This is where your **Values** are demonstrated.

- *Example:* "Instead of panicking, I just looked at the front row and admitted I was human. I told them I'd forgotten the next part, and we all just laughed for a minute. That moment of honesty actually ended up being the highlight of the talk."

4. The Resolution (The "Lesson")

What did you learn? How did this event shape the man you are today?

- *Example:* "It taught me that people don't actually want you to be perfect; they just want you to be real. I've carried that into everything I do since then."

The Four Character Archetypes

To ensure your "Story Bank" is balanced, you should have at least one story for each of these four archetypes. These represent the different facets of a High-Value Man.

1. The Protector (Compassion & Strength)

- **Goal:** To show you care about things beyond yourself.
- **Story Idea:** A time you stood up for someone who couldn't stand up for themselves, or a time you took responsibility for a major mistake to protect your team.
- **The Subtext:** "I am a man of integrity who uses his power for good."

2. The Seeker (Curiosity & Adventure)

- **Goal:** To show you are not stagnant; you are growing.
- **Story Idea:** A travel mishap, a time you tried a hobby you were terrible at, or a time you moved to a new city with nothing but a suitcase.
- **The Subtext:** "Life is an adventure, and I am an active participant in it."

3. The Resilient (Grit & Perspective)

- **Goal:** To show you don't crumble under pressure.
- **Story Idea:** A professional failure, a fitness goal that seemed impossible, or navigating a personal loss.
- **The Subtext:** "I am the captain of my own ship, regardless of the weather."

4. The Creative/Playful (Humor & Wit)

- **Goal:** To show you don't take yourself too seriously.
- **Story Idea:** A "social fail," a misunderstanding that led to a hilarious situation, or a quirky tradition you have with your friends.
- **The Subtext:** "I am comfortable in my own skin and fun to be around."

Tactical Delivery: Pacing and Presence

The best story in the world will fail if it is delivered like a grocery list. Storytelling is an oral tradition; it requires **Performance.**

1. The Power of the Pause

Silence is the "punctuation" of storytelling. Use a 2-second pause right before the "climax" of your story to build tension. Use a 3-second pause after the "lesson" to let the emotion sink in.

2. Sensory Language (VAK)

To trigger neural coupling, use words that appeal to the senses:

- **Visual:** "The sky was that specific shade of bruised purple right before a storm."
- **Auditory:** "The only sound was the rhythmic *thump-thump* of the helicopter blades."
- **Kinesthetic:** "I could feel the grit of the sand in my teeth and the heat radiating off the pavement."

3. Eye Contact and Expression

Don't stare at her intensely for the whole story. Look away during the "thoughtful" parts as if you are re-living the memory, then lock eyes during the "emotional" parts. Your face should mirror the emotion of the story. If you're talking about something funny, your eyes should be "smiling" before your mouth does.

The "Hero Trap" and How to Avoid It

A common mistake men make is always casting themselves as the "Flawless Hero" of their stories.

- *The Story:* "The boss was wrong, I was right, I saved the company, everyone clapped."

This is a rapport-killer. It creates a wall between you and the listener.

The High-Value Correction: Be the "Flawed Hero." Make yourself the "butt of the joke" in the beginning. Describe your confusion, your fear, or your mistakes. When you eventually succeed (or at least learn something), the win feels earned rather than braggy. True confidence is the ability to admit you were once a fool.

Vulnerability: The Kintsugi of Character

In Japanese culture, there is an art form called **Kintsugi**, where broken pottery is repaired with gold lacquer. The philosophy is that the piece is more beautiful *because* it was broken and repaired.

Your stories should be your "Golden Cracks." Sharing a vulnerability—a time you were heartbroken, a time you felt lost, or a time you doubted yourself—is the highest form of social value. It proves that you are so secure in your current state that your past "brokenness" doesn't threaten you.

The Rule of Vulnerability: Always share from a "scar," not a "wound."

- **A Wound:** An ongoing problem you haven't resolved (e.g., "I'm still so depressed about my ex"). This feels heavy and needy.

- **A Scar:** A past struggle that is now a part of your strength (e.g., "Going through that breakup was the hardest year of my life, but it taught me how to find happiness on my own"). This feels inspiring and high-value.

The "Spike and Bridge": Transitions

How do you get in and out of a story without it feeling awkward?

1. The "Spike" (The Entry): Wait for a keyword. If she mentions "family," don't just say "I have a brother." Say, "Family is such a wild dynamic. My brother and I actually didn't speak for two years until a very strange encounter in a hospital waiting room changed everything..."

2. The "Bridge" (The Exit): Always turn the spotlight back to her immediately after the story ends.

- "...and that's why I never trust a GPS in the mountains anymore. Have you ever had one of those moments where technology just completely betrayed you?"

This ensures the conversation remains a **dialogue**, not a lecture.

Building Your "Story Bank"

You shouldn't be making stories up on the fly. You should have a curated "Bank" of 5–7 stories that you have refined and practiced.

The Exercise: The Narrative Audit

1. **Recall:** Write down ten significant moments from your life (good, bad, or weird).

2. **Filter:** Which ones demonstrate a core value (Resilience, Humor, Curiosity)?

3. **Structure:** Apply the Hook-Conflict-Pivot-Resolution framework to three of them.

4. **Edit:** Cut out the "boring" details. Does she need to know the name of the street? No. Does she need to know how you *felt*? Yes.

5. **Rehearse:** Tell the story to a friend or record yourself on your phone. Listen for "umms," "ahhs," and places where the pacing drags.

Conclusion: The Man Behind the Narrative

Sharing stories is the ultimate act of "Generosity." You are giving her a map of your soul. When you do it correctly—with humor, vulnerability, and a focus on character—you aren't just "talking." You are creating an emotional experience that she will remember long after she forgets your name or your job.

Chemistry is not found in the facts of our lives. It is found in the **resonance** of our journeys.

Take a breath. Look back at your life. Find the gold in your cracks. And when the moment is right, tell her a story.

CHAPTER 5

USE YOUR VOICE AND TONALITY TO LEAD

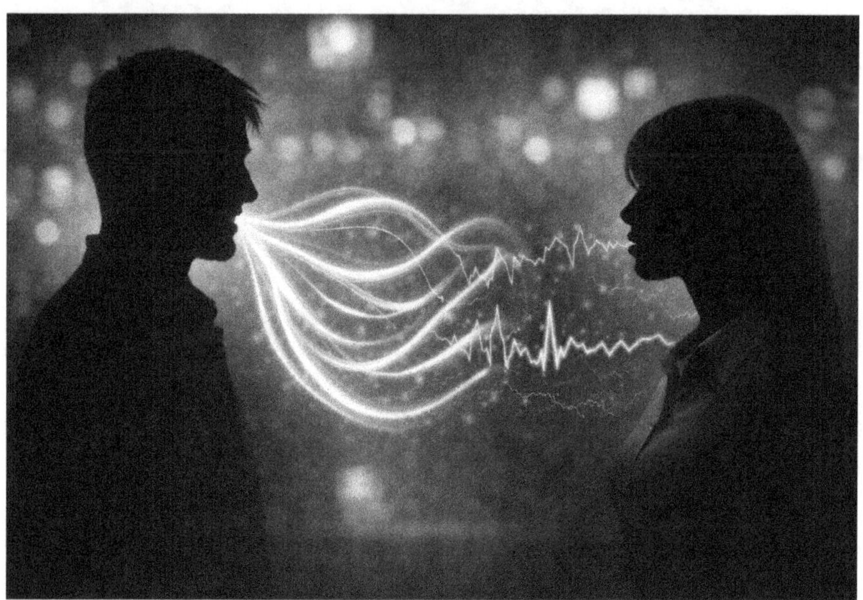

The Invisible Command

If Book 1 was your "Packaging" and the previous chapters of Book 2 were your "Script," Chapter 5 is your **Soundtrack**.

Imagine watching a high-stakes thriller film—a moment of intense connection between two leads—but the music playing in the background is a high-pitched, frantic circus theme. No matter how perfect the actors' faces are, or how brilliant the dialogue is, the "vibe" is destroyed. You wouldn't feel tension; you would feel a jarring sense of mismatch.

Most men spend their entire lives focusing on the "What"—the specific words, the clever lines, the perfect stories—but remain completely unconscious of the "How." They approach an attractive woman with a high-value observation, but their voice is thin, nasal, and high-pitched. They deliver a witty tease, but their voice trails off at the end like a question, signaling a desperate need for her approval.

Your voice is a biological instrument that bypasses her logical brain and speaks directly to her limbic system—the part of the brain that processes emotion, status, and "gut feelings." To lead an interaction and spark chemistry, you must master the mechanics of your voice. You must learn to use tonality to project authority, warmth, and sexual tension. In this chapter, we will deconstruct the physics, the psychology, and the practical training required to transform your voice into a tool of leadership.

The Bio-Mechanics of the High-Value Voice

Sound is a physical wave. When you speak, you are literally moving the air between you and her. The qualities of that wave determine how you are perceived before her brain even finishes decoding the meaning of your words.

1. The Physics of Frequency and Pitch

In the animal kingdom and human society, lower-frequency sounds are almost universally associated with larger physical size, higher testosterone levels, and greater social authority. This is not mere social conditioning; it is evolutionary biology.

The fundamental frequency of a voice (f_0) is determined by the vibration of the vocal folds within the larynx.

$$f = \frac{1}{T}$$

Where f is frequency and T is the period of the vibration. When you are nervous or seeking approval, your throat muscles (the laryngeal muscles) constrict. This tension shortens the period and raises the pitch. This signals "submissiveness" or a "threat response." Conversely, when you are relaxed and grounded, your vocal folds remain elongated and relaxed, producing a lower, more resonant frequency that signals "dominance" and "safety."

2. Resonators: The "Chest Voice" vs. The "Nose Voice"

Resonance is the amplification of sound in your body's cavities. Think of your body as a guitar: the vocal cords are the strings, but the "body" of the guitar determines the richness of the sound.

- **Nasality (The Head Voice):** When sound is trapped in the sinuses and the back of the throat is constricted, it sounds "whiny." This is often associated with the "Nice Guy" archetype—someone who is trying to be non-threatening.

- **The Chest Voice:** High-value tonality comes from the chest and the "mask" (the area around the mouth and nose, but supported by a deep throat). It carries a "vibrational weight" that a woman can actually feel in her own body if she is standing close to you. This is the "bass" of authority.

The Three Tonalities: Seeking, Reporting, and Breaking Rapport

This is the most critical concept in vocal leadership. There are three primary ways to "inflect" your sentences, and each one tells a completely different story about your status relative to the person you are speaking to.

1. The Upward Inflection (Seeking Rapport)

This is when your voice goes up in pitch at the end of a sentence, making a statement sound like a question. It is often referred to as "uptalking."

- **The Subtext:** "Am I okay? Do you like me? Am I allowed to be here?"
- **The Effect:** It signals high anxiety and a "lower-status" position. It is the sound of a subordinate reporting to a boss.

  Example: "Hi, I'm Mark? I thought you looked really nice today?"

  Even though these are statements of fact, the tone makes them sound like requests for validation. If you speak this way, you are essentially asking her for permission to keep talking to her. This is the fastest way to kill chemistry.

2. The Flat Inflection (Reporting Rapport)

The pitch stays level throughout the sentence, with no significant rise or fall at the end.

- **The Subtext:** "I am sharing facts. I am neutral. I am a professional."
- **The Effect:** It is professional and safe, but it rarely sparks chemistry. It is the voice of a news anchor, a professor, or a coworker. It lacks "color" and emotional depth. While it won't necessarily "hurt" you like upward inflection does, it won't "help" you build tension.

3. The Downward Inflection (Breaking Rapport)

The pitch of your voice drops slightly on the final syllable of the sentence.

- **The Subtext:** "I am certain of what I am saying. I do not need your approval. I am the leader of this moment."
- **The Effect:** This is the most attractive tonality. It creates an aura of "Amused Mastery." It signals that you are the "Anchor" in the social environment. It suggests a "calm confidence" that doesn't need to rush or explain itself.

The Engine: Diaphragmatic Breathing and Support

You cannot have a powerful, resonant voice without a powerful air supply. Most men are "chest breathers." When they get nervous, their breathing becomes shallow, their shoulders rise, and their voice loses its "floor." This results in a voice that sounds thin and easily "cracked."

To lead with your voice, you must breathe from your **diaphragm**—the dome-shaped muscle at the base of your lungs.

The Mechanics of Support:

- **Inhalation:** Your belly should expand, not your chest. This pulls the diaphragm down, creating a vacuum that fills the lowest part of your lungs.
- **The "Support":** As you speak, you use your abdominal and intercostal muscles to control the steady release of that air. This gives your voice "projection" without you having to shout. It is the difference between a speaker that is simply "loud" and a speaker that has "substance."

Temporal Leadership: The Luxury of Pacing

The speed at which you speak is a direct indicator of your perceived social value.

- **Fast Speaking:** Signals that you are afraid of being interrupted. It implies that you don't think your words are worth the other person's time, so you have to "rush" to get them out before they lose interest. This is a "low-status" signal.

- **Measured Pacing:** Signals that you are comfortable taking up "temporal space." It implies that you expect people to listen. It suggests that your thoughts are well-formed and that you are in no hurry to please.

The "High-Value Pause"

The most powerful tool in tonality is not a sound at all—it is **silence**.

1. **The Pre-Statement Pause:** Pausing for one second before you say something important builds anticipation. It draws her in.

2. **The Mid-Sentence Pause:** Breaking a sentence into "chunks" makes you sound more thoughtful and less like you are reciting a rehearsed script.

3. **The Post-Question Pause:** After you ask her something, **wait**. Do not fill the silence if she doesn't answer immediately. The man who can "hold the silence" without fidgeting or "explaining away" his question is always the one in control of the frame.

Vocal Subtext: The "Hidden" Conversation

Every time you speak, you are sending two messages: the **Text** (the words) and the **Subtext** (the feeling). Chemistry is sparked almost entirely by the Subtext.

Consider the sentence: *"You're quite the troublemaker, aren't you?"*

- **Subtext A (Upward Inflection/Fast Pacing):** "I hope you're not mad that I'm teasing you, please laugh so I know I'm safe."

- **Subtext B (Downward Inflection/Low Pitch/Slow Pacing):** "I see through your polite exterior, and I find the real you very intriguing."

The words are identical, but the **feeling** is the difference between a "friend" and a "lover." When you use a "Warm, Deep, Downward" tonality, you are communicating that you are a "Sexual Man" rather than just a "Friendly Stranger." This is how you avoid the "Friend Zone" before you even finish your first sentence.

Vocal "Pollution": What to Eliminate

To lead effectively, you must identify and eliminate "Vocal Pollution"—the habits that undermine your authority.

1. **Vocal Fry:** This is the "creaky" or "raspy" sound at the end of a breath when you run out of air. While sometimes used for effect, excessive vocal fry sounds tired, uninspired, and low-energy. It lacks the "ping" of a healthy, vibrant voice.

2. **Nasality:** As mentioned before, speaking "through the nose" signals a lack of physical grounding. It often results from a tight jaw or "clenched" teeth.

3. **Filler Words (Um, Uh, Like, You Know):** These are "vocal tics" that fill the silence because the speaker is afraid of it. They break the rhythm of your leadership and signal that your brain is struggling to keep up with your mouth.

The "Vocal Gym": A 30-Day Training Protocol

Your voice is a physical instrument. You must train it outside of social situations so that it becomes your "default" when you are under the pressure of an attractive woman's presence.

Exercise 1: The "Humming" Resonance Drill

Close your lips and hum the lowest note you can comfortably hit. Focus on feeling the vibration in your chest and your lips.

- **The Goal:** Once you feel that vibration, try to maintain it while saying "Hello" or "My name is..."
- **Practice:** 5 minutes every morning to "place" your voice in your chest resonator rather than your throat.

Exercise 2: The "Downward" Statement Drill

Record yourself on your phone saying 10 neutral sentences (e.g., "The weather is quite nice today," "I'm heading to the gym later").

- **Rep 1:** Say them with an upward inflection (like a question).
- **Rep 2:** Say them with a downward inflection (like a command/statement of fact).
- **The Goal:** Develop the muscle memory of the downward drop. Listen to the recordings and notice how much more "powerful" and "certain" you sound in Rep 2.

Exercise 3: The "Straw" Technique

Blow through a drinking straw into a half-full glass of water while making a consistent "u" sound (a low-pitch hum).

- **The Goal:** The resistance of the water helps balance the pressure above and below the vocal folds, reducing tension and increasing vocal "ping."

Exercise 4: The "Slow Motion" Reading

Read a page of a book out loud, but speak at 50% of your normal speed. Over-enunciate every consonant. Use the "High-Value Pause" at every comma and period.

- **The Goal:** Train your brain to be comfortable with a slower, more deliberate conversational tempo.

Leading the Vibe: The Final Integration

When you master your tonality, you become a "Vocal Anchor." In a loud, chaotic bar or a busy cafe, your calm, resonant, downward-inflected voice creates a "Vacuum of Attention." She will naturally lean in to hear you, not because you are shouting, but because your voice feels "steady" and "grounded" amidst the noise.

You are no longer just "talking" to her. You are **submerging** her in your reality. Your voice says: *"I am here, I am grounded, and I am leading this moment."* This is the essence of vocal leadership. It is the soundtrack to the chemistry you are building.

CHAPTER 6

CREATE TENSION THROUGH PUSH AND PULL

The Friction of Desire

You have mastered the foundation. You look the part, you have broken the ice, you have listened deeply, and your voice carries the weight of authority. But there is a final, vital ingredient required to transform a "good conversation" into "palpable chemistry."

That ingredient is **Tension**.

Most men are terrified of tension. They spend their entire lives trying to diffuse it. They want the interaction to be "smooth," "comfortable," and "easy." They agree with everything she says, they laugh at every joke (even the unfunny ones), and they ensure there are no awkward silences. They believe that by removing all friction, they are making it easier for her to like them.

They are wrong.

Comfort without tension leads to the "Friend Zone." Tension without comfort leads to "Threat." Chemistry is the electric spark that happens in the middle. To create this spark, the High-Value Man uses the most powerful social tool in existence: **Push and Pull.**

Push and Pull is the art of alternating between showing interest (Pull) and showing a lack of interest or challenging her (Push). It is the verbal and physical representation of the "Chase." By moving between these two poles, you prevent the conversation from "flatlining." You keep her nervous system engaged, her dopamine levels spiked, and her attention locked on you.

The Neurobiology of the "Chase"

To master Push and Pull, we must understand why the human brain responds to it so intensely. It is rooted in the concept of **Intermittent Reinforcement.**

1. The Dopamine Spike of Uncertainty

In the 1950s, psychologist B.F. Skinner discovered that lab rats would press a lever more frequently if the reward (food) was given *unpredictably* rather than every time. This is known as a Variable Ratio Schedule.

In dating, if you are "All Pull" (constantly complimenting her, always available, always agreeable), your "reward value" drops to zero because you are 100% predictable. The brain stops releasing dopamine because there is no mystery. However, when you "Push" (tease her, disagree, or physically lean back), you introduce **Uncertainty**. When you follow that with a "Pull" (a sincere look, a touch, or a deep question), the dopamine spike is ten times more powerful because it was "earned."

2. The Probability of Attraction

We can model the "Tension Curve" using a simple relationship between **Validation** and **Investment**. If V is the validation you give and I is her level of investment:

$$\text{Tension} \propto \frac{dI}{dV}$$

True tension is created when her investment increases while your validation remains "fluctuating." If you give too much validation (V) for too little investment (I), the tension collapses.

The Mechanics of the "Push"

A "Push" is any action that signals you are not 100% "sold" on her yet. It communicates that you have standards and that her beauty alone is not enough to win you over.

Important Note: A "Push" is never an insult. It is never mean-spirited. It is always delivered with the **"Amused Mastery"** and the **"Selective Smirk"** we discussed in previous chapters.

Types of Verbal Pushes:

1. **The Playful Disqualification:** * *"You're cute, but I feel like you're probably a lot of trouble. I'm not sure I can handle you."*
   - *"We were getting along so well until you said you liked [X]. I think we have to break up now."*

2. **The "Challenge" Push:**
   - *"You're very articulate. Is there actually a brain behind those eyes, or is this all just a clever act?"*

3. **The Role Reversal:** * *"Stop trying to pick me up. I told you, I'm a respectable man."*

Types of Physical Pushes:

1. **The Lean Back:** Just as the conversation gets intense, physically lean back in your chair or take a half-step away. This creates a "void" that she will naturally want to fill by leaning in.

2. **The "Eye-Break":** Break eye contact first, looking away as if you've been distracted by something more interesting in the room for a split second.

The Mechanics of the "Pull"

A "Pull" is an act of warmth, intimacy, or validation. It rewards her for "investing" in the conversation or for handling your "Push" with grace. Without the Pull, you are just an arrogant jerk. The Pull is what makes the interaction feel "safe" and romantic.

Types of Verbal Pulls:

1. **The Sincere Compliment:** * *"All joking aside, I really love the way your mind works. You're incredibly sharp."*

2. **The Vulnerability Pull:** * *"I don't usually tell people this, but..."*

3. **The "We" Language:** * *"I feel like we're the only two people in this room who actually get what's going on right now."*

Types of Physical Pulls:

1. **The Lean In:** Dropping your voice and leaning into her "bubble" to share a secret.

2. **The Prolonged Eye Contact:** Locking eyes and holding the gaze for 2–3 seconds *after* the talking has stopped.

3. **The Gentle Touch:** A brief touch on the arm or shoulder during a laugh.

The "Golden Ratio" of Tension

The secret to Push and Pull is not the individual moves, but the **Transitions**.

Think of it like a rubber band. If you only "Pull," the rubber band is limp (No Tension/The Friend Zone). If you only "Push," the rubber band snaps (Too much Pressure/Rejection). The High-Value Man keeps the rubber band stretched just enough to feel the energy, but never enough to break it.

The Sequence of the Spark:

A perfect Push-Pull sequence often looks like this:

1. **Pull:** You have a deep, 2-minute conversation about her passions (Building Comfort).

2. **Push:** You playfully tease her about a dorky detail in her story (Creating Tension).

3. **Push:** You lean back and look at her skeptically (Increasing Uncertainty).

4. **Pull:** You smile, lean in, and say, *"Actually, that's the most interesting thing I've heard all night"* (Releasing Tension/Rewarding her).

The Result: She experiences an emotional "rollercoaster." Her brain associates you with high-arousal emotions. She feels like she is "winning" you over, which is far more attractive to a woman than a man who simply "gives up" his interest for free.

Advanced Technique: Future Projection

Future Projection is a high-level Push-Pull tool that involves "imagining" a future together—usually one that is absurd or doomed to fail. This allows you to "Pull" (by talking about a future) and "Push" (by making the future ridiculous) simultaneously.

- *"We are going to have a great life together. We'll have a house in the suburbs and two dogs. But I'm taking the dogs in the divorce because you're clearly going to be the one who forgets to feed them."*

Why it works: It forces her to visualize a romantic connection with you, but the "Push" at the end keeps it playful and prevents it from feeling "heavy" or "creepy."

Calibration: When to Push and When to Pull

The most common mistake men make is using Push-Pull like a robot. You must **Calibrate** based on her response.

If She Is...	You Should...	Why?
Leaning in, laughing, and touching you.	**Push.**	She is already high-interest; a "Push" will increase the challenge and keep the value high.
Looking distracted, giving short answers.	**Pull (Then Exit).**	She doesn't have enough comfort yet. Use a "Pull" to build rapport. If she doesn't respond, use the False Time Constraint (Chapter 2) to leave.
Teasing you back aggressively.	**Push Harder.**	She is playing the game. This is "Banter Battle." Match her energy to show you aren't intimidated.
Becoming quiet or looking offended.	**Hard Pull.**	You pushed too far. Pivot immediately to a sincere "Pull" to restore the safety of the interaction.

Push and Pull only works if the "Vibe" is playful. If you "Push" with a flat, serious face, it feels like a genuine rejection. This is why the **"Selective Smirk"** from Book 1 is your most important non-verbal asset. Your eyes must always say, *"I'm having fun with you,"* even when your words are "Pushing" her away.

The "Nice Guy" Correction: If you find yourself constantly apologizing after a tease, you are killing the tension. An apology is a "White Flag." It tells her you are afraid of her reaction. Instead of apologizing, simply "Pull" with a warm smile.

Exercises: Mastering the Pendulum

1. The "Disqualification" Workout

In your next three conversations, practice "disqualifying" yourself or her as a romantic partner.

- *"You're way too [Adjective] for me. My mom warned me about girls like you."*

- *Goal:* Notice how her interest actually *increases* when you suggest that you might not be a "match."

2. The "Physical Elastic" Drill

Practice the "Lean Back." During a conversation, wait for her to say something interesting. Instead of leaning in, slowly lean back in your chair, look her in the eye, and wait 2 seconds before responding.

- *Goal:* Feel the "Social Pressure" building and notice her urge to fill the space.

3. The "Future Projection" Script

Write out three "Future Projections"—one involving a vacation, one involving a career, and one involving a mundane activity (like grocery shopping). Make each one end in a playful "Push" or "Divorce."

- *Goal:* Internalize the structure so you can use it naturally in the flow of conversation.

The essence of Push and Pull is the communication of **High Value**. A man who is "All Pull" says, *"I need you."* A man who is "All Push" says, *"I'm better than you."*

The High-Value Man says, *"I'm interested in you, but I'm not sold on you. Impress me."*

By creating tension, you are inviting her into a dance. You are providing an emotional experience that is rare, exciting, and deeply memorable. You are no longer just another face in the crowd; you are the man who makes her heart race, her mind wonder, and her spirit engage.

CHAPTER 7

CONCLUSION: CEMENTING THE CONNECTION

The Final 10 Percent

In the previous chapters of *Spark Chemistry*, you have learned the art of the entrance, the depth of active listening, the power of character-based storytelling, and the electric friction of Push and Pull. You have successfully ignited a spark. However, many men who master the "art of the interaction" stumble at the finish line. They build immense chemistry, only to let it evaporate through a clumsy exit or a desperate attempt to "climb" for a result.

The transition from a high-energy conversation to a phone number or a confirmed date is the "Bridge." If the bridge is built too early, it feels flimsy and intrusive. If it is built too late, the fire has already burned out. This chapter is dedicated to the **Mechanics of the Bridge**. We will explore how to use the "Peak-End Rule" to your advantage, how to qualify her so that the connection feels earned, and how to execute a "High-Value Close" that leaves her eager for the next encounter.

The Psychology of the Exit: The Peak-End Rule

To understand why the final moments of your interaction are more important than the beginning, we must look at the research of Nobel laureate **Daniel Kahneman**. His work on the **Peak-End Rule** suggests that the human brain does not remember experiences as a mathematical average of every second spent. Instead, we remember two specific snapshots:

1. **The Peak:** The moment of highest emotional intensity (positive or negative).
2. **The End:** How the experience concluded.

The Trap of the "Nice Guy" Exit

Most men are terrified of the conversation ending. Because they are enjoying the chemistry, they "cling" to it. They stay in the conversation until the energy naturally dips, until they run out of things to say, or until the woman begins looking for her friends. By staying until the energy fades, they ensure that the "End" of the memory is **stagnant**. No matter how amazing the "Peak" was, her brain will categorize the encounter as "initially fun, but ultimately a bit draining."

The High-Value Exit Strategy

The High-Value Man exits while the energy is still high. You want to walk away when you are both laughing, when you've just shared a deep insight, or when the tension is at its thickest.

Why this works: It creates what psychologists call the **Zeigarnik Effect**—the tendency of the brain to remember uncompleted or interrupted tasks better than completed ones. By leaving while things are still "great," you create a psychological "Open Loop." Her brain will naturally want to close that loop, which manifests as her thinking about you after you're gone.

High-Value Qualification: Turning the Table

Before you ask for a way to stay in touch, you must perform the final "Test." In the early chapters, you demonstrated your value. Now, you must allow her to demonstrate hers. This is **Qualification**.

If you ask for a woman's number simply because she is beautiful, you are signaling that your standards are purely superficial. This lowers your value. A High-Value Man is selective. He wants to know if the woman behind the beauty has the character, intelligence, or humor to warrant more of his time.

The Shift from "Do You Like Me?" to "Do I Like You?"

Qualification is a power shift. It moves you from the "Suitor" role to the "Evaluator" role.

The Mechanics of the Qualification Question:

A good qualification question should be playful but pointed. It should ask her to reveal something about her internal world.

- *"You're obviously very charming, but I have to ask—are you actually a kind person, or is this just a very well-rehearsed social mask?"*

- *"I usually get along best with people who are a bit rebellious. What's the most impulsive thing you've done in the last six months?"*

- *"You seem like you have your life very much together. Tell me one thing about you that is completely disorganized."*

Processing the Answer

When she answers, do not just nod and agree. Listen for the **Value** behind her words.

- **If she gives a shallow answer:** Use a "Push" (Chapter 6). *"That's the 'interview' answer. I'm looking for the real one."*

- **If she gives a genuine answer:** Use a "Pull." Lean in, look her in the eye, and say, *"I didn't expect that. I actually really respect that."*

By making her "earn" your validation, you make the eventual connection feel like a prize she has won, rather than a favor she is granting you.

The Logistics of the Exchange

Once the qualification is met and the energy is at a peak, it is time to build the physical bridge. This is the part men overthink, yet it is the simplest part if the chemistry is present.

1. Seeding the Future (The Soft Close)

A "Hard Close" (asking for a number out of nowhere) is jarring. A "Soft Close" involves "seeding" an activity you could do together based on the conversation you've already had.

> Example: You've been talking about your mutual love for old jazz records.

> The Seed: "You know, there's this tiny, hidden record shop in the North End that has a secret lounge in the back. We should definitely go there and see if we can find that rare Coltrane pressing you were talking about."

By using the word **"We,"** you are testing her response to a shared future. If she smiles and agrees, the bridge is already half-built.

2. The Statement of Intent

Do not ask: "Can I have your number?" This is a "Subordinate" request.

Instead, use a Statement of Intent.

- *"I've actually got to get back to my friends, but I've really enjoyed this. Let's exchange numbers. I'll send you the details for that record shop."*

This is leading. You are stating what is going to happen, assuming that she is just as interested as you are. This "Assumptive Close" is a massive indicator of confidence.

3. The Phone Exchange

When she agrees, do not fumble with your phone. Hand it to her with the "New Contact" screen already open. This is a non-verbal "command" that is smooth and high-value.

The 24-Hour Momentum: Digital Chemistry

The "Bridge" doesn't end when you walk away. It continues through the first few digital interactions. Many men build a 10/10 connection in person and then kill it with 2/10 texting.

The "Callback" Text

Your first text should arrive within 24 hours (the "wait three days" rule is an outdated myth that signals games and insecurity). The first text should be a **Callback** to a specific, unique moment from your conversation—ideally a "Push" or a shared joke.

- **Low-Value Text:** *"Hey, it was nice meeting you. What's up?"* (Boring, requires her to do the work).
- **High-Value Callback:** *"I just walked past a bookstore and saw a cover that looked exactly like your 'troublemaker' expression. I think the universe is warning me. Hope your night ended well!"*

The Law of Reciprocity in Texting

Texting is a game of "Match and Mirror."

- If she sends short, functional texts, do not send paragraphs.
- If she takes four hours to reply, do not reply in four seconds.

You must maintain your "Temporal Value." If you are always available to text, it implies you have nothing else going on in your life. A High-Value Man is busy with his mission; his phone is a tool for logistics, not a substitute for his social life.

The Probability of the Second Meeting

We can actually visualize the likelihood of a second meeting based on the relationship between **Investment (I)** and **Time (T)**.

The "Attraction Decay" can be modeled by:

$$A(t) = A_0 e^{-kt}$$

Where A_0 is the initial chemistry, k is the decay constant (how fast she forgets the "vibe"), and t is the time elapsed.

To prevent $A(t)$ from dropping to zero, you must "Reinforce" the connection with high-value pings that remind her of the **Peak** and the **End**.

Advanced Tactics: Dealing with "Resistance"

Sometimes, despite great chemistry, a woman might hesitate at the exchange of numbers. This is often not a rejection of *you*, but a "Safety Check."

- **She says:** *"I don't usually give my number out."*
- **The High-Value Response:** *"I don't usually ask for them. But I think we're both smart enough to realize this wasn't a 'usual' conversation. If it makes you feel better, I promise only to use it for good, never for evil."* (Delivered with a smirk).

If she still refuses, **Outcome Independence** is your greatest weapon.

- *"Totally understand. It was great meeting you anyway. Have a killer night."*

By walking away without bitterness or "pleading," you maintain your status. Frequently, this "High-Value Exit" in the face of rejection is so attractive that she will actually stop you and give you the number anyway.

The Mindset of Abundance

The ultimate "Bridge" is built on the foundation of Abundance.

If you feel that this is your "only chance" to meet a woman like this, you will leak "Neediness." Neediness is a scent that women can detect from a mile away. It makes your tonality go up (Chapter 5), it makes you overstay your welcome (Chapter 7), and it makes you "All Pull" (Chapter 6).

To cement a connection, you must truly believe that you are a man of value and that if this doesn't work out, there are thousands of other incredible women you will meet. You are the **Prize**. You are the **Selector**.

Summary of the Bridge Protocol

1. **Identify the Peak:** Wait for the moment of highest laughter or connection.
2. **Qualify:** Ask a "Challenge" question to see if she meets your standards.
3. **Seed the Future:** Mention a shared activity based on a previous topic.
4. **Statement of Intent:** Lead the exchange of contact info with confidence.
5. **Exit on Top:** Walk away immediately after the exchange to preserve the "Peak-End" memory.
6. **Callback Text:** Send a high-value text within 24 hours that references a shared joke.

1. The "Standard" Audit

Write down three things you actually value in a person that have nothing to do with looks. Next time you're in a conversation, ask a question to see if she has one of those things.

- *Goal:* Move from "Being Selected" to "Selecting."

2. The "Assumptive Close" Drill

In a low-stakes environment (like talking to a barista or a coworker), practice leading the end of the conversation. Instead of saying "Goodbye," say, "I've got to run, but let's chat more about [Topic] later."

- *Goal:* Normalize the act of leading the transition.

3. The "Callback" Brainstorm

Think of the last three people you met. What was one specific, "weird" or "funny" detail they mentioned? Write a text for each person using that detail as a callback.

- *Goal:* Train your brain to "Curate" details for future rapport.

Conclusion: The Start of the Journey

Book 2 has been about **Sparking Chemistry**. You have the tools to ignite interest, build trust, and create tension. By mastering the "Bridge," you ensure that the sparks you create don't just flicker and die in the night, but grow into something substantial.

Chemistry is the fuel, but **Leadership** is the engine. A man who can lead a woman from a crowded room to a shared future is a man who understands the deepest levels of social dynamics.

Remember: You aren't just "getting a number." You are inviting an interesting person into your already incredible life. Act accordingly.

CHAPTER 8

REFLECTION QUESTIONS

The Laboratory of Social Dynamics

We have reached the end of *Book 2: Spark Chemistry*.

You have been exposed to a significant amount of data. You now understand the neurobiology of active listening, the narrative architecture of a high-value story, the physics of vocal tonality, the friction of push-pull dynamics, and the psychological principles of the "High-Value Exit."

But data is not skill. Reading a book about swimming does not prevent you from drowning when you hit the water. To transform this information into **Instinct**, you must move from the "Classroom" to the "Laboratory." You must audit your current behaviors, identify your "Nice Guy" leaks, and rigorously test these new principles in the real world.

This chapter is designed as a **Self-Audit Protocol**. It is not meant to be read quickly. It is meant to be studied. Take a pen and a notebook. Be honest with yourself. The goal here is not to be perfect; the goal is to be **conscious**.

Most men believe they are good listeners. Most men are wrong. They are simply "polite waiters"—waiting for their turn to speak. Chapter 3 challenged you to become a "Social Alchemist" who transforms raw conversation into trust.

The Diagnostic Questions:

1. **The "Internal Monologue" Check:**

   - *Question:* In your last three conversations, can you recall exactly what you were thinking while the other person was speaking? Were you visualizing their story, or were you rehearsing your next line?

   - *The Pivot:* If you were rehearsing, you were in **Level 1 Listening**. How much emotional data did you miss because you were focused on your own performance?

2. **The "Fixer" Reflex:**

   - *Question:* Think of the last time a woman (or anyone) complained to you about a problem. Did you offer a solution within the first two minutes?

   - *The Pivot:* How did the energy shift when you offered the solution? Did she seem relieved, or did she shut down? True chemistry requires empathy before logistics.

3. **The Silence Tolerance Test:**

   - *Question:* On a scale of 1–10, how anxious do you feel when there is a pause in conversation?

   - *The Pivot:* Do you fill the silence with "nervous chatter" or "filler words" (um, like, so)? The High-Value Man can sit in silence for 4 seconds without fidgeting.

The Field Drill: "The Journalist"

For the next 24 hours, enter every conversation with the goal of finding out one specific emotion the other person is feeling. Do not offer advice. Do not tell a related story about yourself yet. Just use "Labels" (e.g., "It sounds like you felt betrayed") and see how deep they go.

Part 2: The Storytelling Audit (Reflecting on Chapter 4)

Chapter 4 argued that facts are forgotten, but stories are felt. Your "Story Bank" is your Resume of Character. If you don't have one, you are relying on luck.

The Diagnostic Questions:

1. **The "Hero" Audit:**
   - *Question:* Review the stories you usually tell at parties. In these stories, are you always the "cool guy" who wins? Or do you allow yourself to look foolish, struggling, or vulnerable?
   - *The Pivot:* A story where you are perfect is a story that creates distance. Where is the "Kintsugi" (the golden crack) in your narrative?

2. **The "Sensory" Check:**
   - *Question:* When you describe a memory, do you describe the *feeling* of the environment? (The smell of the rain, the bass of the music, the knot in your stomach).
   - *The Pivot:* Without sensory details, neural coupling cannot happen. You are just listing events.

3. **The "Why" Factor:**
   - *Question:* Why are you telling the story? Is it to impress her (Outcome Dependence) or to reveal a value (Self-Expression)?
   - *The Pivot:* If you stripped away the "cool" parts of your story, what does the core conflict say about your character? (e.g., *"I value loyalty," "I am resilient," "I am curious"*).

The Field Drill: "The 90-Second Arc"

Take one of your "rambling" stories and cut it down to 90 seconds.

- **0-15s:** The Hook (Why it matters).
- **15-45s:** The Conflict (The struggle/The low point).
- **45-75s:** The Pivot (The choice you made).
- **75-90s:** The Resolution (The lesson).
- *Action:* Record yourself telling it. If it's boring to you, it's boring to her.

Part 3: The Vocal Presence Audit (Reflecting on Chapter 5)

Your voice is the soundtrack of the interaction. You cannot lead with a voice that asks for permission.

The Diagnostic Questions:

1. **The "Uptalk" Infection:**
   - *Question:* Do you end your sentences with an upward inflection? (e.g., *"Hi, I'm John?"*).
   - *The Pivot:* This is the #1 killer of authority. It signals submissiveness. Are you asking her to accept your reality, or are you stating your reality?

2. **The Speed Trap:**
   - *Question:* When you get nervous or excited, does your rate of speech increase?
   - *The Pivot:* Fast talking signals that you believe your time is limited and you might be interrupted. Slowing down signals that you believe you are worth listening to.

3. **The "Chest vs. Throat" Check:**
   - *Question:* Place your hand on your chest while you speak. Do you feel a vibration? Or is the sound coming entirely from your throat/nose?
   - *The Pivot:* A "throat voice" triggers a "flight or fight" response in others because it mimics the sound of anxiety. A "chest voice" triggers safety.

The Field Drill: "The Slow-Motion Order"

The next time you order coffee or food, make a conscious effort to speak 30% slower than you think is normal. Use a downward inflection on your order. ("I'll have a black coffee." -> Drop the pitch at "coffee"). Notice if the cashier treats you with more attention or respect.

Part 4: The Tension Audit (Reflecting on Chapter 6)

Push and Pull is the art of creating the "Spark." Without it, you are just a "nice friend."

The Diagnostic Questions:

1. **The "Nice Guy" Baseline:**

    ○ *Question:* Do you agree with everything she says? If she says she hates a movie you love, do you backpedal?

    ○ *The Pivot:* Agreement without friction is boring. Are you afraid that if you disagree, she will stop liking you? That fear is what makes you unattractive.

2. **The "Insult vs. Tease" Calibration:**

    ○ *Question:* When you try to "Push," does it come off as mean? Or do you use the "Selective Smirk" to show it's playful?

    ○ *The Pivot:* A "Push" without warmth is an insult. A "Push" with warmth is a tease. Check your eye contact—are you smiling with your eyes?

3. **The "All Pull" Danger:**

    ○ *Question:* Are you constantly leaning in, complimenting, and validating?

    ○ *The Pivot:* If you are "All Pull," you are a fan, not a peer. Where can you introduce a playful disqualification? (e.g., *"You're too much trouble for me"*).

The Field Drill: "The Disqualification"

In your next low-stakes conversation, find a reason to playfully "disqualify" the other person or yourself. ("Oh no, you're a cat person? We can't be friends."). Watch their reaction. Do they laugh? Do they try to defend themselves? That is the spark of tension.

The "Bridge" is how you cement the memory. If you fumble the exit, you lose the game.

The Diagnostic Questions:

1. **The "Lingering" Problem:**

    ○ *Question:* Do you stay in conversations until they run dry? Do you wait for the "awkward pause" before you say goodbye?

    ○ *The Pivot:* This violates the Peak-End Rule. You are training people to associate you with "draining energy."

2. **The Qualification Gap:**

    ○ *Question:* Do you ask for numbers just because she is hot? Or do you actually care about who she is?

    ○ *The Pivot:* If you don't ask a "Qualification Question" (e.g., *"What are you passionate about?"*), your interest is cheap. Why should she value your attention if you give it to everyone?

3. **The "Ask" Anxiety:**

    ○ *Question:* Do you get sweaty palms when it's time to ask for the number? Do you make it a "big deal"?

    ○ *The Pivot:* It should be a "Statement of Intent" (*"Let's continue this"*), not a request for a favor (*"Can I please...?"*).

The Field Drill: "The Peak Exit"

Leave a conversation (even a phone call with a friend) when you are laughing the hardest. Say, "I gotta run, but this was great. Talk soon." Hang up. Notice how much more energy you feel, and how they will likely text you shortly after to continue the joke.

Integration: The "Spark Chemistry" Scorecard

Use this scorecard to rate your interactions over the next week. Be brutal.

Metric	Low Value Behavior (Score 1-3)	High Value Behavior (Score 4-5)	Your Score
Listening	Waiting to talk; checking phone; offering solutions immediately.	4-second pauses; labeling emotions; full body orientation.	
Storytelling	Fact-based; bragging; boring details; "Hero" mode.	Vulnerable; sensory details; clear "Pivot"; humor.	
Tonality	High pitch; fast pace; uptalking; nasal resonance.	Chest resonance; slow pace; downward inflection; silence.	
Tension	100% Agreeable; afraid to offend; "Nice Guy" energy.	Playful teasing; push-pull dynamics; breaking eye contact first.	
The Close	Lingering too long; awkward "ask"; no qualification.	Leaving at the peak; "Assumptive Close"; callback texting.	

Total Score Analysis:

- **0-10:** You are in the "Friend Zone" or "Invisible Zone."
- **11-18:** You are pleasant, but forgettable.
- **19-25:** You are a High-Value Man who sparks genuine chemistry.

You have mastered the art of sending the right messages. You know how to package yourself (Book 1) and how to spark the interaction (Book 2).

But communication is a two-way street. As you are deploying these strategies—the eye contact, the push-pull, the tonality—she is constantly broadcasting data back to you. She is telling you exactly how she feels, whether she is attracted, whether she is bored, or whether she is testing you.

Most men are blind to this data. They miss the subtle "Green Lights" of attraction and plow through the "Red Lights" of discomfort. To truly master social dynamics, you must learn to decode the silent language of the female nervous system.

You must learn to see what isn't being said.

This leads us to **Book 3: Read Her Signals**.

BOOK THREE
READ HER SIGNALS

INTRODUCTION: THE SILENT LANGUAGE OF ATTRACTION

The Invisible Broadcast

If Book 1 was your **Hardware** (your presentation and environment) and Book 2 was your **Software** (your communication and stories), then Book 3 is your **Radar**.

In the previous two volumes, we focused almost exclusively on your output—the signals you are sending to the world. We optimized your appearance, refined your tonality, and structured your narratives to project the highest possible value. But social intelligence is a feedback loop. A radio transmitter is useless if it cannot receive the signal coming back from the tower.

Most men navigate the world of dating and social interaction while virtually "blind." They are so focused on their own performance—what they should say next, how they look, whether they are "winning"—that they miss the torrent of data being broadcast by the woman standing three feet in front of them.

She is constantly speaking to you. Even when her mouth is closed, her nervous system is shouting. She is communicating her comfort levels, her sexual attraction, her skepticism, and her boundaries through a complex, ancient, and mostly subconscious language of biological signals.

To become a truly High-Value Man, you must move beyond the "guessing game." You must learn to read the silent language of attraction. By the end of this book, you will no longer wonder if a woman is interested; you will **see** it in the dilation of her pupils, the angle of her feet, and the subtle shifts in her vocal prosody.

The Biological Imperative: Why Signals Exist

To decode attraction, we must first understand why humans communicate through "signals" rather than just direct statements. Why doesn't a woman simply say, *"I find your genetic profile compatible and I am experiencing a surge of dopamine in your presence"*?

1. The Evolutionary "Safety Net"

For most of human history, a woman's choice of partner was a high-stakes survival decision. Choosing a low-value or dangerous man carried the risk of physical harm or the loss of resources for herself and her offspring. Direct, overt expressions of interest were (and often still are) socially risky. They make her vulnerable to unwanted attention or social judgment.

Subconscious signals—often called **IOIs (Indicators of Interest)**—allow a woman to "test the waters." They provide a way to invite a man to lead without the social "cost" of being rejected or appearing "easy." They are a form of plausible deniability. If a man doesn't respond to her hair-flip or her lingering gaze, she hasn't "lost face"; she was just fixing her hair or looking around the room.

2. The Limbic System vs. The Prefrontal Cortex

The signals we are going to study in this book are primarily generated by the **Limbic System**—the oldest part of the brain responsible for emotions, territoriality, and survival instincts.

When a woman feels attraction, her limbic system triggers involuntary physiological responses before her logical prefrontal cortex can even form a sentence. These include:

- **The Autonomic Nervous System (ANS):** Triggers changes in heart rate, skin flushing (vasodilation), and breathing patterns.

- **The Endocrine System:** Releases oxytocin (the bonding hormone), dopamine (the reward chemical), and norepinephrine (the "excitement" chemical).

Because these responses are involuntary, they are the most honest form of communication. Her mouth can lie to be polite, but her capillaries and her pupils cannot.

The Three Pillars of Signal Detection

Before we dive into specific cues in the coming chapters, we must establish the "Heads-Up Display" (HUD) through which you will view every interaction. To avoid "Confirmation Bias"—the tendency to see what you *want* to see—you must follow the three pillars of signal detection:

Pillar I: Baseline (The Normal)

You cannot identify a signal of attraction if you don't know what her "Neutral" state looks like. This is the biggest mistake men make—they see a woman being friendly and assume it's attraction.

- **The Rule:** Observe how she interacts with others (the bartender, her friends, the waiter). Is she naturally touchy? Does she always maintain heavy eye contact? That is her **Baseline**. Any deviation from that baseline when she speaks to *you* is a signal. If she is quiet with others but animated with you, that is a Green Light.

Pillar II: Clusters (The Rule of Three)

A single signal is a fluke. A woman touching her hair might just have an itchy scalp. A woman leaning in might just be trying to hear you over the music.

- **The Rule:** Never act on a single signal. Look for **Clusters**. True attraction manifests as three or more signals occurring in a short window of time (e.g., she leans in, touches her neck, and maintains prolonged eye contact).

Pillar III: Context (The Environment)

Signals must be filtered through the environment.

- **The Rule:** A woman crossing her arms in a cold park is simply freezing; a woman crossing her arms in a warm, comfortable lounge is likely "defensive" or "closed." Always account for the physical and social context before interpreting a gesture.

The Spectrum of Engagement

Attraction is not a binary "On/Off" switch. It is a spectrum of physiological and psychological arousal. As a leader, your job is to identify where she is on this spectrum so you know whether to "Push" or "Pull" (referencing Book 2, Chapter 6).

Stage	Biological State	Common Physical Signals
1. Neutral	Parasympathetic dominance.	Relaxed posture, scanning the room, "Reporter" tonality, no mirroring.
2. Curiosity	Slight dopamine spike.	"Head tilt," prolonged eye contact, feet and torso pointed toward you.
3. Attraction	Norepinephrine / Adrenaline.	Pupil dilation, "Preening" (fixing hair/clothes), mirrored movements, flushing.
4. Intimacy	Oxytocin / Vasopressin surge.	Breaking the "touch barrier," whispered tonality, lowering of defensive barriers.

The Feedback Loop: Calibration

The ultimate goal of reading signals is **Calibration**.

Calibration is the ability to adjust your behavior in real-time based on the feedback you are receiving. It is the difference between a man who is "creepy" and a man who is "charming."

- **If you see Green Lights (IOIs):** You should escalate. Lean in, use a more intimate story, or move closer.
- **If you see Yellow Lights (Compliance):** She is listening but not yet "invested." You need more "Tension" or better "Storytelling."
- **If you see Red Lights (IODs - Indicators of Disinterest):** You must de-escalate immediately. Lean back, give her space, or change the topic.

A High-Value Man never "forces" an interaction. He reads the signals and flows with them. If a woman is broadcasting "Red Lights," the High-Value response is to gracefully exit or give her so much space that she feels safe again. This paradoxically often makes you *more* attractive because it shows you aren't "thirsty" or desperate.

The Ethical Responsibility of the Radar

Mastering the silent language of attraction gives you a form of "X-ray vision." You will see things that most men—and even many women themselves—are not consciously aware of.

With this power comes an ethical mandate. Reading signals is not about "manipulation"; it is about **Empathy**. By reading her signals, you are becoming more attuned to her comfort and her desires. You are ensuring that you never overstay your welcome and that you only escalate when you have her subconscious "consent."

The most attractive man in the room is the one who understands a woman better than she understands herself in that moment—the man who can see she is overwhelmed and gives her a "False Time Constraint" to relax her, or the man who sees she is burning with attraction and has the courage to lead the interaction forward.

1. The "Baseline" Observation Exercise

Go to a public place (a park, a mall, a coffee shop). Pick a stranger and observe them for 3 minutes.

- How do they stand?
- How often do they touch their face?
- What is their "neutral" expression?
- When someone approaches them, what changes?
- *Goal:* Train your brain to identify "Baselines" quickly and objectively.

2. The "Cluster" Hunt

Watch a romantic movie or a reality dating show. Instead of listening to the dialogue, mute the sound entirely.

- Can you tell when one person is attracted to the other just by their body language?
- Identify at least 3 signals occurring at once.
- *Goal:* Learn to see "Clusters" without the distraction of words and clever dialogue.

3. The "Mirror" Check

In your next conversation (with anyone), consciously notice if the other person starts to "Mirror" your posture. If you lean back, do they lean back? If you take a sip of your drink, do they take a sip of theirs?

- *Goal:* Identify the first signs of subconscious "Rapport" and neural coupling.

You have spent years listening to what people say. From this moment forward, you are going to watch what they **do**.

The silent language of attraction is a 24/7 broadcast. It is happening all around you, in every cafe, every office, and every bar. Once you learn to see it, the world becomes a much clearer, much more navigable place. You will no longer feel like you are walking through a dark room; you will feel like you have finally turned on the lights.

In the next chapter, we will focus on the most powerful "broadcaster" of the human body: **The Eyes**.

CHAPTER 2

DECODE EYE CONTACT AND FACIAL MICRO - EXPRESSIONS

The Windows to the Limbic System

The human face is the most sophisticated communication suite on the planet. While the body communicates general "vibes"—comfort, nervousness, or aggression—the face provides the high-definition details. Specifically, the eyes are the only part of the human central nervous system that is directly visible to the outside world.

When you look into a woman's eyes, you are looking at a direct readout of her autonomic nervous system. Because the muscles of the face and the dilation of the pupils are largely controlled by the involuntary nervous system, they are nearly impossible to fake. A woman can tell you she's having a great time while her eyes are darting toward the exit and her pupils are constricted—her words are a social courtesy, but her face is a biological confession.

The limbic system—the emotional center of the brain—processes social information at a speed that far outpaces the logical prefrontal cortex. This creates a phenomenon known as "emotional leakage." Even when a person is trying to mask their feelings, the truth leaks out in the form of micro-gestures. To lead effectively, you must become a "Micro-Expressionist." You must learn to look past the surface-level smile and decode the flickering signals that last only a fraction of a second. In this chapter, we will break down the mechanics of the gaze, the science of pupil dilation, and the "Micro-Expressions" that signal true attraction versus polite engagement.

The Mechanics of the Gaze: Direction and Duration

The way a woman looks at you—and where she looks—tells you exactly how she has categorized you in her social hierarchy. Most men assume that if she is looking at them, she is interested. This is a dangerous oversimplification. We must analyze the "geometric path" of the eyes.

1. The Three Types of Gazes

In social psychology and behavioral analysis, we categorize gazes based on the triangular patterns the eyes follow during interaction. Understanding these allows you to gauge her level of "arousal" versus "assessment."

- **The Power Gaze:** In this pattern, her eyes move in a triangle between your eyes and your forehead. This is the gaze of a boss, a negotiator, or someone who is evaluating you from a position of detached authority. There is no sexual tension here; there is only "assessment." She is checking for competence or threat, but she is not visualizing intimacy. If you find yourself on the receiving end of a Power Gaze for too long, you have likely failed to disrupt her "shield" (referencing Book 2, Chapter 1).

- **The Social Gaze:** This is the most common pattern. Her eyes move in a triangle between your eyes and your mouth. This signals comfort, rapport, and active listening. She is engaged in the exchange of information. While it is a positive sign, it does not necessarily signal sexual attraction. Many men get stuck in the "Friend Zone" because they mistake a steady Social Gaze for a sign that they should escalate.

- **The Intimate Gaze:** This is where the spark lives. The triangle extends below the face. Her eyes move from your eyes, down to your chest or body, and back up. Crucially, if she is highly attracted, you will see her eyes flicker down to your lips while you are speaking. This is a subconscious visualization of kissing. In more intense moments, the "Intimate Gaze" becomes "heavy"—the eyelids drop slightly, and the gaze lingers on your eyes for an extra beat.

2. The Duration of Contact and the "Golden Ratio"

The length of eye contact is a powerful indicator of status and interest. In a neutral social setting, eye contact is usually intermittent. However, attraction changes the rules of duration.

- **The Golden Ratio (60-70%):** High-value interaction thrives when you maintain eye contact for about two-thirds of the conversation. This shows you are confident enough to hold her gaze but not so obsessed that you are staring her down like a predator.

- **The 40% Threshold (The Submissive Signal):** If she holds eye contact for less than 40% of the time, she is either extremely socially anxious, distracted by something more interesting, or signaling a lack of respect.

- **The "Lingering Look":** When a woman is highly attracted, she will often hold your gaze for 2–3 seconds longer than is "socially necessary" after a sentence ends. This is the biological "invite." She is waiting to see if you have the confidence to hold that tension. If you break it too soon, you signal a lack of internal power.

The Pupil: The Truth Machine

The pupil's primary job is to regulate light, but its secondary job is to signal **Arousal**. This is governed by the Dilator Pupillae muscle, which is controlled by the Sympathetic Nervous System (the "Fight, Flight, or Fornicate" system).

The Science of Mydriasis (Dilation)

When the brain perceives something it desires—whether it is a delicious meal, a beautiful work of art, or an attractive mate—it releases a surge of norepinephrine. This causes the pupils to dilate to take in as much of the "rewarding" stimulus as possible.

- **The "Green Light":** If her pupils are significantly enlarged in a moderately lit room, she is experiencing a biological "Arousal Spike." Her nervous system is signaling that she is stimulated by your presence. This is one of the most reliable indicators of interest (IOI) because it is impossible to fake.

- **The "Red Light" (Miosis):** Conversely, constricted pupils in the same lighting can signal "Disgust," "De-arousal," or hostility. It indicates that her system is trying to "shut out" the stimulus.

The Context Filter: Always account for lighting. If you are in a dark bar, everyone's pupils will be dilated. The High-Value Man looks for the *change*. Do her pupils dilate further when you move closer? Do they expand when you drop your voice to a lower register? That delta is where the truth lies.

Decoding Facial Micro-Expressions

Dr. Paul Ekman's research into universal micro-expressions revealed that certain facial movements are hardwired into our species. These "flickers" happen in 1/15th to 1/25th of a second—too fast for the conscious mind to catch without training, but perfectly readable once you know what to look for.

1. The Duchenne Smile vs. The Pan-Am Smile

A "fake" smile (The Pan-Am Smile, named after the polite but forced smiles of flight attendants) only involves the Zygomatic Major muscles—the ones that pull the corners of the mouth up. It is a social mask.

A "real" smile (The Duchenne Smile) involves the **Orbicularis Oculi** muscles—the muscles that surround the eyes.

- **The Indicator:** Look for the "Crow's Feet." If her mouth is smiling but the skin at the corners of her eyes remains smooth and "still," she is performing a social duty. If the eyes crinkle and the cheeks lift significantly, she is genuinely enjoying the moment. This is a sign of true "Rapport" (referencing Book 2, Chapter 2).

2. The "Flash" of Recognition (The Eyebrow Raise)

When we encounter something we find pleasant or intriguing, we involuntarily raise our eyebrows for a fraction of a second. This "Eyebrow Flash" opens the eyes wider, signaling "Welcome" and curiosity.

If you approach a woman and she gives you a quick eyebrow flash before she even speaks, you have been granted "social permission." If her eyebrows remain flat or knitted together (The Corrugator Frown), she is in a defensive state.

3. The "Lip Press" vs. The "Lip Part"

The mouth is a gateway for both communication and consumption. Its tension levels reveal her comfort.

- **The Lip Press:** Tightening the lips into a thin line (disappearing lips) is a universal sign of suppressed emotion. It signals disagreement, disapproval, or a desire to leave. It means her "Shield" is fully raised.

- **The Lip Part (The Slack Jaw):** When a woman is attracted, her facial muscles—particularly around the jaw—begin to relax. Her mouth may hang slightly open. This is caused by a shift to parasympathetic dominance and an increased breathing rate. It is a high-level sign of physical comfort and arousal.

The "Preening" Reflex

While not a micro-expression in the classic sense, "Preening" is a series of facial and head gestures that signal a desire to appear more attractive to a specific male. These are limbic responses to the presence of a high-value man.

1. **The Hair Flip/Stroke:** This is a multi-layered signal. It exposes the neck (a vulnerable area), flashes the underside of the wrist (another vulnerability), and releases pheromones from the hair into the air between you.

2. **The Collarbone Touch:** By touching her neck or collarbone, she is subconsciously drawing your eyes to her chest and neck—areas associated with high intimacy.

3. **The Ear Tuck:** This is a "clearing" gesture. She is removing obstacles (hair) so that she can see you better and, more importantly, so that you can see her eyes and face more clearly.

If these gestures occur in **Clusters** (referencing Book 3, Chapter 1)—for example, she tilts her head, fixes her hair, and smiles with her eyes—she is "setting the stage." She is subconsciously preparing for a deeper connection.

Calibration: The "Eye-Break" Test

The High-Value Man does not just observe; he leads. You use your own eye contact to "ping" her nervous system and see how she responds.

The Drill: During a high-point in the conversation (after a joke or a deep story), lock your gaze on her eyes for 3–4 seconds. Do not look away. Maintain a slight, amused smirk. Then, slowly break eye contact by looking to the side (horizontally).

- **The Positive Response:** She holds your gaze until you break it, or she looks slightly "flustered" (blushing or looking down then back up immediately). This shows she is affected by your presence.

- **The Negative Response:** She breaks eye contact immediately, looks at her phone, or looks "relieved" when you turn away. This indicates that the tension was "unearned" or that her comfort level is still too low.

Warning: Never break eye contact by looking down. Looking down is a universal sign of submission in the animal kingdom. If you break eye contact, look to the side as if you've been distracted by a thought or something in the distance.

Advanced Oculesics: Reading "The Triangle"

If you want to know if a woman is thinking about kissing you, watch her eyes during a silence. If her gaze drops to your mouth, stays there for a second, and then darts back to your eyes, she has just "mentally rehearsed" a kiss. This is the ultimate "Green Light." At this point, the "Software" of Book 2 has done its job, and it is time for the "Bridge" of Book 2, Chapter 7.

1. The "Pupil Watch" (Low Stakes)

Practice looking for pupil dilation in people you already know—friends, family, or coworkers. Observe how their pupils change when they talk about a topic they love versus a topic they find boring.

- **Goal:** Train your eyes to notice "Mydriasis" automatically without having to stare or feel awkward.

2. The "Silent Film" Study

Watch 10 minutes of a high-quality drama (like *Mad Men*, *Succession*, or *The Crown*) on mute. Focus entirely on the eyes and mouth of the characters during a romantic or tense scene.

- **Goal:** Identify the "Intimate Gaze" and "Duchenne Smiles" in professional actors who are trained to mimic these biological truths.

3. The "Mirror" Micro-Check

In front of a mirror, practice a fake "polite" smile (mouth only) versus a genuine smile (eyes and cheeks). Feel the difference in the muscles. Then, practice the "Eyebrow Flash."

- **Goal:** Build "proprioception"—the ability to feel what your own face is broadcasting so you can control your own "output."

Summary: The Face Doesn't Lie

The eyes and face provide the "Real-Time Analytics" of your interaction. While words are filtered through the "social editor" of the prefrontal cortex, the face is a direct cable to the limbic system.

- **Triangular Gaze to Mouth** = High Rapport/Social Comfort.
- **Triangular Gaze to Lips/Body** = Sexual Interest.
- **Pupil Dilation** = Biological Arousal.
- **Eye Crinkles (Duchenne)** = Sincerity and Joy.
- **Lip Press** = Resistance or Discomfort.

By learning to read these signals, you move from "guessing" to "knowing." You can see the attraction building long before she says a word, allowing you to lead with absolute confidence and perfect timing.

CHAPTER 3

RECOGNIZE PHYSICAL PROXIMITY AND TOUCH CUES

The Geography of Attraction

If the face (Chapter 3, Chapter 2) provides the "high-definition" details of attraction—the micro-flickers of the eyes and the dilation of the pupils—then the body's position in space provides the "topography." In the animal kingdom, territory is everything. From the pride lands of the Serengeti to the crowded floor of a metropolitan lounge, the management of physical distance is a primary survival and mating mechanism. Humans are no different. We carry with us an invisible, psychological bubble known as "Personal Space." Who we allow into that bubble, how we behave when we are there, and how we react when someone else enters it is the ultimate indicator of trust, power, and sexual tension.

Most men are "space-blind." They operate with a lack of spatial awareness that consistently sabotages their results. They either invade a woman's space too quickly—triggering her amygdala's "flight or fight" response and being categorized as a "creep"—or they stay too far away for too long, signaling a lack of confidence and ensuring the interaction remains "platonic" and safe. To lead effectively, you must understand **Proxemics** (the study of human space) and the **Haptic Loop** (the science of touch).

In this chapter, we will explore the four zones of proximity, the psychological "Point of No Return" in physical distancing, and the subtle "Touch Cues" that women use to signal they are ready for you to escalate. By mastering the geography of attraction, you stop guessing if she wants you closer and start reading the undeniable map her body is drawing.

Proxemics: The Four Zones of Space

The term "Proxemics" was coined by anthropologist Edward T. Hall in 1963. He discovered that humans maintain four distinct "distance hidden dimensions" depending on the level of intimacy and the nature of the social transaction. Understanding these zones is the foundation of **Calibration** (Book 3, Chapter 1). You must know which zone you are currently in to know which social tools to use.

1. The Public Zone (12 to 25 Feet)

This is the distance of a speaker to an audience or a passerby on a sidewalk. It is the zone of "Total Stranger." In a social setting like a bar or a party, if a woman remains in this zone, she is not yet "in" the interaction with you. If you attempt to communicate from this distance, you must use high-volume **Vocal Tonality** (Book 2, Chapter 5) and broad gestures. Any attempt to "read signals" here is premature; she is simply a person in the room.

2. The Social Zone (4 to 12 Feet)

This is the distance for "safe" interaction—the space we keep between ourselves and coworkers, waiters, or new acquaintances. At this distance, you are broadcasting that the interaction is purely functional or introductory. There is no "Spark" (Book 2) at four feet because there is no physical threat or intimacy. If you spend the entire night talking to a woman from 5 feet away, her body will never register you as a romantic prospect. You are effectively "background noise."

3. The Personal Zone (1.5 to 4 Feet)

This is where friendship, rapport, and the initial stages of attraction happen. This is the "Bubble of Connection." When you are in this zone, you can see the micro-expressions of her face (Chapter 2) and smell her perfume. This is the zone of **Stage 1 Attraction**. If a woman allows you to enter and stay in this zone without subconsciously adjusting her feet to move away, she has granted you "Social Clearance."

4. The Intimate Zone (0 to 18 Inches)

This is the "Red Zone." This space is traditionally reserved only for lovers, close family, and the most trusted of friends. It is a high-stakes area. When you enter this zone, her brain performs an immediate "Safety and Arousal Audit." If you move into this zone and she does not stiffen her shoulders, lean back, or create a barrier, the physical "Shield" is officially down. You have successfully navigated the transition from "Social" to "Sexual."

Reading Proximity Signals: The Truth of Movement

How a woman manages the distance between you reveals her internal "Comfort Level" far more accurately than her words. Watch for these three primary proximity shifts:

1. The "Lean-In" (The Vacuum Effect)

The human body is a heat-seeking missile for things it desires. When we are genuinely interested in a person or an idea, we subconsciously move our center of gravity toward the source of interest.

- **The Signal:** If you are talking and she leans forward—perhaps resting her elbows on the table, tilting her torso toward you, or shifting her weight to the balls of her feet—she is literally "drawn in."

- **The High-Value Response:** Resist the urge to lean in to meet her. This is the "Nice Guy" mistake; it closes the gap too quickly and kills the tension. Instead, stay exactly where you are or even lean back slightly. Let her occupy your space. By forcing her to "reach" for you, you create a powerful **Pull** dynamic (Book 2, Chapter 6).

2. The "Torso Shielding" vs. "The Open Path"

The torso contains our most vital organs (heart, lungs, stomach). When we feel threatened or disinterested, we subconsciously "Shield" them.

- **The Red Light:** If she places her purse, a drink, a cushion, or even her own crossed arms directly between your torso and hers, she is creating a physical barrier. She is signaling that her "Intimate Zone" is closed for business.

- **The Green Light:** If she moves her drink to the side, takes off her jacket, or clears the space on the table between you, she is "Clearing the Path." She is removing the barricades to intimacy, signaling that she is comfortable with the visual and physical "vulnerability" of being open to you.

3. Directional Alignment (The Rule of Feet)

The brain's limbic system controls the feet more honestly than the face. Because the feet are responsible for "Flight" in the face of danger, they are the first to point where the mind truly wants to go.

- **The Check:** Look at her feet and knees. If she is facing you but her feet are angled toward the exit or toward her group of friends, she is "mentally checked out." She is prepared to leave.

- **The IOI:** If her feet and knees are pointed directly at you—even if she is looking away momentarily—her "Intent" is fully focused on you. In a group setting, if you notice her knees are pointed toward you despite her talking to someone else, you are the person she is most interested in.

The Haptic Loop: The Science of Touch

Touch (Haptics) is the most potent "accelerant" for chemistry. While eye contact builds rapport, touch triggers a massive neurological event: the release of **Oxytocin** (the bonding hormone) and **Dopamine**. However, because touch is so intimate, it is also the area where most men fail through lack of calibration.

1. The "Accidental" Touch (The Probe)

A woman who is interested will often "test" your reaction with a touch that provides her with "plausible deniability." This is a "Probe."

- **The Signal:** Her arm brushes yours while you are walking. Her foot knocks against yours under the table and she doesn't immediately withdraw it. She "accidentally" touches your hand while reaching for her drink.

- **The Interpretation:** She is checking your "Physical Baseline." She wants to see if you are a "Safe" and "Stable" leader. If you flinch, jump back, or apologize profusely, you signal low-value and insecurity. If you remain calm, acknowledge the touch with a look, and "hold" the contact for a half-second longer than necessary, you signal dominance and high-value comfort.

2. Compliance Touching (The Break-Through)

This is when she touches you to emphasize a point or because her emotions (usually laughter) have lowered her social guard.

- **The Signal:** She taps your forearm when you say something funny. She "pushes" you playfully when you tease her. She touches the fabric of your shirt to "check the material."

- **The Interpretation:** This is a high-level **Indicator of Interest (IOI)**. She has broken the "Touch Barrier." In her limbic system, the "Intimate Zone" is now open. This is your green light to begin your own calibrated escalation of touch.

3. Self-Touching (Autocontact and Pacifying)

Sometimes, her attraction manifests as a "redirected" touch.

- **The Signal:** Stroking her own forearm, playing with a necklace, or rubbing the back of her neck.

- **The Interpretation:** This is often a "pacifying" gesture. It means she is feeling internal "Tension." To determine if it's good tension (sexual) or bad tension (anxiety), look at the face (Chapter 2). If she is smiling or maintaining eye contact while stroking her neck, it is a high-level sexual signal. She is subconsciously mimicking the touch she wants to receive.

Calibration: The "Space-Invader" Test

A High-Value Man never "asks" for permission to be intimate; he **tests** for it. To know if she is ready for the "Intimate Zone," you must perform a calibrated "Space Test."

The Drill: While the conversation is at a high-energy peak (you are both laughing or sharing a "High-Value Story"), move slightly closer—about 6 to 8 inches. Do not make a grand gesture of it; just shift your weight or slide your chair slightly.

- **The Positive Response:** She stays put, remains relaxed, or—the ultimate green light—moves slightly closer to "close the gap" you created. Her nervous system is signaling "Compliance."

- **The Negative Response:** She subtly leans back, shifts her chair away, or creates a "Shield" with her arms.

- **The High-Value Pivot:** If you get a negative response, **immediately** move back *further* than your original starting point. This is a "Push." It shows you are highly calibrated to her boundaries and that you aren't "thirsty" for her space. Paradoxically, this "pulling away" often makes her feel a sense of loss, causing her to lean back in toward you to regain the rapport.

The Biology of "The Lean": Passing the Safety Audit

Why is proximity so powerful? It comes down to **Biological Vulnerability**. By allowing you into her intimate zone, her brain is performing a "Risk Assessment." Because her limbic system can detect pheromones and body heat at this range, she is gathering data that words cannot provide.

If you move in and your **Vocal Tonality** (Book 2, Chapter 5) remains calm, your breath is steady, and your hands are relaxed, you pass the "Safety Test." You are broadcasting that you are a man who is comfortable with intimacy. If you are shaking, stuttering, or "leaning in" with desperate energy, you fail the test. Attraction is a byproduct of safety plus tension.

The "Departure" Signal: Pre-emptive Proximity

One of the most overlooked proximity signals is what I call the "Pre-emptive Close."

- **The Signal:** When a woman is about to leave a group or a venue, she will often move physically closer to the man she is interested in *before* saying her goodbyes.

- **The Interpretation:** She is creating one last "Peak" (Book 2, Chapter 7) of intimacy. She is giving you a final window to "build the bridge" and exchange contact information. If you miss this proximity shift because you are too busy talking to your friends, you miss the date.

Exercises: Mastering the Geography of Space

1. The "Zone" Audit

The next time you are out in a social setting (a coffee shop, office, or bar), consciously identify which "Zone" you are in with every person you interact with. Try moving 6 inches closer to a friend during a story and notice the exact moment their body language shifts.

- **Goal:** Develop an "Internal Radar" for spatial boundaries that operates automatically.

2. The "Barrier" Observation

At a restaurant, watch other couples. Count how many "objects" (phones, salt shakers, bags) are placed between them. Can you identify who is on a first date versus who has been together for years based purely on the "Clarity of the Path" between their torsos?

- **Goal:** Train your brain to see "Shielding" behavior and "Path Clearing" as if it were written in neon lights.

3. The "Knee Point" Check

In your next three conversations, look down at your own feet first. Are they pointing at the door (suggesting you're in a rush) or at the person? Then look at hers.

- **Goal:** Practice the "Rule of Feet" until you can read a person's true intent without ever looking at their face.

Summary: The Space Between

Attraction is a game of "Closing the Gap." Every inch of space between you and a woman is a piece of data.

- **Leaning in** = Active Engagement and "Vacuum" Interest.
- **Pointing knees toward you** = Total Intent and Emotional Focus.
- **Clearing barriers** = Subconscious Invitation for Intimacy.
- **Touching the forearm** = The Breaking of the Social Shield.

A High-Value Man never "pounces" on space. He invites her into his "Personal Zone," monitors her comfort with a "Space-Invader Test," and leads the physical progression with the steady, calibrated hand of a professional. You are the architect of the geography; she is the one choosing to inhabit it.

CHAPTER 4

IDENTIFY VERBAL INDICATORS OF INTEREST

Decoding the Auditory Layer

If the face is the "high-definition" detail (Chapter 2) and the body is the "topography" (Chapter 3), then the spoken word is the **narrative engine** of attraction. However, a significant gap exists between what is said and what is communicated. Most men listen strictly to the *content* of what a woman says while remaining completely deaf to the *intent* and *subtext* behind her delivery.

In the realm of high-value social dynamics, words are often used as a smoke screen. A woman can say, *"I really hate this song,"* but if she says it while leaning into your personal space, maintaining 70% eye contact, and looking at your lips, the "hate" for the song is a secondary data point. The primary message is: *"I am using this song as an excuse to get closer to you."* Conversely, she can say, *"That is so interesting,"* but if her torso is angled away and she's scanning the room for her friends, the words are merely a social mask for boredom.

To be a High-Value Man, you must develop an **"Auditory Radar."** You must train your brain to filter out the "noise" of polite conversation and listen for **Verbal Indicators of Interest (VIOIs)**—the subtle linguistic shifts, investment markers, and tonal changes that signal she is moving from a passive observer to an active participant in your reality. In this chapter, we will break down the "Investment Scale," the psychological power of the "Qualification Statement," and the neurobiology of "Linguistic Mirroring."

In every interaction, there is an invisible "balance sheet" of effort. The person who is working harder to sustain the dialogue—asking the most questions, providing the longest explanations, and reviving dead topics— is the one who is currently more invested. We measure verbal interest by tracking the **Ratio of Effort**.

Level 1: The Information Gap (Low Interest/Reactive)

At this level, the woman is in "Safe Mode." She is responding to your leads but offering nothing in return.

- **The Signal:** You ask a question, and she gives a one-word or short-phrase answer. You tell a high-value story, and she responds with "Cool," "Wow," or "That's crazy." She provides no "hooks" for you to grab onto.

- **The Diagnosis:** This is **Reactive Speech**. She is fulfilling the social contract of being polite, but she has not yet decided if you are worth her mental energy.

- **The High-Value Response:** Stop pushing. If you continue to ask questions here, you become a "Social Waiter." Pull back, use a **False Time Constraint** (Book 2, Chapter 7), and see if she steps up to fill the silence.

Level 2: Thread Expansion (Curiosity/Engagement)

This is the first true "Green Light." It indicates that she has moved from a passive listener to a co-creator of the conversation.

- **The Signal:** She takes a small piece of information you gave her—a "thread"—and expands on it without being prompted.

- **Example:** You mention you recently visited Japan. Instead of saying "Nice," she says, *"I've always wanted to go to Kyoto. Did you make it to the bamboo forest, or did you stay mostly in Tokyo?"*

- **The Diagnosis:** She is "building the bridge." By asking a follow-up or sharing a related experience, she is signaling that she wants the interaction to continue. She is offering you a path to keep the "Software" (Book 2) running.

Level 3: Direct Inquiry and Vetting (High Investment)

This is the "Deep Dive." At this stage, she is no longer just being friendly; she is performing a **Value Audit**.

- **The Signal:** She begins asking "High-Level" questions about your character, your past, your ambitions, or your "why."

- **Example:** *"So, what actually drives you to do what you do?"* or *"You seem very confident, were you always like this, or did you have to learn it?"*

- **The Diagnosis:** She is looking for the man beneath the "Packaging" (Book 1). When a woman asks "vetting" questions, she is subconsciously determining if you are a long-term prospect or just a passing conversation. This is a massive VIOI.

The "Qualification" Indicator: Fighting for Approval

One of the most profound shifts in an interaction occurs when a woman begins to **Qualify Herself** to you. In social hierarchy, the person with the higher status is the one who "judges," and the person with the lower status is the one who "seeks approval."

- **The Signal:** She subtly (or overtly) brags about her skills, her traits, or her background in response to a value you expressed.

- **The Psychology:** If you mention, *"I really value people who are adventurous,"* and she immediately responds with, *"Oh, I actually went skydiving last month and I love solo traveling,"* she is **Qualifying**.

- **The Interpretation:** She has accepted your "Frame." She is no longer just talking to you; she is "applying" for your attention.

She wants to ensure that you see her as a high-value match.

Pro-Tip: When you catch a qualification, acknowledge it with a "Reward." A simple smirk and a statement like, *"I didn't take you for a risk-taker; I like that,"* solidifies your position as the leader of the interaction.

Future Pacing: The "Mental Rehearsal" of Intimacy

"Future Pacing" is a linguistic phenomenon where the mind projects itself into a hypothetical future. In the context of attraction, it is a sign that her subconscious has already accepted the idea of seeing you again.

- **The Signal:** She starts using the words **"We"** or **"Us"** in a future-tense context, often framed as a joke or a challenge.

- **Example:** *"We would be such a disaster if we ever went to an escape room together"* or *"You'd probably hate my favorite dive bar, it's way too loud for you."*

- **The Interpretation:** Her brain has simulated a "Date 2" or "Date 3." By placing you in her future reality, she is signaling that the barriers of "Stranger" have been dismantled.

Vocal Prosody and the "Arousal" Pitch

The *sound* of her voice—the pitch, the tempo, and the "breathiness"—is a biological readout of her autonomic nervous system.

1. The "Pitch Drop" (The Bedroom Voice)

Research in evolutionary psychology and acoustics suggests that while men are attracted to slightly higher-pitched feminine voices, women's voices actually **drop in pitch** when they are speaking to a man they find sexually attractive.

- **The Science:** When a woman is aroused, her vocal cords relax due to a surge in oxytocin and a decrease in cortisol (stress). This creates a "breathier," lower, more intimate tone.

- **The Check:** Compare how she speaks to the waiter versus how she speaks to you when you are in the **Intimate Zone** (Chapter 3). If her voice becomes lower and more rhythmic, she is broadcasting biological attraction.

2. The Laughter Bias

Is she laughing at your jokes, or is she laughing at *you*?

- **The Signal:** You make a mediocre, "dad-joke" level comment, and she gives a genuine, full-body laugh.
- **The Interpretation:** Laughter is a "social lubricant" and a submission signal. It signals that she feels safe enough to lose control momentarily. If the "Laughter Frequency" is high, she is using it as a way to build rapport and lower the tension between you.

Linguistic Mirroring: The "Echo" of Rapport

When two nervous systems begin to sync (a state known as **Neural Coupling**), their communication styles begin to converge. This is a subconscious attempt to build "sameness" and safety.

- **The Signal:** She starts adopting your specific vocabulary, slang, or cadence. If you use a specific metaphor (e.g., calling something "a total chess move"), and she uses that same metaphor ten minutes later, you are in a state of **High Rapport**.
- **The Diagnosis:** This "Echo Effect" is her limbic system saying, *"I am like you; we are on the same team."* It is one of the strongest indicators that your "Software" (Book 2) has successfully integrated with hers.

Calibration: The "Topic Pivot" Test

A High-Value Man does not wait for signals to fall into his lap; he **pings** the environment to see what comes back. To determine if her interest is deep or just surface-level politeness, use the **Pivot Test**.

The Drill: During a comfortable, lighthearted part of the conversation, suddenly pivot to a "Vulnerability Question."

- **The Script:** *"You seem like you have everything figured out, but what's the one thing people always get wrong about you?"*
- **The Positive Response:** She pauses, thinks, and gives an "Invested" answer. She welcomes the challenge.
- **The Negative Response:** She deflective with a joke, gives a shallow answer, or tries to pivot back to "Safe" topics like work or the weather.

1. The "Investment Ratio" Audit

In your next three social interactions, mentally keep score.

- Who asked the last question?
- Who is speaking 70% of the time?
- **Goal:** Learn to recognize the "Information Gap" in real-time so you know when to pull back and let her work.

2. The "Pitch" Comparison

Listen to a woman talk to a group of her girlfriends, and then notice the change in her voice when a man she is interested in joins the circle.

- **Goal:** Train your ear to detect the "Pitch Drop" and "Vocal Fry" associated with attraction.

3. The "We/Us" Tracker

In any interaction, pay close attention to the first time the word "We" is used to describe a shared hypothetical.

- **Goal:** Identify the exact moment "Future Pacing" begins.

A High-Value Man listens with his whole brain, filtering for **Subtext**.

- **Short, reactive answers** = Low Investment (You are over-pursuing).
- **Expanding on threads** = Curiosity (The "Software" is working).
- **Qualifying herself** = High Attraction (She sees you as high-status).
- **Future Pacing** = Deep Rapport (The "Bridge" is built).

When you master the auditory layer, you gain a massive advantage. You no longer get "blindsided" by a rejection later in the night, because you heard the lack of investment an hour ago. Conversely, you will have the confidence to escalate when you hear the "Pitch Drop" and the "Qualification" markers that tell you she is ready for the next level of intimacy.

CHAPTER 5
DISTINGUISH BETWEEN POLITENESS AND ATTRACTION

The Great Social Delusion

The most common trap for men—and the source of the most "friend-zone" frustrations—is the inability to distinguish between **Social Politeness** and **Genuine Attraction**.

We live in a civilized society governed by unspoken rules of decorum. Most women are socially conditioned from a very young age to be agreeable, kind, and accommodating. This "Politeness Mandate" is a survival mechanism; it is designed to minimize friction, avoid unwanted conflict, and maintain social harmony. Consequently, a woman may smile at your jokes, ask you follow-up questions, and maintain steady eye contact simply because she is a high-value, polite person—not because she wants to date you.

A High-Value Man does not let his ego blind him to this reality. He does not see a friendly smile and automatically assume he's "in." He understands the fundamental neurological divide: **Politeness is a Social Duty** mediated by the Prefrontal Cortex, whereas **Attraction is a Biological Compulsion** mediated by the Limbic System.

If you misread politeness as attraction, you come across as socially uncalibrated, "thirsty," and lacking in empathy. You become the guy who doesn't know when to leave. Conversely, if you misread attraction as mere politeness, you miss your window of opportunity to lead the interaction to a meaningful conclusion. In this chapter, we will break down the subtle "Stress Tests" and signal filters that allow you to determine if she is being "Nice" or if she is "Interested."

The "Service Industry" Fallacy

Before we dive into spontaneous social interactions, we must address the most common mistake made by men globally: misreading the "Customer Service" persona.

Whether it is a waitress, a bartender, a flight attendant, or a brand ambassador, these women are literally **paid to be charming**. Their livelihood depends on their ability to make you feel comfortable and important.

- **The Rule:** If a woman is in a professional environment where her role involves hospitality, her baseline is "High-Level Politeness."
- **The Filter:** You must assume she is just excellent at her job until she provides a signal that is **outside her professional duty**.
  - *Example:* A bartender being "nice" is part of the job. A bartender writing her personal number on the back of your receipt without you asking—or staying fifteen minutes after her shift ends specifically to talk to you—is an indicator of interest.

If you cannot distinguish between a professional "mask" and a personal "signal," you will consistently find yourself in awkward situations that damage your social reputation.

Politeness vs. Attraction: The Comparison Table

To refine your "Radar," you must stop looking at the broad gestures and start looking for the **Micro-Deltas**—the small, involuntary differences in how she uses her body and voice.

Feature	Social Politeness (The Mask)	Genuine Attraction (The Truth)
Eye Contact	**Static.** She looks at you because it is polite to listen. The gaze is steady but lacks "heat."	**Lingering.** Her gaze is "heavy." She looks at you even during silences or when others are talking.
Smiling	**The "Pan-Am" Smile.** The zygomatic major muscles pull the mouth up, but the eyes remain "cold."	**The "Duchenne" Smile.** Orbicularis oculi muscles engage; her whole face "lights up" with genuine warmth.
Body Angle	**V-Shape.** Her torso is pointed toward you to be polite, but her feet are pointed away.	**Closed Circuit.** Torso, hips, and feet are all "locked in" on your position.
Touch	**Functional.** Brushing past you or a polite handshake. No lingering contact.	**Testing.** "Accidental" brushes or playful pushes. She seeks excuses to break the touch barrier.
Investment	**Reactive.** She answers your questions but offers no "hooks" to continue.	**Proactive.** She asks *you* questions and qualifies herself to keep the conversation alive.

Politeness is a performance that is easy to maintain when things are going well. The truth of her intent comes out when you introduce a small amount of **Social Friction**. A woman who is just being polite will try to "smooth over" friction to return to safety; a woman who is attracted will lean into the tension.

1. The Gentle Tease (The Playful Push)

A High-Value Man uses "Teasing" (Book 2, Chapter 4) as a primary diagnostic tool for interest.

- **The Polite Response:** She laughs politely, perhaps looks a bit confused, and quickly tries to change the subject back to a "safe" topic. She is uncomfortable with the tension and wants to maintain the "Social Mask."

- **The Attracted Response:** She teases you back. She "challenges" your frame. She might lean in, roll her eyes playfully, and give you a light "shove." This indicates "Neural Coupling"—she is comfortable enough to engage in the "mating dance" of push and pull.

2. The "Opinion" Challenge

State a slightly controversial (but not offensive) opinion. For example, *"I honestly think that most popular 'must-read' books are a waste of time."*

- **The Polite Response:** She avoids conflict at all costs. She nods and says, *"That's an interesting way to look at it,"* or *"I can see why some people might feel that way."* She is being a "Pleaser."

- **The Attracted Response:** She shows you her "Real Self." She either passionately agrees or playfully disagrees with her own counter-points. She values your interaction enough to risk a small disagreement.

The Proximity Filter: The "Lean Back" Test

As discussed in Chapter 3, physical space is the ultimate "Truth Serum." Words can lie, but the nervous system's reaction to proximity is almost impossible to mask.

The Drill: During a neutral part of the conversation, subtly move into her personal space—by about 4 to 6 inches. Do not make it a dramatic move; just shift your weight or slide your glass.

- **The Result (Politeness):** She will subtly (and politely) shift her weight or lean back to re-establish the standard "Social Zone." She won't make a scene because that would be "rude," but her body is signaling a clear "Boundary."

- **The Result (Attraction):** She will remain exactly where she is, or she will lean in even further to close the gap you left. Her body is signaling "Compliance" and a desire for intimacy.

Investment: The "Silicon Valley" Rule

In the world of high-growth startups, venture capitalists say: *"If they aren't paying, they aren't customers; they're just window shoppers."* In the world of dating, the rule is: **"If she isn't investing her energy, she isn't interested; she's just being nice."**

Polite Conversation is a transaction of information.

Attracted Conversation is an investment of energy.

1. Check the "Hooks"

Does she leave "Hooks" in her sentences for you to follow?

- **Polite:** "I work in marketing." (End of sentence. No path forward).

- **Attracted:** "I work in marketing, which mostly means I spend all day trying to figure out why people buy things they don't need. It's actually kind of fascinating. Do you find yourself falling for good ads?" (Multiple hooks provided).

2. The "Silence" Test

When a natural pause occurs in the conversation (The "Lull"), who works to break it?

- **Polite:** She lets the silence hang until it becomes awkward, or she uses the silence as an excuse to look at her phone or signal her friends. She is relieved the "duty" of talking is over.

- **Attracted:** She feels the tension of the silence and tries to "save" the interaction by asking a new question or bringing up a new topic. She is actively fighting to keep you engaged.

Sometimes, a woman is *extremely* friendly, high-energy, and talkative, but the interest is purely platonic. This is often more confusing than simple politeness because the "Investment" is high, but the "Direction" is wrong. Look for these **Anti-Attraction** signals:

1. **The "Sibling" Frame:** She compares you to a brother or a "best friend" early in the conversation.

2. **The "Unfiltered" Zone:** She is *too* comfortable. She talks about "unsexy" topics like messy breakups, medical issues, or other men she is currently pursuing. There is no "Preening" (Chapter 2) because she isn't trying to impress you.

3. **The "Wingwoman" Effect:** She tries to introduce you to her friends or asks for your "guy's perspective" on someone else she is dating.

Calibration: The Graceful De-escalation

A High-Value Man does not get defensive or angry when he realizes a woman is "just being polite." He is not a "Nice Guy" who expects a reward for his time. He respects the social contract.

If your "Radar" detects that she is in "Polite Mode" and is not responding to your "Stress Tests," the high-value move is to **De-escalate immediately**.

- Give her more physical space.
- Direct your attention to other people in the group or the room.
- End the conversation on a high note: *"It was great meeting you; I'm going to go catch up with my friends."*

Paradoxically, by being the man who can "read the room" and give her space when she is only being polite, you actually **increase your perceived value**. It proves you are socially intelligent, outcome-independent, and not desperate for her validation. Frequently, this "Pull-Back" makes her wonder why you stopped pursuing, which can trigger attraction where there was none before.

Exercises: Sharpening the Filter

1. The "Barista" Observation

Go to a busy, high-end coffee shop. Watch the lead barista interact with a string of customers.

- Identify their "Social Mask" (The Polite Smile).
- Observe how they interact with a regular customer they *actually* like. What changes in the micro-expressions around their eyes?
- **Goal:** Learn to identify the "flicker" between professional duty and personal warmth.

2. The "Five-Second" Silence Drill

In your next three conversations, when a natural pause occurs, do not speak. Count to five in your head while maintaining a relaxed, friendly expression.

- Notice if the other person feels the need to "invest" to keep the conversation going.
- **Goal:** Measure the other person's "Investment Level" objectively.

3. The "Frame" Test Comparison

Tease a female friend (someone you have a zero-sexual relationship with) and then tease a woman you are interested in.

- Compare the "vibe" of the reactions. Is the laughter polite and deflective, or is it challenging and lingering?
- **Goal:** Learn to feel the "Spike" in tension that only exists when attraction is present.

Summary: Trust the Biology, Not the Words

- **Politeness** is a choice made by the **Social Brain**. It is a mask of agreeableness.
- **Attraction** is a reaction made by the **Biological Brain**. It is a compulsive pull.

If she is smiling but her pupils are normal, her feet are pointed away, and she is "Shielding" her torso, she is being polite. If she is challenging you, leaning in, "Preening," and asking questions to keep the interaction alive, she is attracted.

Stop listening to the "Nice" things her social conditioning makes her say. Start watching the **Compulsive** things her biology forces her to do.

CHAPTER 6

SPOT RED FLAGS AND SIGNS OF DISINTEREST EARLY

The Art of the Strategic Withdrawal

In the complex journey toward becoming a High-Value Man, your progress is measured as much by your restraint as by your action. We often focus on the "push"—the art of escalation, the boldness of the approach, and the skill of maintaining eye contact. However, knowing when to "push" is only half the battle. The other—and arguably more critical—half is knowing exactly when to stop.

A significant portion of what is labeled "creepiness" in modern social dynamics isn't caused by a lack of good intentions or a lack of charm; it is caused by a profound lack of **Calibration** (Book 3, Chapter 1). When a man fails to recognize that the energy in an interaction has shifted from "curious" to "closed," he begins to over-invest. He pushes harder to compensate for her lack of interest, which in turn creates a feedback loop of discomfort.

A man who cannot read the signs of disinterest is like a pilot who ignores the flashing warning lights on his dashboard; eventually, the plane is going to crash. Whether that "crash" takes the form of a blunt, public rejection, a damaged social reputation within your circle, or simply hours of your life wasted on a dead-end pursuit, it is entirely avoidable. To protect your status and your sanity, you must sharpen your **"Negative Signal Radar."**

Disinterest in a civilized social setting is rarely broadcast through a megaphone. Because of the "Social Politeness" mandate discussed in Chapter 5, women will rarely say, "I am not interested in you, please leave." Instead, disinterest is whispered through micro-gestures, spatial distancing, and the construction of verbal "walls."

A High-Value Man is never a beggar for attention. He understands that his time and his masculine energy are his most precious currencies. If the **"Biological Buy-in"** isn't there, he doesn't take it personally. He recognizes the signal early, de-escalates gracefully, and moves his attention elsewhere. In this chapter, we will decode the "Red Flags" of the limbic system, the mechanics of "Social Distancing," and the specific behaviors that signal her "Shield" is not just up, but reinforced.

The Limbic "Freeze" and "Flight" Responses

As we established in the earlier chapters, the limbic system—the brain's emotional survival center—governs the involuntary spark of attraction. However, it is also the system responsible for **rejection and avoidance**. When a woman feels a lack of chemistry, a lack of alignment, or a lack of safety, her brain enters a subtle, socially-masked version of the "Freeze, Flight, or Fight" response.

1. The "Freeze" (The Social Paralysis)

When a woman is disinterested but feels "trapped" in a conversation by social norms or physical surroundings (like being in a corner of a bar or in a shared office space), she will subconsciously "Freeze."

- **The Signal:** Her face becomes a "mask" of static politeness. She maintains a tight-lipped smile, but the "Duchenne" crinkle in her eyes (Chapter 2) is missing—her eyes are effectively "dead."

Most tellingly, she stops nodding, stops using hand gestures, and her body becomes stiff and rigid.

- **The Neurobiology:** This is a "low-arousal" avoidance tactic. By minimizing her physical and verbal output, she is trying to become "invisible" to you. She is providing the bare minimum amount of social data required to keep the peace until she can find a socially acceptable exit strategy.

- **High-Value Move:** If you feel the energy "flatline," do not try to "reanimate" the conversation by asking more personal questions or telling longer stories. This is the moment to provide "Space" (Chapter 3). Pull back immediately.

2. The "Flight" (The Subtle Exit)

This is the most frequent form of disinterest. She isn't literally running for the door, but her body's navigation system is already "mentally" leaving the room.

- **The Signal:** Look at the "Rule of Feet" from Chapter 3. Her feet and knees are pointed toward the exit, the bar, or her group of friends, even if her face is still looking at you. She begins checking her watch or her phone frequently.

- **The "Horizon Scan":** While you are speaking, her eyes will frequently "break" from yours to scan the room over your shoulder. She is looking for a "Social Lifeboat"—a friend to wave over or an excuse to move.

- **The Interpretation:** Her intent is no longer on the "Current Reality" (the interaction with you); it is focused entirely on the "Next Reality" (the act of leaving).

Physical Red Flags: The "Closed" Body

In Chapter 3, we discussed the "Geography of Attraction" and how a woman "clears the path" for intimacy. Now, we must look at the **"Geography of Rejection."** When the limbic system rejects a suitor, it subconsciously tries to "shrink" the body's profile or create physical barriers.

1. Torso Shielding and the "Double Arm Cross"

The front of the human torso—containing the heart, lungs, and stomach—is our primary "vulnerability zone."

- **The Red Flag:** If she crosses her arms tightly across her chest, or if she holds an object (a purse, a drink, a cushion) like a shield against her stomach, she is "Blocking."

- **The Nuance:** Context matters. If it's 60°F in the room, she might just be cold. However, if she is "Shielding" while simultaneously leaning her torso away from you, it is a definitive sign that her "Intimate Zone" is strictly off-limits. She is creating a physical wall to protect her personal space.

2. The "Lint-Picking" Displacement

When humans feel social anxiety, boredom, or a desire to leave, they often engage in "displacement behaviors"—performing small, meaningless tasks to distract themselves from the discomfort of the interaction.

- **The Signal:** She starts picking non-existent lint off her clothes, obsessively checking her fingernails, or rearranging the napkins and glasses on the table between you.

- **The Interpretation:** She is using her "focal point" to block you out. By obsessing over a minute physical task, she is signaling that her internal world (or even a piece of lint) is more interesting and worthy of her attention than the external interaction with you.

3. Eye Contact Deflection (The "Staccato" Gaze)

In Chapter 2, we spoke about the "Intimate Gaze" and how it builds a bridge between two people. The opposite is the **"Staccato Gaze."**

- **The Signal:** She looks at you for the briefest possible second when you speak—just enough to acknowledge she heard you— and then immediately flicks her eyes away at a wall, the floor, or her drink.

- **The Interpretation:** Eye contact creates "Neural Coupling." She is subconsciously avoiding this coupling because she does not want to build rapport or "lead you on." She is keeping the interaction strictly "Transactional."

When a woman is disinterested, her verbal output shifts from "Invested" to **"De-invested."** She stops co-creating the reality and starts providing "dead ends."

1. The "Monosyllabic Barrier"

The hallmark of a disinterested woman is the "Closed Response."

- **The Signal:** You ask a high-quality, open-ended question designed to build rapport, and she shuts it down with a one-word answer.
    - *You:* "You seem like someone who has traveled a lot. What's the most adventurous thing you've done lately?"
    - *Her:* "Nothing." or "Not much."
- **The Interpretation:** She is refusing to give you "Hooks." She is making it as cognitively difficult as possible for you to continue. She is hoping you will get bored and leave so she doesn't have to be the "bad guy" who ends it.

2. The "Polite Interruption"

This is a sophisticated social tool used to break the "Frame" of a story.

- **The Signal:** She interrupts your story not to add a "Thread Expansion" (Chapter 4), but to "close" the interaction.
- **Example:** *"Oh, that's so crazy. Anyway, I think my friends are looking for me, it was nice meeting you!"*
- **The Interpretation:** She is using a "Social Out" to prevent the conversation from reaching a state of "Flow."

3. The "We/Us" Absence

Pay attention to pronouns. As we learned in Chapter 4, an attracted woman will eventually start using "We" or "Us" (Future Pacing). A disinterested woman will do the opposite. She will emphasize **"I," "Me,"** and **"My Friends."** She is maintaining a strict "Identity Boundary" to ensure you don't think you are part of her group or her future.

In the 21st century, the smartphone is the ultimate social weapon. It is the "Escape Hatch" we all carry in our pockets.

- **Level 1 (Passive Disinterest):** She has her phone on the table, face up, and her eyes constantly dart to notifications while you are speaking. This shows you do not have her full attention.

- **Level 2 (Active Disinterest):** She picks up the phone and starts scrolling or replying to texts while you are in the middle of a sentence. This is a clear signal of low respect and zero attraction.

- **Level 3 (The Tactical Exit):** She uses the phone to pretend she has an urgent "call" or a "text from her ride" that requires her to leave immediately.

The High-Value Rule: If a woman checks her phone more than once during a 10-minute interaction without apologizing or offering a valid reason (e.g., "I'm so sorry, I'm waiting for a work emergency call"), your current value in her eyes is lower than her digital feed. Do not try to "win" her attention back. **Gracefully walk away.**

Distinguishing "Playful Disinterest" from "True Disinterest"

Sometimes, a woman will act disinterested as a **"Hard-to-Get" Test** (Book 2, Chapter 4) to see if you have the confidence to persist. If you walk away during a "Test," you fail. If you stay during "True Disinterest," you become the "Creep." You must distinguish between the two.

Feature	Playful/Testing Disinterest	True/Biological Disinterest
Eyes	She "rolls" her eyes but maintains a smirk or "Heavy Gaze."	Her eyes are flat, "dead," and scanning for an exit.
Proximity	She says "You're trouble" but stays in your space.	She physically steps back or angles her torso away.

Feature	Playful/Testing Disinterest	True/Biological Disinterest
Touch	She pushes you playfully or "hits" your arm.	She flinches or stiffens if you accidentally touch her.
Voice	High energy, sarcastic, teasing, or "sing-song" tone.	Low energy, flat, monotone "customer service" tone.

The "Friend-Zone" Red Flags: The "Safety" Trap

This is the most dangerous form of disinterest because it feels like "Interest." She is very engaged, she talks to you for hours, and she seems to "value" you. However, she sees you as a **non-sexual support system**.

1. **The "Man-Hating" Rant:** She talks to you about how "all men are trash" or details the problems she's having with her "toxic" ex. She is using you as an emotional dumping ground.

2. **The "Zero-Tension" Zone:** She is *too* comfortable. She mentions "unsexy" topics like her digestion, her messy apartment, or her skincare routine for acne. There is no **"Preening"** (Chapter 2) because she isn't trying to attract you; she has already categorized you as "Safe/Platonic."

3. **The "Wingman" Request:** She asks for your "honest guy opinion" on a man she is currently obsessed with. This is the ultimate "Negative Signal."

Calibration: The Graceful Exit (The "Eject" Button)

The most attractive and high-value thing you can do when a woman shows genuine disinterest is to **believe her immediately.**

A Low-Value Man tries to "convince" her of his worth. He tells more jokes, talks louder, and becomes "thirstier." This only confirms her limbic system's decision to reject him.

A High-Value Man sees the lack of interest, acknowledges the "Warning Lights" on the dashboard, and withdraws his attention instantly.

The Script for a High-Value Exit:

- *"It was great meeting you, I'm going to go catch up with my friends. Have an amazing night."*

- *"You seem a bit distracted/busy, I'll let you get back to your night. Take care."*

By exiting first, you regain the **Power Position**. You demonstrate that you were there to *share* your high-value energy, and if she isn't "buying," you are perfectly happy to "sell" elsewhere. You leave with your dignity intact and your social reputation preserved.

Exercises: Mastering the Radar

1. The "Exit Scan"

Go to a crowded social environment (a bar, lounge, or networking event). Do not listen to the conversations. Just watch the **feet and hips**. Try to predict which interactions will end in the next 60 seconds based purely on who is "leaning out" or pointing at the door.

- **Goal:** Sharpen your "Spatial Intelligence" so you can feel the "Exit Energy" before it's spoken.

2. The "Phone-Check" Empathy Drill

In your own life, pay close attention to the physiological "drop" in your chest when someone you are talking to pulls out their phone. Now, look for that same energy in the women you approach. If you see it, acknowledge that the "Connection" has been severed.

- **Goal:** Develop an intuitive "Radar" for the modern social disconnect.

3. The "Silence" Test (Negative)

If you suspect a woman is "just being polite" (Chapter 5), stop talking for five full seconds during a lull.

- If she looks relieved and uses the time to turn away or check her phone, she is disinterested.

- If she looks slightly panicked and tries to restart the talk, she was just shy or overwhelmed.

- **Goal:** Use silence as a diagnostic tool to save yourself hours of wasted time.

Summary: Your Time is Your Currency

Attraction is, at its core, a "Yes" or "No" game played by the nervous system.

- **"Yes"** looks like: Leaning in, pupil dilation, "Thread Expansion," and "Preening."
- **"No"** looks like: "Shielding," "Staccato" gaze, "Phone Shields," and feet pointed at the door.

A High-Value Man does not waste his precious currency (time) trying to turn a biological "No" into a "Maybe." He reads the signals, respects the boundary, and maintains his status by being the one to end the interaction. When you stop chasing the "No," you finally have the energy and the calibration to find the "Yes."

CHAPTER 7

CONCLUSION: ACTING ON WHAT YOU SEE

The Transition from Analyst to Architect

You have traveled through the high-definition nuances of the face (Chapter 2), the topography of physical space (Chapter 3), the narrative engine of verbal investment (Chapter 4), and the critical filters of politeness versus genuine interest (Chapters 5 and 6). You now possess the most sophisticated "Social Radar" available to the modern man. However, knowledge without application is merely a burden. In the world of high-value dynamics, there is no prize for being the smartest observer in the room if you remain paralyzed by analysis. To "Read the Signals" is a passive skill; to **Act on What You See** is an active leadership trait.

The difference between a "Social Analyst" and a "Social Architect" is the ability to move. An analyst sits in the corner of the room, correctly identifying that the woman at the bar is showing ventral openness and dilated pupils, yet he never leaves his stool. He has the data, but he lacks the execution. An architect, however, uses that data to build a bridge. He sees the "Green Light" and immediately shifts his energy to lead the interaction toward a conclusion.

This concluding chapter is about **Synthesis**. It is about taking the disparate "blips" on your radar—a dilated pupil here, a pointed foot there, a qualifying statement in the middle of a laugh—and weaving them into a coherent strategy for escalation or withdrawal. We will explore the "Golden Rule of Three," the "Calibration Loop," and the psychological blueprint for the **Perfect Move**.

The "Golden Rule of Three": Moving Beyond the Single Signal

The biggest mistake a "Novice Reader" makes is reacting to a single indicator. This is often driven by "Confirmation Bias"—the tendency to look for signals that support what we *want* to believe. If a man is desperate for a woman to like him, he will see her move a stray hair behind her ear and convince himself it's a high-level grooming signal. In reality, she might just have an itch.

A High-Value Man understands the **Biological Law of Probability**. A single signal is an anomaly; two signals are a coincidence; but **three signals are a Cluster.**

1. The Principle of Biological Triangulation

To accurately diagnose the "State of the Union" in an interaction, you must triangulate. This means identifying at least three indicators from different physiological or linguistic categories that all point toward the same emotional state.

If you see a woman laugh at your joke (Category: Verbal/Vocal), but her arms are crossed (Category: Space/Blocking) and her feet are pointed toward her friends (Category: Navigation), the "Cluster" is actually negative. The laugh was a social mask. However, if she laughs, uncrosses her arms to touch your forearm, and leans her torso into your personal space, you have a **Positive Cluster**.

2. The High-Interest Cluster Example

Let's look at a "Triple-Green" scenario where action is not just suggested, but mandatory for the High-Value Man:

1. **Face (Limbic):** She maintains a "Heavy Gaze," frequently dropping her eyes to your lips during lulls in the conversation.
2. **Space (Proxemics):** She has cleared the "Barriers" (moving her drink or purse to the side) and has moved into your **Personal Zone** (within 18 inches) without you initiating the move.
3. **Verbal (Investment):** She uses "Future Pacing" or "Qualifying" statements, such as, *"I'm actually a really great cook; we should have a bake-off sometime."*

The Diagnosis: The biological and psychological evidence is overwhelming. Her limbic system has accepted you. At this point, failing to escalate—whether through a more intimate touch, a deeper vocal tone, or a direct invitation—is a sign of low-value hesitation.

The "Cross-Pollination" of Signals: Resolving the Congruence Gap

In many interactions, you will encounter a "Congruence Gap"—where her words say one thing, but her body says another. A woman might say, *"I'm having such a great time talking to you,"* while her torso is angled 45 degrees away and she is scanning the room for her friends.

The Rule of Biological Primacy: In cases of conflicting data, always trust the **lower-brain signals** (the feet, the hips, and the space) over the **higher-brain signals** (the words and the polite smile).

Words are mediated by the Prefrontal Cortex; they can be faked, rehearsed, and masked. The feet and the ventral (front) of the body are mediated by the Limbic System; they are the "Truth Tellers" of human interaction. If she is "Qualifying" herself verbally but her feet are pointed at the exit, she is likely feeling a "social obligation" to be nice while her body is screaming for an escape. A High-Value Man sees this, respects the biological truth, and initiates the exit first to maintain his dignity.

The Calibration Loop: The OODA Process in Social Dynamics

In military strategy, the OODA loop (Observe, Orient, Decide, Act) is a four-stage cycle for making decisions in fast-moving, high-stakes environments. As a High-Value Man, you apply this same process to the social "battlefield" to ensure you are always one step ahead of the interaction.

Phase 1: Observe (The Raw Data Acquisition)

In this phase, you are the "Radar." You are constantly scanning for the signals we have discussed throughout Book 3. You aren't staring or acting like a predator; you are practicing "Diffused Attention." You notice the micro-dilations of the pupils, the shift in her vocal pitch, the way she holds her glass, and her proximity to the exit. You are gathering the "Blips."

Phase 2: Orient (The Context Filter)

This is the most critical phase. You filter the raw data through the **Context of the Environment**.

- Is she leaning in because she likes you, or because the music in this club is 110 decibels and she literally can't hear you?

- Is she crossing her arms because she's disinterested, or because the air conditioner is blasting directly on her shoulders?

- Is she checking her watch because she's bored, or because she mentioned earlier she has an early flight?

Orientation prevents "False Positives." You adjust your reading for the "Baseline" of the room. A High-Value Man is never a victim of his own optimism; he is a realist who understands environment.

Phase 3: Decide (The Strategic Selection)

Based on the clusters you've identified and the context you've filtered, you choose your "Next Move."

- **Cluster is Positive:** "I will move into the Intimate Zone and test for a Haptic response (touch)."

- **Cluster is Neutral/Polite:** "I will use a 'Topic Pivot' or a 'Tease' (Chapter 5) to test if I can spark a biological reaction."

- **Cluster is Negative:** "I will perform a 'Graceful Exit' (Chapter 6) before the energy becomes awkward."

Phase 4: Act (The Decisive Execution)

You execute the move with 100% conviction. High-value action is never tentative. If you decide to lead her to a quieter part of the bar, you do it with a steady hand and a calm, authoritative voice. If you decide to end the conversation, you do it without looking back for approval. Tentative action smells like insecurity; decisive action smells like leadership.

The Science of "The Perfect Move"

Acting on signals is not about "pouncing" on a woman the moment you see a green light. It is about **Invitation and Leadership.** It is a dance of pressure and release. When you identify a high-interest cluster, your "Action" should follow the **Lead-and-Wait protocol.**

1. The Lead (The Escalation)

You initiate a subtle change in the dynamic. This could be physical (moving 6 inches closer), vocal (lowering your pitch and slowing your tempo), or emotional (moving from small talk to a "vulnerability pivot").

2. The Wait (The Calibration Gap)

After you "Lead," you must pause for 2–3 seconds. This is the "Calibration Gap." You are giving her nervous system time to process the new level of intimacy and decide how to respond. Most men skip the wait; they push and push until the woman feels overwhelmed. A High-Value Man is comfortable in the silence.

3. The Confirmation (The Compliance Signal)

You look for the response.

- **Compliance:** She stays in the new space, her pupils dilate further, or she touches you back. You have moved the "Bridge" forward.

- **Resistance:** She subtly leans back or creates a verbal barrier. If you get resistance, you de-escalate without ego. You simply return to the previous level of intimacy as if nothing happened. This "calibration" makes you feel safe to her, which paradoxically often leads to her reciprocating later.

Overcoming the "Analysis Paralysis": The Three-Second Rule

Many men fail in social dynamics because they become "Social Scientists." They spend so much time "reading" and "decoding" that they forget to actually **interact**. They become the man who can spot a "Duchenne Smile" from forty yards but can't hold a three-minute conversation.

Analysis Paralysis is a biological state where the Prefrontal Cortex over-calculates the risks of rejection, leading to a "Freeze" response in the man. To break this, you must implement the **"Three-Second Rule of Action."**

Once your "Radar" detects a high-value cluster (three positive signals), you have exactly three seconds to take the next step in escalation.

- If she touches your arm and qualifies herself—count: *One, Two, Three*—and then you must move closer or lead the topic deeper.

By acting within three seconds, you bypass the "Fear Center" of your brain. You act before your ego has time to tell you "What if she says no?" You become a man of **Actionable Intelligence**.

Acting on Disinterest: The "Phantom" Strategy

What do you do when the clusters are consistently negative? Most men view this as a personal failure. They try "one more joke" or "one more drink" to turn the "No" into a "Yes." This is low-value behavior; it signals that your self-worth is dependent on her approval.

When you see a "Rejection Cluster" (Shielding, Staccato Gaze, Monosyllabic answers), your action should be an **Instant Strategic Withdrawal.** We call this the **"Phantom Strategy."**

1. **Detach Mentally:** Realize this is a biological mismatch, not a character flaw.

2. **De-value the Interaction:** Subtly shift your focus away from her. Look at the room, check the time, or engage with someone else in the group.

3. **The Graceful Exit:** Use the scripts from Chapter 6. *"It was great meeting you; I'm going to go find my friends. Have a good night."*

By acting decisively on disinterest, you prevent the "Creep" label. More importantly, you signal to your own subconscious that your time is too valuable to spend on someone who isn't "invested." This builds **Internal Frame** (Book 2), which makes you significantly more attractive to the *next* woman you encounter, because you are no longer carrying the "stink" of a man who stayed too long at a party where he wasn't wanted.

Synthesizing the Chapters: The Master Intelligence Checklist

Before you close this book and step out into the world, run through this **Final Intelligence Checklist** for every interaction you enter. This is your "Pre-Flight" check for social mastery.

- **The Eyes (Chapter 2):** Have I seen "The Flare" or the "Intimate Scan"? If the gaze is strictly social (eyes-to-eyes), I stay in the "Acquaintance Frame."

- **The Proximity (Chapter 3):** Is she "Clearing the Path"? If her purse is still between us, I have not yet earned her trust.

- **The Investment (Chapter 4):** Is she using "Future Pacing" (We/Us)? If the pronouns are all "I" and "You," the bridge is not yet built.

- **The Filter (Chapter 5/6):** Is this "Biological Attraction" or "Social Politeness"? Am I mistaking her "Barista Smile" for a "Bedroom Smile"?

- **The Action (Chapter 7):** Have I identified a **Cluster of Three**? Am I moving with **100% Conviction**, or am I hesitating like a "Social Waiter"?

Exercises: The Synthesis Drills

To turn this knowledge into an instinct, you must perform these three "Drills" in the real world.

1. The "Cluster Hunt" (Non-Participant Observation)

Go to a high-traffic social area—a hotel lobby, a busy park, or a lounge. Pick three "target" groups. For each group, identify a "Signal Cluster." Do not stop until you have identified at least three distinct signals (Face, Space, and Verbal) for each interaction.

- **Goal:** Train your brain to see "Triangles" rather than "Dots." Stop reacting to single signals and start seeing patterns.

2. The "OODA" Speed Drill

In your next three social interactions, consciously walk yourself through the OODA loop.

- *Observe* the baseline.

- *Orient* to the room.

- *Decide* on an escalation.

- *Act* within the three-second window.

- **Goal:** Decrease the "Lag Time" between your eyes seeing a signal and your feet or hands acting on it.

3. The "Decisive Withdrawal" Challenge

In an interaction where you feel the interest is "Lukewarm" or "Polite," practice being the **first person to leave.** Do it while the conversation is still "good" but not "great." Notice how it feels to be the one who controls the "Exit Frame."

- **Goal:** Eradicate the fear of "Negative Signals" by realizing they are simply data points for a strategic move.

Summary: The Power of the Calibrated Man

You are now a master of the **Geography of Attraction**. You no longer navigate the social world by "vibes," "luck," or "hope." You navigate by **Intelligence**.

A man who can read the silent language of the face, the secret intent of the feet, and the hidden investment in the voice is a man who cannot be easily manipulated, ignored, or "friend-zoned." He is a man who leads with empathy but acts with dominance. He knows exactly where he stands at all times because he is listening to the language the body cannot help but speak.

The signals are the map, but you are the driver. Use the map to find your destination, but never forget to enjoy the journey. Social intelligence is not about "winning"; it's about **alignment**. When you are aligned with the signals, you find the women who are actually looking for a man like you.

CHAPTER 8

REFLECTION QUESTIONS

The Final Audit: Mastery Through Self-Reflection

You have completed the technical curriculum of Book 3. You have learned to decode the micro-expressions of the face, the silent geography of proximity, the subtext of verbal investment, and the critical distinction between social masks and biological truth. However, as we have emphasized throughout this series, high-value status is not a destination; it is a process of constant calibration.

The world's most sophisticated radar systems require regular maintenance to ensure they aren't producing "ghost signals." Your social intuition is no different. If your internal state is clouded by ego, desperation, or past trauma, you will misread even the most obvious signals.

This final chapter is designed to be your **Internal Audit**. These reflection questions are not merely academic; they are designed to strip away the "Social Delusions" we discussed in Chapter 5 and force you to look at your interactions with surgical objectivity. To get the most out of this chapter, I recommend writing your answers in a private journal. The act of externalizing your thoughts into writing forces the Prefrontal Cortex to engage, moving you from "Vibe-based" thinking to "Logic-based" mastery.

Section 1: The Mindset of the Observer

Before you can read her signals, you must be able to read your own. Your internal "Baseline" dictates the frequency of your radar.

1. Am I Reading Reality or My Own Projections?

When you enter an interaction, do you find yourself looking for "Green Lights" because they are actually there, or because you *need* them to be there to validate your ego?

- **The Psychology:** Confirmation Bias is the enemy of calibration. If you feel "thirsty" or low-value, your brain will hallucinate signs of interest to protect you from the pain of rejection.

- **The Deep Reflection:** Recall your last three "failed" interactions. In hindsight, were the red flags present from the beginning? Why did you choose to ignore the "Staccato Gaze" or the "Torso Shielding"? What were you hoping to gain by staying?

2. What is My Baseline "Vocal and Physical Tonality"?

A High-Value Man understands that he is a "Signal Generator" as much as a "Signal Receiver."

- **The Psychology:** Through **Emotional Contagion**, your state will influence hers. If you are anxious, she will feel a subtle "Threat Response" in her limbic system, causing her to close her body language.

- **The Deep Reflection:** If you were to watch a video of yourself approaching a woman, would you see a man who is grounded and outcome-independent, or a man who is "leaning in" too far and seeking approval? How does your body feel in the first 30 seconds of an approach—is it tight or relaxed?

3. Am I Truly Comfortable with "No"?

Is your "Graceful Exit" (Chapter 6) a tactical move, or a genuine expression of your value?

- **The Psychology:** Outcome independence is the ultimate high-value signal. If you can walk away from a "No" with the same smile you had during a "Yes," you prove that your value is internal, not external.

- **The Deep Reflection:** When you sense disinterest, do you feel a "Sting" of rejection, or a sense of "Information Gathering"? Can you honestly say that you value your time enough to be happy when a woman reveals she isn't interested early?

Section 2: Auditing the Visual and Facial Domain

The face is the most complex social canvas. These questions ensure you aren't just looking, but actually *seeing*.

4. Can I Distinguish Between a "Social Mask" and a "Limbic Truth"?

How many times have you mistaken a "Pan-Am Smile" (Chapter 2) for genuine attraction?

- **The Psychology:** Social conditioning makes women experts at "The Mask."

- **The Deep Reflection:** Think of a woman who was "just being nice" to you (perhaps a waitress or a polite colleague). What were the micro-signals that revealed her true state? Did her eyes lack the Duchenne crinkle? Were her feet pointed away while her mouth was smiling? How will you use this "Micro-Delta" to calibrate in the future?

5. Am I Tracking the "Micro-Flicker"?

In Chapter 2, we discussed the "Visual Flare." Are you present enough to catch the split-second signals that happen before the conscious mind takes over?

- **The Psychology:** Micro-expressions last less than 1/25th of a second. They are the only time the "True Self" is visible before social conditioning "buffers" the response.

- **The Deep Reflection:** In your next five interactions, make it your primary goal to watch for the **initial reaction** when you say something bold or teasing. What did her face do in the first half-second? Did she flinch, or did her pupils dilate? What does your ability (or inability) to catch these flickers tell you about your level of presence?

Section 3: Auditing Space and Proximity (Proxemics)

The geography of an interaction tells the story of power and intimacy.

6. Do I Own My Space, or Am I "Leaking" Energy?

In Chapter 3, we discussed "Ventral Openness." Are you presenting a "High-Value Silhouette"?

- **The Psychology:** A man who "fidgets" or "shrinks" his body is signaling that he feels lower in status than the person he is talking to.

- **The Deep Reflection:** When you are in a high-stakes social environment, what is your "Resting Posture"? Do you find yourself crossing your arms (Blocking) or checking your phone (Shielding)? How can you consciously expand your "Physical Footprint" to signal dominance and comfort?

7. How Do I React to the "Invisible Wall"?

When you move 4 inches closer and she subtly leans back (The Proximity Test, Chapter 5), what is your immediate internal response?

- **The Psychology:** The "Lean Back" is a biological boundary.

- **The Deep Reflection:** Do you feel the urge to "chase" her into that space to regain the connection? Or can you immediately de-escalate and give her double the space back? Which response signals higher value?

Section 4: The Investment and Verbal Audit

Words are the secondary language; investment is the primary one.

8. Am I Working Harder Than She Is?

Look at your recent text threads or look back at your recent conversations. Who is providing the "Hooks"?

- **The Psychology:** The person who is more "Invested" is the person with the lower perceived value in the interaction.

- **The Deep Reflection:** Do you find yourself asking "Interview Style" questions to keep a dying conversation alive? When she provides a "Monosyllabic Answer" (Chapter 6), do you try to "save" her, or do you let the silence hang to see if she will invest? Why are you afraid of the silence?

9. Can I Spot the "Brother/Safe" Frame Before It Becomes a Trap?

In Chapter 6, we discussed the "Friend-Zone" red flags. Are you ignoring "Platonic Signals" because you're addicted to her attention?

- **The Psychology:** Many men accept "Platonic Validation" as a consolation prize for "Sexual Attraction." This is low-value behavior that wastes your most precious resource: time.

- **The Deep Reflection:** Is there a woman in your life right now who is "too comfortable" with you? Does she talk about her periods, her exes, or her messy life without "Preening"? If so, why are you still in her "Safe Zone"? What would happen if you withdrew your attention today?

Section 5: Tactical Synthesis (The OODA Loop)

Reading is nothing without action. These questions audit your ability to execute.

10. Do I Act, or Do I Analyze?

When you see a "Cluster of Three" (Chapter 7), do you move within three seconds, or do you enter "Analysis Paralysis"?

- **The Psychology:** Hesitation is a signal of low-confidence. Women can "smell" the moment a man decides to do something and then hesitates.

- **The Deep Reflection:** What is the specific thought that stops you from escalating when you see a "Green Light"? Is it fear of rejection, or fear of "being a creep"? How does the "Three-Second Rule" (Chapter 7) solve this problem for you?

11. How High is My "Signal-to-Noise" Ratio?

Are you focusing on the right data points, or are you getting distracted by the "Noise" (the music, her friends, your own thoughts)?

- **The Psychology:** Selective attention is a limited resource. You must learn to ignore the "Social Noise" to focus on the "Limbic Signals."

- **The Deep Reflection:** In a crowded room, can you maintain "Neural Coupling" (Chapter 4) with her, or are you constantly looking around to see if other people are watching you? Who is the "Lead" in your reality—you or the crowd?

Section 6: The Long-Term Calibration

Mastery is a lifetime pursuit. These questions focus on your growth over time.

12. How Has My "Success Rate" Changed Since I Started Reading Signals?

Don't define "Success" as just getting a phone number. Define it as **Efficiency**.

- **The Metric:** Success = (Total Interactions) / (Time Wasted on Disinterest).

- **The Deep Reflection:** Are you getting "Rejected" faster? High-value men get rejected quickly because they don't linger in "Neutral" zones. They find the "No" early and move on. Are you becoming more efficient at finding the "No"?

13. Am I Developing "Social Empathy" or "Social Manipulation"?

There is a thin line between "Reading Signals" to build a bridge and "Using Signals" to force an outcome.

- **The Philosophy:** A High-Value Man uses his "Radar" to find **Mutual Alignment**. He wants to find the women who *want* to be found by him.

- **The Deep Reflection:** Do you use this knowledge to "trick" women into liking you, or to find the women who already have a biological spark with you? Which path leads to a high-value life, and which leads to a low-value "game" mentality?

Exercises: The Reflection Lab

1. The "Interaction Autopsy"

Take your most recent "Cold Approach" or date. Spend 20 minutes writing down every signal you remember.

- Categorize them into Face, Space, Verbal, and Haptic.
- Did they form a Cluster?

- Did you act on that Cluster?
- If you could go back, what was the "Pivot Point" you missed?

2. The "Mirror Drill"

Spend 5 minutes in front of a mirror practicing your "Neutral High-Value Baseline."

- Relax your brow.
- Maintain "Ventral Openness."
- Speak one sentence out loud and listen to your "Vocal Tonality." Is it "Seeking" (rising at the end) or "Telling" (dropping at the end)?

3. The "Outcome Independence" Challenge

For the next 48 hours, your goal is to get three "Graceful Rejections." Go into interactions with the express goal of finding a "No" as quickly as possible. Notice how your anxiety vanishes when the "No" becomes the target.

- **Goal:** Desensitize your ego to rejection so your "Radar" can function without emotional interference.

Summary: The Unfair Advantage

You now have a framework for self-correction that 99% of men will never possess. Most men will go through their entire lives wondering why they were "Friend-Zoned," why she "ghosted," or why the "vibe" felt off. They are flying blind in a storm of biological data.

You, however, are a **Calibrated Observer**. You know that her eyes tell the truth, her feet point the way, and her investment dictates the value. But more than that, you know that **you** are the one in control of the interaction. You are the architect.

The questions in this chapter are your "Maintenance Manual." Revisit them every few months. As you grow in value, your baseline will shift, and your radar will become even more sensitive.

BOOK FOUR
MAKE HER WANT YOU

CHAPTER 1

INTRODUCTION: WHY WE CHASE WHAT WE CAN'T EASILY CATCH

The Paradox of Desire

In the previous three books, we have focused on the foundation: building your internal state, understanding the dynamics of value, and learning to read the silent language of attraction. You have learned how to be "present," how to calibrate your energy, and how to decode her signals with surgical precision. But now, we move into the most provocative phase of your transformation. We move from the **Passive Observer** to the **Active Catalyst**.

Book 4 is about **Desire**.

Not just "interest" or "attraction," but the deep, visceral pull that makes a woman think about you when you aren't in the room. It is about the psychological mechanics that turn a "pleasant acquaintance" into a "necessary obsession." And to understand desire, we must first confront a fundamental, often uncomfortable truth of human psychology: **We value most what we have to work for.**

We are biologically wired to equate "easy" with "low value" and "difficult" with "high value." This is the paradox of the human heart. While we claim to want peace, stability, and "nice" things, our nervous systems are designed to chase the challenge. In this chapter, we will dismantle the "Why" behind this phenomenon. We will explore the neurobiology of dopamine, the economics of the mating market, and the evolutionary blueprints that dictate why we chase what we can't easily catch.

The Neurobiology of the Chase: Dopamine and the Skinner Box

To understand why a woman (or any human) becomes more interested when you aren't constantly available, we have to look at the brain's reward system. Specifically, we have to look at **Dopamine.**

Contrary to popular belief, dopamine is not the "pleasure" chemical; it is the **"anticipation"** chemical. It is the neurotransmitter of *wanting*, not *having*.

1. The Reward Prediction Error

In the late 20th century, researchers discovered something fascinating about the way mammals respond to rewards. If a reward is 100% predictable—if you press a button and a treat appears every single time—the dopamine spike eventually flattens out. The brain becomes bored. The reward is "guaranteed," so it no longer requires focused attention or high valuation.

However, when the reward is **intermittent**—if the treat appears only *sometimes* after the button is pressed—the dopamine spikes reach massive levels. The brain enters a state of hyper-focus. Because the outcome is uncertain, the "value" of the reward skyrockets in the subject's mind.

2. Application to Dating

When a man is "too easy"—when he texts back within seconds every time, when he is available for every date, and when he expresses total devotion before the first week is over—he becomes a **Predictable**

Reward. He has effectively "killed" the dopamine response in her brain. There is no mystery, no tension, and therefore, no chase.

A High-Value Man, as we will explore in this book, is not "playing games." He is simply living a life that is **Naturally Intermittent**. Because he has a passion and purpose outside the relationship (Chapter 2) and prioritizes his own schedule (Chapter 4), his "availability" is a rare and precious resource. This creates the "Anticipation Loop" that fuels desire.

The Scarcity Principle: Economics of Attraction

In economics, the law of supply and demand is absolute. When the supply of a commodity is high, the price drops. When the supply is low and the demand is high, the price—and the perceived value—soars. Human attraction follows this exact economic curve.

1. The "Precious Metal" Identity

Consider the difference between gold and sand. Chemically, they are both just arrangements of atoms. But you can find sand on any beach. It requires zero effort to obtain. Gold, however, is buried deep. It requires mining, refining, and luck. Because gold is scarce, it is used to symbolize status, love, and power.

A man who is always available, always "pursuing," and always seeking validation is "Social Sand." He is everywhere, and therefore, he is worth very little. A High-Value Man is "Social Gold." He is selective about who he spends time with, and he doesn't give away his attention for free.

2. The Scarcity Equation

We can model this value mathematically. Let V represent Perceived Value, B represent the Benefit of the interaction, and A represent Availability:

$$V = \frac{B}{A}$$

As Availability (A) approaches infinity (meaning you are always there), the Perceived Value (V) approaches zero, regardless of how great the Benefit (B) is. To increase your value, you must decrease your availability to a level that reflects your actual status as a busy, high-purpose individual.

Evolutionary Psychology: The "Busy Mating" Signal

Our ancestors did not live in a world of Tinder and Instagram. They lived in small tribes where survival was the only metric. In that environment, a man who was always "hanging around" the camp, doing nothing but seeking the attention of women, was a liability. He wasn't hunting, he wasn't protecting, and he wasn't building.

1. Survival Capacity as Attraction

From an evolutionary standpoint, a woman's "Mating Radar" is designed to find a man with **Resource Capacity**. A man who is deeply invested in his mission (his "hunt") is naturally less available than a man who has no mission. Therefore, "Busy-ness" and "Preoccupation" became evolutionary proxies for **Success and Competence**.

When you are "hard to catch," you are subconsciously signaling: *"I have other things that demand my attention—things that are vital to my survival and status."* This makes you a much more attractive "Genetic Bet" than the man who has nothing better to do than wait for a text reply.

2. The "Pre-Selection" Effect

Why is a man who is "taken" or who has many female friends often more attractive than a man who is single and "hunting"? It's the same principle. If other women want him, he is "Pre-Selected." His value is "Socially Validated." He is hard to catch because he is already in demand. Throughout Book 4, we will learn how to generate this "Pre-Selection" energy through your lifestyle choices, not through deception.

The "Investment Effect": Why We Value What We Build

There is a psychological phenomenon known as the **"IKEA Effect."** People value furniture they assembled themselves significantly more than the same furniture they bought pre-assembled. Why? Because we infuse our own labor into the objects we work for. Our "Investment" creates a sense of ownership and value.

1. Making Her Invest

If you make a relationship "too easy" for a woman, you are depriving her of the opportunity to **Invest** in you. If you do all the planning, all the driving, all the paying, and all the emotional lifting, she has no "Labor" in the interaction.

To make her *want* you, she must be allowed to contribute. She must "earn" your attention. When she has to work to fit into your busy schedule, or when she has to qualify herself to meet your boundaries (Chapter 3), she is investing her time and emotional energy. The more she invests, the more she will value you.

2. The Danger of the "Gift" Mentality

The "Nice Guy" error is to treat himself like a gift that he is trying to give away for free. The High-Value Man treats himself like a **Prize** that must be won. A gift is nice, but it is often taken for granted. A prize is celebrated.

Playing Games vs. High-Value Reality

At this point, you might be thinking: *"Isn't this just playing hard-to-get? Isn't this just 'The Game'?"*

It is vital to make a distinction here. A Low-Value Man **pretends** to be busy. He waits exactly 20 minutes to text back because he read it in a book. He acts disinterested while staring at his phone, waiting for her to call. This is "Playing Games," and it is transparent. Eventually, the facade cracks, and his true "Needy" nature is revealed, causing the attraction to evaporate.

A High-Value Man **is** busy. He waits 20 minutes to text back because he was actually finishing a workout, leading a meeting, or reading a book. He is "hard to catch" because he is actually **moving fast** in the direction of his goals.

The goal of Book 4 is not to teach you how to "act" like a high-value man; it is to teach you how to **become** one so that these psychological principles happen automatically. You don't have to "try" to be scarce when your life is full of passion and purpose (Chapter 2).

The Architecture of Book 4

In the coming chapters, we will break down the specific pillars of creating desire:

- **Chapter 2: Passion and Purpose.** We will explore how your external mission creates an "Attraction Halo" that pulls women toward you.

- **Chapter 3: Healthy Boundaries.** You will learn that "No" is the most attractive word in the English language when used correctly.
- **Chapter 4: Your Schedule.** We will discuss the logistics of "High-Value Availability."
- **Chapter 5: Vulnerability Without Weakness.** How to be a human being without losing your masculine "Edge."
- **Chapter 6: Anticipation and Tension.** The mechanics of the "Slow Burn" and escalation.

Summary: The Prize Mindset

If you take nothing else from this introduction, remember this: **Desire cannot exist without Space.** If you are always there, if you are always easy, if you are always "yours," there is no space for her to miss you. There is no space for her to wonder about you. There is no space for her to **want** you.

To become the High-Value Choice, you must step back into your own life. You must become the man who is chasing his own potential, not the man who is chasing a woman. When you stop being the "Chaser," you create the vacuum that allows her to become the "Seeker."

CHAPTER 2

DEMONSTRATE PASSION AND PURPOSE OUTSIDE THE RELATIONSHIP

The Gravity of the North Star

One of the most pervasive and damaging lies sold to modern men by cinema, pop music, and romantic literature is the **"Romantic Center" fallacy**. We are conditioned from a young age to believe that the ultimate expression of love—the "pinnacle" of masculine devotion—is to make a woman the absolute center of our universe. We are told to make her our "everything," our "reason for breathing," and our "sole focus." We are taught that a man who sacrifices his hobbies, his friends, and his career goals to spend every waking second with a woman is a "hero" of romance.

In reality, for a High-Value Man, this is the fastest way to kill desire. It is a biological death sentence for attraction.

Desire, at its core, requires a certain amount of **Gravitational Pull**. In celestial terms, a planet doesn't orbit a vacuum; it orbits a sun—a massive, burning center of energy that has its own trajectory, its own internal fusion, and its own purpose. When you make a woman your "everything," you effectively extinguish your own fire. You stop being the sun and start being a satellite. You lose your "mass," your "heat," and eventually, you lose your "orbit."

A man without an external mission is a man who is "floating." He has no weight. Because he has no weight, he becomes easily moved by her moods, her whims, and her emotional fluctuations. This lack of stability is terrifying to the female limbic system. Paradoxically, the more a man makes a woman his "world," the less she wants to live in it.

To be truly magnetic, a man must have an **External North Star**. He must have a mission, a passion, or a purpose that exists entirely independent of his romantic life. This isn't about ignoring her or being cold; it's about having a "Mental Fortress" that she can admire, support, and occasionally visit, but never fully occupy. When a woman sees you pursuing something that challenges you, she sees a man who is capable of leading. When she sees that you have goals that are more important than a Tuesday night text thread, she realizes that your time is a limited, high-value resource.

In this chapter, we will explore why purpose is the ultimate aphrodisiac, the neurochemistry of "The Winner Effect," and how to build a life that is so compelling that a woman feels lucky to be a part of it.

The "Halo Effect" of Competence

Psychologically, humans are prone to the **Halo Effect**—a cognitive bias where our overall impression of a person influences how we feel and think about their character in specific areas. If we perceive someone as highly competent in one domain, our brains subconsciously "fill in the blanks" and assume they are competent in others.

1. Competence as a Proxy for Survival

From an evolutionary perspective, competence is a signal of **"Resource Acquisition Potential."** In the ancestral environment, a man who was the best hunter, the most skilled toolmaker, or a strategic leader was a man who could ensure survival. Even in our modern, safe world, the limbic system still reads "He is great at his craft" as "He is a high-capability male."

When you demonstrate mastery—whether it is scaling a business, mastering a martial art, or becoming a virtuoso at an instrument—you are signaling to her biology that you are an "Expert Navigator" of reality. This creates a sense of safety and trust. She doesn't have to "mother" a man who is a master of his own domain.

2. The "Obsession" Factor and the Flow State

There is something deeply attractive about a man in a **"Flow State."** Flow, a term coined by psychologist Mihaly Csikszentmihalyi, is the state of total immersion in a task where time seems to disappear. When you are deeply immersed in your passion, your body language changes. Your focus is singular, your movements are efficient, and you radiate a sense of **"Unfazed Presence."**

This is the opposite of the "Needy" energy we discussed in Book 1. A man who is obsessed with his mission doesn't have the "cognitive bandwidth" to worry about whether she liked his last Instagram post or why she took two hours to reply. That indifference—born of genuine preoccupation—is incredibly magnetic. It signals that you are the protagonist of your own story, rather than a supporting character in hers.

Self-Expansion Theory: Why She Wants Your World to Be Big

Social psychologist Arthur Aron developed **Self-Expansion Theory**, which suggests that one of the primary motivations for humans to enter and stay in relationships is the desire to "expand" the self. We seek partners who bring new perspectives, skills, identities, and "worlds" into our lives. We want to be "more" because of the person we are with.

1. The Danger of the "Closed System"

If your life is small—if it consists only of your job and your relationship—you offer very little room for her to "expand" into. You become a **"Closed System."** Within a few months, she has mapped out your entire "territory." There are no more mountains to climb, no more mysteries to uncover. This leads to the "Stagnation of the Familiar," which is a primary killer of long-term desire.

2. The "Piggyback" Growth Model

However, if you have a vibrant passion, a circle of high-achieving friends, and a purpose that takes you into new territories, she gets to "piggyback" on your growth. When you learn a new skill, she feels the excitement of your progress. When you move up in your career, she feels the expansion of her own social status. She isn't just dating you; she is gaining access to the **"World of You."**

The High-Value Rule: Never stop being the adventurer she fell in love with. The moment you "settle" and make the relationship your only hobby, the expansion stops, and the boredom begins. To keep her wanting you, you must keep growing.

The Neurochemistry of Purpose: The "Winner Effect"

There is a biological reason why successful, purpose-driven men seem to have an "aura" of attraction. It's called **The Winner Effect**, a phenomenon well-documented in both animals and humans.

1. The Testosterone Feedback Loop

When a man sets a goal and achieves it—no matter how small—his brain releases a surge of dopamine and testosterone. Testosterone isn't just about muscle mass; it's the hormone of **Status, Challenge, and Confidence**. Research shows that "winners" in athletic or professional competitions experience a sustained lift in T-levels.

This creates a positive feedback loop:

1. **Win:** Your T-levels rise.
2. **Hormonal Shift:** You become more confident and less sensitive to cortisol (stress).
3. **Behavioral Change:** You take more calculated risks and lead more effectively.
4. **Attraction:** This state of "High T / Low Cortisol" is the gold standard for masculine attraction.

2. Pheromones and Presence

This biological shift isn't just internal; it is perceptible to others. Higher testosterone levels literally change your "Social Presence." It makes your voice deeper and more resonant, your eye contact steadier, and your scent—literally, through pheromones—more attractive to women, especially during their fertile window.

When you spend your day chasing your purpose and "winning" in your own arena, you bring that **"Winning Energy"** back into the relationship. You don't need her to validate you because your "Wins" have already done the job. You are "fed" by your mission, which allows you to be "generous" with your affection rather than "hungry" for her approval.

Masculine Mission vs. Emotional Availability

A common counter-argument to the "Mission First" mindset is: *"But shouldn't I be emotionally available and present for her? Won't I lose her if I'm always working?"*

This is where many men misunderstand the concept of **Presence**. Presence is not the same as **Permanence**.

A High-Value Man is **100% Present** when he is with her, but he is **100% Gone** when he is on his mission.

1. The Trap of the "Grey Zone"

The problem most modern men face is "The Grey Zone." They are physically with their woman, but they are mentally checking work emails or scrolling through social media. Conversely, they are at work, but they are constantly texting her, seeking her attention throughout the day. This is the worst of both worlds. It makes you a "Low-Focus" man. You are never fully "with her" and never fully "at work."

2. Creating the "Passion Gap"

By setting **"Non-Negotiable Mission Hours,"** you create what we call a **"Passion Gap."** This gap is the space where the **Anticipation** we discussed in Chapter 1 lives. When you say, *"I'm going into 'deep work' mode for the next four hours to finish this project; I'll call you when I'm out,"* you are setting a boundary that signals: *"My mission is my priority."* Counter-intuitively, this makes the time you *do* spend with her feel more valuable. It is "earned" time. She knows she has the attention of a man who is capable of intense focus, which makes your focus on *her* feel like a significant prize.

Identifying Your Purpose: The "Ikigai" of the High-Value Man

If you don't currently have a "North Star," you are in a state of **Social Vulnerability**. Without a mission, you will inevitably default to making the woman your mission. You will become the "Chaser" because you have nothing else to run toward.

Your purpose doesn't have to be "saving the world" or being a billionaire. It just has to be something that:

- **Challenges you:** It must push your "Edge" and force you to grow.
- **Requires mastery:** It must be something you can get better at over time.
- **Has an external goal:** It must involve building, creating, or winning in the real world.

The Production vs. Consumption Audit

A High-Value Man is primarily a **Producer**. A Low-Value Man is primarily a **Consumer**.

Category	Low-Value "Placeholder" (Consumption)	High-Value "Purpose" (Production)
Fitness	Going to the gym just to "look good" for others.	Training for a specific goal (Marathon, BJJ Blue Belt, Powerlifting total).
Career	"Clocking in" and waiting for the weekend.	Mastering a specific skill to become the top 1% in your industry.
Hobby	Consuming media (Gaming for 20 hours a week, Netflix).	Producing something (Woodworking, Coding an app, Writing a book).
Social	Hanging out to "kill time" and drink.	Leading a community, mentoring others, or building a network.

The "Fortress of Solitude" Strategy

Every High-Value Man needs a **"Fortress of Solitude"**—a physical or mental space where he goes to build his empire and commune with his own thoughts. Historically, men had "Man Caves," workshops, or libraries. These weren't just for storage; they were for the preservation of the masculine "Self."

1. The Psychology of Strategic Absence

When you are in your "Fortress," the relationship—for all intents and purposes—does not exist. This is not out of malice; it is out of **Necessity**. You are recharging your masculine battery.

2. Strength vs. Compliance

- **The "Nice Guy" Move:** He has a scheduled gym session or a night in his workshop. His girlfriend calls and says she's "bored" or "misses him." He cancels his plans to go over to her house. **Result:** He feels a subtle resentment, and she feels a subtle loss of respect. He has proven that his goals are secondary to her whims.

- **The High-Value Move:** He says, *"I miss you too. I'm in the middle of my session/project right now, and I'm finishing up at 8:00 PM. I'll come over then and give you my full attention."* **Result:** He stays strong in his mission, and she feels a surge of desire for the man who won't be swayed. She realizes that her "pull" is strong, but his "North Star" is stronger.

Exercises: Building Your External World

To shift from "Satellite" to "Sun," you must take practical steps to rebuild your external world.

1. The "Time Audit" (Surgery for your Schedule)

For one week, track every hour of your time with brutal honesty.

- How much time is spent in **"Mission Mode"** (building, learning, winning)?

- How much is spent in **"Maintenance Mode"** (scrolling, chasing her attention, waiting for a reply)?

- **Goal:** Shift at least 10 hours a week from "Maintenance" to "Mission." Use that time to start a project you've been putting off.

2. The "Passion Pitch" (Finding Your Fire)

If someone asks you, *"What are you working on right now?"* and your only answer is *"Oh, you know, just the usual work stuff,"* you are failing the "Purpose Test." You sound like a man who is bored with his own life.

- Find one project, skill, or goal you are currently obsessed with.
- Practice speaking about it for 60 seconds with genuine fire.
- **Goal:** Your eyes should light up when you talk about your mission, not just when you talk about her.

3. The "Non-Negotiable" Boundary

Identify one activity that is vital to your growth (e.g., Tuesday night boxing, Saturday morning coding, Sunday morning hiking). Make it a **"Non-Negotiable."** * Even if the woman you are dating invites you to something "better," you stick to your mission.

- **Goal:** Demonstrate to yourself—and to her—that your "North Star" is fixed, not floating. This builds your "Internal Frame" and earns her long-term respect.

Summary: The Magnetic Mission

A man without a purpose is a man who is "drifting." And a woman, in her deepest biological and psychological core, does not want to be the "Anchor" for a drifting man. Being an anchor is exhausting; it's a burden. She wants to be the "Clipper" ship that sails alongside a man who knows exactly where he is going and has the "wind" of his own purpose in his sails.

When you demonstrate passion and purpose outside the relationship, you solve three major attraction problems simultaneously:

1. **You eliminate "Neediness":** You are already fulfilled by your own achievements.
2. **You trigger the "Halo Effect":** Your competence in the world makes you more attractive in the bedroom.
3. **You create "Space":** By being busy, you allow her the space to miss you, which is the only environment where desire can grow.

Stop trying to "Make Her Want You" by focusing on her. That is like trying to make a fire by staring at the wood. You must strike the match of your own ambition. Focus on your mission, become the sun in your own universe, and her wanting to be in your orbit will be the natural, unavoidable byproduct.

CHAPTER 3

SET HEALTHY BOUNDARIES TO EARN RESPECT

The Architecture of Respect

In the modern dating landscape, there is a pervasive and toxic myth that "niceness" is the primary currency of attraction. We are told that if we are just agreeable enough, accommodating enough, and supportive enough, respect and desire will follow as a natural reward. This is a fundamental misunderstanding of human psychology.

While "niceness" is a social lubricant, it is not an aphrodisiac. In fact, excessive agreeableness often signals a lack of core values. A man who never says "No" is a man who stands for nothing. And a man who stands for nothing can never be respected.

Respect is the "Floor" of attraction. You can have chemistry, shared interests, and physical sparks, but without respect, the structure will eventually collapse. Respect is earned through the setting and

212

enforcement of **Boundaries**. Boundaries are the "Walls" of your identity. They define where you end and the rest of the world begins. They protect your time, your energy, and your dignity.

In this chapter, we will dismantle the "Nice Guy" fear that boundaries drive women away. We will explore the evolutionary necessity of "Testing," the different types of boundaries every High-Value Man must possess, and the specific scripts for enforcing those boundaries with calm, masculine authority.

The Boundary Paradox: Why "No" Creates Desire

To the uninitiated, setting a boundary feels like a risk. The "Low-Value" mindset fears that saying "No" to a woman—refusing a late-night demand, calling out disrespectful behavior, or sticking to a prior commitment—will make her leave.

The **Boundary Paradox** states that the more you are willing to risk the relationship to protect your standards, the more she will want to stay in it.

1. The Respect-Desire Equation

We can conceptualize the relationship between respect (R), boundaries (B), and desire (D) through a simple (though non-literal) psychological formula:

$$D = \frac{A \times R}{C}$$

Where:

- A is initial Attraction (physical/personality).
- R is Respect (earned through B).
- C is Compliance (the degree to which you "bend" to her whims).

As Compliance (C) increases toward 100%, the denominator grows, and Desire (D) begins to shrink. Conversely, when Respect (R) is high because you have strong Boundaries (B), Desire remains elevated. A woman cannot truly desire a man she can manipulate. Manipulation leads to contempt, and contempt is the ultimate killer of attraction.

2. The Search for the "Unmovable Object"

From an evolutionary perspective, women are biologically wired to seek out "The Unmovable Object." In a chaotic world, a man who cannot be easily swayed by emotional pressure or social manipulation is a man who can provide genuine security.

When a woman "tests" your boundaries, she isn't usually trying to get her way; she is checking to see if you are a "Solid Pillar" or a "Straw Man." If you fold the moment she shows a little bit of attitude or pressure, you have failed the safety check. You have proven that you are not strong enough to lead her or protect her from the world, because you can't even protect your own standards from *her*.

The Three Pillars of High-Value Boundaries

A High-Value Man does not set boundaries because he is "mean" or "controlling." He sets them because he has a **Standard of Quality** for his life. There are three primary domains where these boundaries must be established.

Pillar 1: Time and Priority Boundaries

Your time is your only non-renewable resource. If you treat your time as "cheap," she will value it accordingly.

- **The Standard:** Your mission, your growth, and your existing commitments come before a last-minute whim.

- **The Encroachment:** She texts you at 9:00 PM on a Tuesday asking you to come over, knowing you have a 6:00 AM presentation.

- **The High-Value Response:** *"I'd love to see you, but I've got a big day tomorrow and I'm already winding down. Let's do Thursday night instead."* * **Why it works:** You are demonstrating that you are a man of **Purpose** (Chapter 2) and that your schedule is not a "Playground" for her convenience.

Pillar 2: Behavioral and Respect Boundaries

This is about how she speaks to you and treats you. Many men let "small" disrespects slide to avoid conflict, only to find themselves in a relationship characterized by constant belittlement.

- **The Standard:** You do not tolerate "Passive-Aggression," "Shouting," or "Public Embarrassment."
- **The Encroachment:** She makes a sarcastic, cutting joke about your career in front of a group of friends.
- **The High-Value Response:** You don't get angry; you get calm. You pull her aside or wait until you are alone and say: *"I'm all for a good laugh, but that comment earlier felt disrespectful. I don't do 'put-downs' in front of people. Let's not have that happen again."*
- **Why it works:** You are communicating that you have an "Internal Judge" of what is acceptable. You are not "punishing" her; you are informing her of the "Price of Admission" to your life.

Pillar 3: Emotional and Value Boundaries

This involves protecting your mental health and your core values.

- **The Standard:** You are not an "Emotional Dumpster" or a "Plan B."
- **The Encroachment:** She only calls you when she is crying about her ex or when her "cooler" plans fall through.
- **The High-Value Response:** *"I'm happy to support you, but I feel like our time together is becoming focused on [Negative Topic]. I'm interested in building something positive here. If you're not in a place to do that, maybe we should take some space."*

The Mechanics of Enforcement: Soft vs. Hard Boundaries

Setting a boundary is 10% words and 90% action. If you set a boundary and then fail to enforce it, you have done more damage than if you had never set it at all. You have essentially taught her that your "Rules" are just "Suggestions."

1. The "Soft Boundary" (The Warning)

Most boundary violations start as "Calibrations." She might not know where your lines are yet. In this phase, use the **O-F-N-A Framework**:

- **Observation:** *"When you cancel our plans at the last minute..."*
- **Feeling:** *"...it feels like you don't value my time."*
- **Need:** *"I need to know that the plans we make are solid."*
- **Action:** *"If this happens again, I'm not going to be able to keep our weekend open for you."*

2. The "Hard Boundary" (The Enforcement)

If the behavior continues, you must move to **Withdrawal**. This is the only language the limbic system truly understands.

- **The Action:** You don't shout. You don't argue. You simply **Remove your Attention.** * You stop texting. You stop calling. You go back to your "Fortress of Solitude" (Chapter 2) and focus on your mission.

You must be willing to let the relationship go to protect the boundary. This is the ultimate "High-Value" move. If she realizes that she can lose you by being disrespectful, she will suddenly find a profound level of respect for you. If she *doesn't* change, then you have successfully filtered out a woman who would have eventually made your life miserable.

Why Women "Test" (And Why You Should Welcome It)

In "The Game" and "Red Pill" communities, these are often called "Shit Tests." I prefer to call them **"Congruence Tests."** A woman tests you to see if the man you are *acting* like is the man you *actually* are. She is looking for the cracks in your armor.

- **The Test:** She might tease you about your outfit, challenge your opinion, or act "difficult" about a date location.
- **The Failed Response:** Becoming defensive, explaining yourself, or getting angry. These all signal that she has "Lowered your Status" and "Moved your Frame."
- **The Passed Response:** Playful Indifference or Calm Assertiveness.
    - *Her:* "Wow, that shirt is... interesting."
    - *You (smiling):* "I know, I make it look good, don't I?"
    - *Her:* "I don't want to go to that restaurant."
    - *You:* "No problem. I'm going there because the food is great. You're welcome to join, or we can catch up another time."

By passing these tests, you are providing her with the "Gift of Certainty." You are proving that you are the captain of the ship and that you won't be knocked off course by a small wave.

Internal Boundaries: The Man in the Mirror

The most important boundaries are the ones you set for yourself. You cannot expect a woman to respect your time if you spend four hours a day scrolling through TikTok. You cannot expect her to respect your body if you eat junk food and skip the gym.

1. Discipline as a Boundary

Self-discipline is essentially a boundary you set against your own lower impulses. A man with high self-discipline radiates a different energy. He is "Self-Governed." This internal order is visible in everything—from the way you keep your apartment to the way you groom yourself.

2. The "Walk-Away" Power

Your ultimate boundary is your ability to walk away from any situation that does not serve your growth or your values. If you are terrified of being alone, you have no boundaries. You are a hostage. A High-Value Man is comfortable in his own company, which gives him the "Nuclear Option" in any negotiation: **The ability to leave.**

Exercises: The Boundary Lab

1. The "Standard List"

Write down five things that you will **no longer tolerate** in your romantic interactions. Be specific.

- *Example: "I will no longer tolerate being ghosted for more than 24 hours without a valid reason."*
- *Example: "I will no longer tolerate being compared to other men."*
- **Goal:** Internalize these as "Hard Filters."

2. The "No" Day

For 24 hours, say "No" to any request that doesn't align with your priorities. Don't over-explain. Don't apologize. Just say, *"I can't do that today,"* or *"That doesn't work for me."*

- **Goal:** Practice the "Muscle" of refusal without the "Guilt" of the "Nice Guy."

3. The "Calm Calling" Drill

Next time someone (anyone—a boss, a friend, a date) crosses a small line, practice calling it out immediately and calmly.

- *"Hey, I don't really like it when you use that tone with me. Let's keep it respectful."*
- **Goal:** Transition from "Suppressed Anger" to "Active Calibration."

Summary: The Fortress of Respect

Boundaries are not a wall to keep people out; they are a gate to ensure that only the right people come in. When you set healthy boundaries, you are not being "difficult"; you are being **Clear**.

A woman of high value is not looking for a "Yes Man." She is looking for a man who has the strength to tell her "No." This strength creates the "Friction" necessary for sexual tension and the "Safety" necessary for long-term love.

Set your standards. Communicate your needs. And most importantly, have the courage to enforce them. Respect is the foundation of the house. Build it with stone, not sand.

CHAPTER 4

PRIORITIZE YOUR OWN SCHEDULE

The Currency of the King

In the hierarchy of human resources, there is one asset that stands above all others. It is not money, for money can be printed, borrowed, or stolen. It is not even status, for status can be manufactured or lost in a single news cycle. The ultimate asset is **Time**.

Time is the only truly non-renewable resource. Every minute you spend is a minute you will never see again. Because of this, how a man manages his time is the most honest indicator of his perceived self-worth. If a man treats his time as "cheap"—if he is available for anyone at any time for any reason—the world, and specifically the women in his life, will perceive him as "cheap."

In Book 4, we are focusing on creating desire. As we established in the introduction, desire cannot exist without **Scarcity**. If you are always available, you are a commodity. If you are difficult to schedule, you are a luxury. In this chapter, we will go beyond the philosophy of "being busy" and dive into the cold, hard logistics of **Schedule Prioritization**. We will discuss why "dropping everything" for a woman is an act of self-sabotage, the "Lead-Time Principle," and how to manage your digital presence so you aren't perceived as a 24/7 "human notification."

The Biology of the "Wait"

There is a psychological phenomenon known as the **Zeigarnik Effect**, which states that humans remember uncompleted or interrupted tasks better than completed ones. This effect is a primary driver of romantic obsession.

1. The Space Where Love Grows

Most men believe that the "bond" is built while they are together. While intimacy is indeed forged during shared moments, **Attraction** is forged in the gaps between those moments. It is during the "Wait"—the time she spends wondering what you are doing, why you haven't texted back yet, and when she will see you again—that her brain processes the interaction and builds a narrative of desire.

If you occupy 100% of her "Mental Real Estate" by being 100% available, you leave no room for the Zeigarnik Effect to take hold. There is no "uncompleted task" for her brain to chew on. You have provided the "Answer" before she even had time to formulate the "Question."

2. The Scarcity-Value Curve

In economics, the price of a good is inversely proportional to its availability. We can render this as a formal relationship:

$$V_{t} = \frac{Q_{i}}{A_{t}}$$

Where:

- V_{t} is the Perceived Value of your time.
- Q_{i} is the Quality of your Interaction.
- A_{t} is your Availability.

If your Availability (A_{t}) is constant and high, the value of your time (V_{t}) plummets. By prioritizing your own schedule—by having a life that is "full"—you naturally decrease A_{t}, which mathematically forces V_{t} to rise.

One of the most common mistakes men make is accepting "Last-Minute Invitations" or "Same-Day Dates." While this may feel like being "spontaneous" or "easy-going," it actually signals to a woman that your calendar is empty and that you have no competing priorities.

1. The 72-Hour Rule

A High-Value Man generally operates on a **72-Hour Lead Time** for primary social engagements. If it is Thursday and you want to see a woman on Saturday, you have waited too long to ask. By Thursday, a man with a "High-Value Schedule" should already have his weekend planned out: his training sessions, his social obligations, and his personal rest.

- **The Low-Value Move:** Texting on Friday at 6:00 PM: *"Hey, what are you doing tonight? Want to grab a drink?"* This signals you had no plans and she is your "Fallback Option."

- **The High-Value Move:** Texting on Tuesday or Wednesday: *"I'm heading to that new gallery on Saturday evening. I'd like you to join me. Does 8:00 PM work for you?"*

2. The "Soft No" for Last-Minute Requests

If a woman texts you on a Tuesday night asking if you want to hang out *tonight*, and you don't actually have a life-or-death commitment, the "Nice Guy" instinct is to say "Yes" because he wants to see her.

The High-Value Man says: *"I'd love to see you, but I've already committed my night to [Project/Gym/Rest]. Let's look at Thursday or Friday."*

This is not a "game." This is **Boundary Setting** (Chapter 3). You are training her to understand that your time must be "booked" in advance because it is in high demand.

The Digital Tether: Breaking the 24/7 Availability

In the age of smartphones, we are all reachable 24/7. This has created a "False Intimacy" where people expect instant replies. For a man trying to build desire, the "Instant Reply" is a catastrophic signal.

1. The "Human Notification" Trap

If you reply to every text within 30 seconds, you are signaling that your phone is the most important thing in your life. It suggests that you are not "In the Flow" (Chapter 2) of any meaningful work.

The High-Value Response Cadence:

- **During Work Hours:** Replies should be minimal or non-existent. You are on a mission.

- **The "Batching" Method:** Check your personal messages only 2-3 times a day.

- **The Depth of Reply:** Your replies should be thoughtful but concise. Avoid "Text Marathons" where you spend three hours ping-ponging back and forth. If a conversation is getting deep, say: *"This is a great topic. Let's dive into it when I see you on Thursday."*

2. The "Read Receipt" Psychology

If you have read receipts on, turn them off. They are a tool for surveillance, not connection. A High-Value Man does not need to prove he is busy; his actions prove it. By removing the "Seen" stamp, you add a layer of mystery. Did he see it? Is he at the gym? Is he in a meeting? This "Mystery Gap" is where her attraction grows.

The Hierarchy of the Calendar

To effectively prioritize your schedule, you must have a clear hierarchy of what comes first. A man who prioritizes a date over his fundamental pillars is a man who is "Building on Sand."

Priority Level	Activity	Negotiability
Level 1: The Pillars	Health (Gym/Sleep), Mission (Work/Business), Core Family.	**Non-Negotiable.** You do not move these for a date.
Level 2: The Growth	Skills (Learning/Hobbies), Social Network (High-Value Friends).	**High Resistance.** Only move for exceptional circumstances.

Priority Level	Activity	Negotiability
Level 3: The Guest	Dating, Casual Socializing, Entertainment.	**Variable.** Scheduled around Levels 1 and 2.

If a woman asks to see you during your "Level 1" time, the answer is always a polite but firm "No." You are the guardian of your own potential. If you sacrifice your "Pillars" for her, you eventually become a lower-value version of yourself—and ironically, the version she will eventually stop being attracted to.

Handling the "U Up?" and the Last-Minute Pivot

As you increase in value, you will encounter "Tests" of your schedule. These often come in the form of "Low-Investment" outreach.

1. The Late-Night Text

If she texts you after 10:00 PM (and you aren't already in a long-term committed relationship with established patterns), she is testing your availability.

- **The Error:** Replying immediately and engaging in a late-night chat. You have signaled that you are "on call."

- **The High-Value Move:** Ignore the text until the next morning. Reply at 9:00 AM or 10:00 AM: *"Caught me while I was out/asleep. Hope you had a good night. Let's touch base later."*

2. The "Cancellation" and the "Reschedule"

If she cancels a date at the last minute without a "Valid Emergency" (e.g., "I'm just tired" or "Something came up"), how you handle your schedule in that moment defines your future respect.

- **The Low-Value Move:** *"Oh, no problem! Want to do tomorrow instead?"* (You have just shown that your Saturday was empty and your Sunday is also empty).

- **The High-Value Move:** *"I understand. I'll jump back into my projects. Let me know when your schedule clears up and we'll see if we can find another window."* **Then, you do not ask her out again.** You wait for her to "Repair" the schedule.

Ultimately, prioritizing your own schedule is the most effective way to internalize an **Abundance Mindset**. When your life is full of things you love—your boxing class, your coding project, your hiking group—you aren't "waiting" for her to make your life exciting. You already have an exciting life; she is simply invited to witness it.

This shift moves you from a "Reactionary" state to a "Proactive" state.

- **Reactionary:** "I hope she texts so I have something to do tonight."
- **Proactive:** "I have a great night planned. If she joins, excellent. If not, I'm still going to have a great night."

Exercises: The Calendar Mastery

1. The "Blackout" Protocol

Select two blocks of 4 hours each week where your phone is in "Do Not Disturb" mode and you are focusing entirely on your Level 1 or Level 2 priorities.

- **The Rule:** You do not check texts. You do not check social media.
- **Goal:** Reclaim your "Deep Work" capacity and prove to yourself that the world doesn't end when you aren't "available."

2. The "Next Week" Planning

On Sunday evening, plan your entire upcoming week. Block out your gym times, your work hours, and your "Fortress of Solitude" time first.

- **The Rule:** Only *after* those are blocked out can you look for "windows" for dating.
- **Goal:** Ensure that you are never "squeezing in" your mission around your dating life.

3. The "Lead-Time" Challenge

For the next two weeks, do not accept any social invitation that is made with less than 24 hours' notice.

- **The Script:** *"That sounds like fun, but I've already got my night planned. Let's do it [Next Available Window] instead."*

- **Goal:** Observe how people's perception of your value changes when they realize you aren't a "last-minute" person.

Summary: The Master of the Clock

A High-Value Man's schedule is a reflection of his priorities. If you want a woman to want you, you must first show her that you want *yourself*— that you value your goals, your health, and your time enough to protect them.

By prioritizing your own schedule, you are not being "busy for the sake of being busy." You are building a life of **Substance**. You are creating the necessary scarcity that fuels desire. You are moving from a man who is "easy to get" to a man who is "worth getting."

Remember: **You are the prize.** The prize doesn't chase the winner; the prize is waiting at the finish line of a very long, very difficult race. Your schedule is that race.

CHAPTER 5

SHOW VULNERABILITY WITHOUT WEAKNESS

The Great Masculine Misunderstanding

In the previous chapters of this book, we have focused heavily on the **"Hard" attributes** of the High-Value Man: his unyielding mission, his iron-clad boundaries, the prioritization of his schedule, and his "Unmovable" nature. These are the structural pillars that create the framework of respect and initial attraction. They represent the "Armor" of the masculine archetype. However, we must confront a vital truth: if a man is *only* hard—if he remains a perpetual stone wall of stoicism, distance, and indifference—he eventually ceases to be a man in her eyes and becomes a caricature. He becomes a "Social Robot" that is impossible to connect with on a deep, visceral, or emotional level.

This brings us to the most nuanced, delicate, and frequently misunderstood tool in the High-Value toolkit: **Vulnerability.**

226

There is currently a dangerous and polarizing binary in our culture regarding male emotion. On one side, the **"Toxic Stoicism"** camp tells men to never show emotion, never admit struggle, and to remain an impenetrable fortress at all times. This school of thought suggests that any crack in the armor is a sign of failure. On the other side, the **"Modern Sensitivity"** camp tells men to "cry more," to share every fleeting insecurity, and to be "totally open" with their partners at all times. They advocate for a total removal of the masculine filter.

Both are paths to attraction-death.

A man who shows **Zero Vulnerability** is eventually perceived as untrustworthy, shallow, or even frightening; a woman cannot truly love or bond with someone she cannot "see." Without a glimpse into your soul, she feels like she is dating a statue. Conversely, a man who shows **Weakness** (which is frequently mistaken for vulnerability) is perceived as an emotional burden. A woman cannot desire a man she feels she has to emotionally "carry" or "mother."

In this chapter, we will define the **"Thin Gold Line"** between these two states. We will explore the "Integration of the Shadow," the psychological difference between "Sharing" and "Dumping," and how to show your scars in a way that makes her want to heal them, not run from them.

Vulnerability vs. Weakness: The Definitive Distinction

To master this chapter, you must first understand the **Direction of Energy**. Vulnerability and weakness may look similar on the surface—both involve the disclosure of sensitive information—but their biological and psychological impact on a woman could not be more different.

1. The Nature of Weakness: Outwardly Dependent

Weakness is characterized by "seeking" energy. It is an emotional state that requires the woman to do "emotional labor" for you. When you display weakness, you are essentially handing her your emotional well-being and asking her to fix it.

- **The Behavioral Profile:** Whining about your boss, complaining that "the world is against you," seeking constant reassurance about your physical appearance or your status, or "trauma-dumping" your past onto her in the hopes that she will provide the therapy you haven't sought elsewhere.

- **The Biological Signal:** Weakness signals to her limbic system: *"I am not capable of handling my own reality. I am overwhelmed by my environment. I need a leader."* * **The Result:** This effectively flips the polarity of the relationship. She moves into the "Masculine" role of the provider/protector, and you move into the "Feminine" role of the seeker. Sexual desire evaporates instantly in this environment because desire requires a tension that weakness collapses.

2. The Nature of Vulnerability: Inwardly Rooted

Vulnerability is characterized by "sharing" energy. It is the act of allowing yourself to be **seen**—including your fears, your history, your failures, and your raw humanity—from a position of **Internal Strength**. You are not asking her to change your state; you are simply allowing her to witness it.

- **The Behavioral Profile:** Admitting a past failure while explaining the wisdom you gained from it; sharing a future dream that genuinely scares you because of the stakes involved; or expressing a deep appreciation for her presence in a way that is honest, grounded, and devoid of desperation.

- **The Biological Signal:** Vulnerability signals: *"I am so secure in my masculine value and my ability to handle my emotions that I do not need to hide behind a mask. I am a complete human being with immense depth."*

- **The Result:** This creates a "Vacuum of Intimacy." By showing her your depths, you invite her to show hers. It builds a bridge of trust that makes the "Hard" attributes of the previous chapters feel safe rather than cold.

The "Safe Harbor" Effect: Why Depth Triggers Devotion

While boundaries and scarcity create **Attraction**, integrated vulnerability creates **Intimacy and Devotion**. In the long run, attraction gets her through the door, but devotion is what keeps her from ever wanting to leave. A woman wants a man who is a "Warrior on the Battlefield"—someone who can handle the world—but she wants to be the unique "Safe Harbor" where that warrior can occasionally set down his shield and be his truest self.

1. The Power of Selective Disclosure

A High-Value Man does not share his depths with everyone. He treats his vulnerability as a **High-Value Asset**, much like his time or his money. If you tell your deepest secrets, your childhood traumas, or your greatest fears to a woman you met three hours ago, you are not being "vulnerable"—you are being "low value." You are over-sharing to create a "False Intimacy" because you lack the patience to build a real one.

However, when you have built a foundation of respect over weeks or months, and you *selectively* share a piece of your internal world, it feels like a monumental gift. It signals to her that she has **"Earned"** a deeper level of access to you. This exclusivity is a powerful driver of desire. She feels like the "Chosen One" who gets to see the man behind the mission.

2. The "Leader with a Heart" Archetype

Psychological research into "Transformational Leadership" shows that the most effective and beloved leaders are those who are perceived as highly competent but also "human." This is known in social psychology as the **Pratfall Effect**.

The Pratfall Effect demonstrates that when a high-status, highly competent person makes a mistake or reveals a flaw, their perceived attractiveness actually **increases**. It makes them relatable and trustworthy. However, if a low-status or incompetent person makes that same mistake, their attractiveness decreases.

The High-Value Rule: You must establish your "High-Status Baseline" (the work we did in Books 1, 2, and 3) *before* your vulnerability becomes an asset. If you lead with your "wounds," you are perceived as a wounded man. If you lead with your strength and then reveal the wounds you have overcome, you are perceived as a **Resilient Man.**

The Shadow and the Scar: How to Share the Past

Every man has a "Shadow"—those parts of his past, his mistakes, or his personality that he is ashamed of or tries to hide from the light. A Low-Value Man either suppresses the shadow entirely (leading to sudden explosions of anger or chronic passive-aggression) or he is consumed by it (leading to the "Weakness" we defined earlier). The Integrated Man **incorporates** his shadow.

1. Own the Narrative (Protagonist vs. Victim)

When you decide to share a "vulnerable" story from your past, the framing is everything. You must always be the **Protagonist**, never the **Victim**.

- **The Victim Narrative (Weakness):** *"My ex-girlfriend really messed me up. She cheated and lied, and now I have major trust issues. I'm just waiting for the next person to hurt me."* * Subtext: "I am broken, please be careful with me and fix my pain."

- **The Protagonist Narrative (Vulnerability):** *"In my last relationship, I lost sight of my own boundaries and ignored red flags because I wanted it to work. It was a painful and humbling lesson, but it taught me exactly what I will and won't tolerate now. It's made me much more selective about who I let into my inner circle."* * Subtext: "I have been through the fire, I have taken responsibility, and I am stronger because of it."

2. The "Done Deal" Rule

A crucial rule for maintaining masculine frame is to never share a vulnerability that you are **currently drowning in**. If you are in the middle of a financial crisis and you are panicked and unsure of your next move, do not go to the woman you are trying to attract for "comfort." Go to your **Council of Men**, your mentor, or your father.

You should only share a vulnerability with a woman once you have **Processed** it. She should see the **"Scar,"** not the **"Bleeding Wound."** * A **Scar** is a sign of healing, survival, and skin that has grown back tougher than before. It is attractive.

- A **Bleeding Wound** is an active emergency that requires her to stop being your partner and start being your medic. This kills the romantic dynamic.

Vulnerability is not just about the words you choose; it is about the **frequency** you emit. It requires a shift in your "Internal Tonality" that signals you are speaking from a place of truth rather than a place of performance.

1. Dropping the "Social Mask" Tonality

Most men spend their day operating in a "Social Mask" tonality. It is generally slightly higher in pitch, faster in tempo, and aimed at "Performing" a certain identity (the "Professional," the "Cool Guy," the "Joker"). To show true vulnerability, you must drop your voice into your lower chest. You must slow your heart rate and your speech.

You must become comfortable with **The Heavy Silence.** When you share something deep, don't rush to fill the silence afterward with a joke or a "just kidding" shrug. Let the weight of the truth sit in the air. This shows you are comfortable with your own depth.

2. The Eye Contact of Truth

In Chapter 7 of Book 3, we discussed the "Intimate Gaze." This is never more important than during a moment of vulnerability. Most men look down at their feet, pick at their nails, or look away when they feel "exposed." This signals shame.

A High-Value Man maintains **steady, soft eye contact**. He is essentially saying: *"I am showing you my truth, I am revealing my humanity, and I am not ashamed of any of it."* This "Unflinching Vulnerability" is one of the most profoundly masculine acts a man can perform. It shows a level of "Internal Frame" that is unshakable.

The "Three-Gate" Filter for Sharing

Before you share something that feels "vulnerable," run it through these three internal gates. This ensures you are staying on the side of strength and not sliding into the territory of weakness.

The Gate	The Question to Ask Yourself	High-Value Indicator
1. The Gate of Purpose	*Why am I sharing this right now?*	You are sharing to build a bridge of understanding or to show her who you truly are. (Not to get pity).
2. The Gate of Resolution	*Have I already done the work to handle this?*	You are sharing a "Scar." You have a plan or have already moved past the struggle. (You aren't asking her to solve it).

The Gate	The Question to Ask Yourself	High-Value Indicator
3. The Gate of Timing	*Has she earned this level of intimacy?*	The depth of the secret matches the depth of the commitment and time spent together.

If the information fails any of these gates, keep it in your journal or discuss it with your male peers. Protecting your "Internal Fortress" is part of your job as a leader.

Vulnerability as a Lead: The "I Value You" Signal

Sometimes, the most powerful and "dangerous" vulnerability has nothing to do with your past or your failures. It is simply being **radically honest about your positive feelings** in the present moment.

In a modern dating world defined by "Ghosting," "Breadcrumbing," and "Playing it Cool," a man who can look a woman in the eye and say, *"I really enjoy our time together; you are a very impressive woman and I find myself thinking about you,"* is taking a massive risk. He is being vulnerable because he is "revealing his hand."

However, because you have already established your **Mission** (Chapter 2) and your **Schedule** (Chapter 4), this honesty doesn't feel like a "trap" or a "plea for love." It feels like a **Selection**. You are not complimenting her to *get* something from her; you are "observing" her value from a position of authority. You are saying: *"I am a man with many options and a busy life, and I have chosen to value you."* That is a high-vulnerability, high-reward move that triggers intense devotion.

Exercises: The Vulnerability Lab

To move from a "Stone Wall" to an "Integrated Man," you must practice these drills in low-stakes environments before applying them to your romantic life.

1. The "Shadow Journal" Drill

Spend 20 minutes tonight writing down three things about yourself or your past that you are "afraid" to tell the woman you are dating.

- For each item, ask yourself: *"Am I afraid because it's a weakness I'm still actively struggling with (Bleeding Wound), or because I'm afraid she will judge my history (Scar)?"*
- If it's a Scar, practice saying the story out loud to a mirror. Notice when your voice goes higher or when you look away. Practice staying grounded until the "shame" dissipates.

2. The "Ex-File" Responsibility Audit

Think about how you describe your past relationships to new people.

- If you find yourself saying all your exes were "crazy" or "toxic," you are operating from a Victim Narrative.
- Rewrite the history of your most painful breakup. Identify **one thing** you were responsible for (e.g., "I stayed too long," "I didn't speak my truth," "I prioritized work over connection").
- **Goal:** Turn the "Wound" into a "Lesson" you can share with authority.

3. The "Unmasked" 10-Minute Window

On your next date, purposefully drop the "Cool Guy" or "Expert" mask for a 10-minute window.

- Share a story about a time you felt completely out of your depth—perhaps your first day at a hard job or a time you traveled and got lost.
- Keep your eye contact steady and your tone low.
- **Observe:** Watch how her body language shifts. Does she lean in? Does she soften? Does she start sharing her own "unmasked" stories? This is the birth of true intimacy.

Summary: The Integrated Man

To make a woman truly **want** you—to make her feel that deep, soul-level pull toward you—you must be a man she can **feel.**

Scarcity, mission, and boundaries create the **"Chasm"** of desire—the space that makes her want to chase you. But **Vulnerability** is the **"Bridge"** that allows her to actually cross that chasm and connect with the man inside.

A High-Value Man is not a hollow suit of armor. He is a living, breathing, complex human being who has the strength to be honest about his humanity. He doesn't hide his scars; he wears them as proof of his resilience. When you master the art of showing **"Vulnerability Without Weakness,"** you become a "Rare Find" in the modern world. You are no longer just another "tough guy" or "nice guy." You are an **Integrated Man**—someone who owns his strength and his shadows in equal measure.

That is the man a woman will not only want—she will fight to keep him.

CHAPTER 6

BUILD ANTICIPATION AND TENSION

The Architecture of the "Ache"

In the modern world of "Instant Gratification," we have collectively forgotten the most essential ingredient of desire: **Anticipation**. We live in an era defined by high-speed internet, overnight shipping, and "on-demand" everything. If we want food, it's at our door in twenty minutes. If we want a movie, it's streaming in seconds. If we want information, it's a thumb-swipe away. This cultural shift toward immediacy has bled into our romantic lives like a slow-acting poison, creating a generation of men who believe that the faster they can get to the "finish line"— whether that's a commitment, a physical encounter, or a confession of love—the better.

In reality, desire is not a sprint; it is a **slow-burning fuse**.

If you want a woman to truly *want* you—to feel that deep, internal, visceral ache that keeps her thinking about you long after you've left the room—you must master the art of building and maintaining tension. Tension is the psychological and physiological state of **"Unresolved Energy."** It is the electric gap between the *wanting* and the *having*. If you close that gap too quickly, the energy dissipates, and the mystery is solved. If you never create the gap in the first place, the energy never starts.

Think of it like a masterfully written thriller novel. If the killer is revealed in the first ten pages, you close the book. The only reason you keep turning the pages is the *unresolved* nature of the plot. In dating, you are the author of the pace. By slowing down the "reveal," you create a vacuum that she will naturally seek to fill with her own thoughts, fantasies, and investment.

In this chapter, we will explore the intricate mechanics of sexual and emotional tension. We will dive deep into the "Rubber Band Theory" of attraction, the neurological power of the "Tactile Pause," and why the most seductive thing you can ever do is be the man who is comfortable enough—and high-value enough—to **wait**.

The Physics of Desire: Rubber Band Theory

To master tension, we must look at the **Rubber Band Theory of Attraction**. This is a mental model that helps you visualize the invisible force field between two people. Imagine a high-tension rubber band connecting you and the woman you are pursuing.

1. The Slack State (The Death of Desire)

When you move toward her too quickly—texting her every morning, agreeing with every opinion she voices, and being available for every last-minute hang-out—the rubber band goes "slack." There is no tension, no pull, and no resistance. In this state, attraction dies a quiet death. You have become a **"Certainty."** Human beings are rarely excited by what is 100% certain. Our brains are hardwired to prioritize the "Variable" and the "Unsolved." When you are too available, you stop being a reward and start being a background feature of her life. The slack state is the hallmark of the "Nice Guy" who wonders why his "perfect" behavior resulted in a "let's just be friends" speech.

2. The Tension State (The Birth of the Pull)

When you move away from her—not out of gamesmanship, but because you are genuinely focused on your **Mission** (Chapter 2) and your **Schedule** (Chapter 4)—the rubber band stretches. This stretch creates a literal psychological "Pull."

Because you aren't constantly in her face, she begins to feel your absence. She wonders what you are doing. She wonders if you are thinking about her. This mental preoccupation is the beginning of investment. To resolve the tension of the stretched rubber band, she must move toward **you** to close the gap. This is the only way to ensure she is a participant in the attraction, rather than just a passive observer of your efforts.

3. The Snap Point: The 90% Rule

The goal of a High-Value Man is to maintain the rubber band at **90% Tension**. You want to be close enough to be a potent, masculine presence in her life, but distant enough that there is always a slight "Pull" exerted on her emotions.

This pull is the physical sensation of **Anticipation**. It's the "butterfly" feeling in the stomach before a date. If you are 100% present all the time, she never gets to feel that pull. By maintaining the 90% mark, you keep the relationship in a state of "Becoming" rather than "Being."

The "Slow-Motion" Strategy: Subverting the Rush

Most men are **"Energy Spillers."** When they are around a woman they find attractive, their nervous system goes into overdrive. They speak faster, they move with twitchy energy, and they try to escalate the interaction as quickly as possible. This "Rushing Energy" is a subtle but powerful signal of low value; it suggests that you don't believe you can hold her attention for long, so you have to "grab" what you can before the opportunity disappears.

A High-Value Man operates in **Slow Motion**.

1. The "Pause" as a Power Move

In conversation, the most powerful tool in your arsenal is the two-second pause. When she asks you a question, or when you finish a point, do not rush to fill the silence.

Wait two seconds longer than is "socially comfortable" before responding. This **"Pregnant Pause"** creates a micro-burst of tension. It forces her to focus entirely on you, to read your eyes, and to wait for your words. It signals that you are the master of your own "Time-Frame" and that you are not intimidated by the vacuum of silence. Silence is only awkward for the man who feels he isn't enough to fill it.

2. The "Nearly" Touch (Somatosensory Anticipation)

Physical tension is not built by the touch itself, but by the **approach** to the touch.

- **The Technique:** While you are sitting near her or walking with her, move your hand close to hers or lean in near her neck while you are speaking. Let the heat from your skin be felt. Let her catch the scent of your cologne. But—and this is the key—**do not make contact.**

- **The Psychology:** Her brain's **somatosensory cortex** (the part of the brain that processes touch) will begin to "fire" in anticipation of the contact. By withholding the actual touch, you keep her in a state of heightened sensory awareness. You are building the "Ache." You are teaching her body to crave your physical presence before you've even laid a finger on her.

Sexual Tension and the "Escalation Ladder"

Sexual tension is a specific, high-voltage subset of anticipation. It is not built through "moves"; it is built through a series of **"Calibrated Risks."** You move one step up the "ladder," check for her response (her "green lights"), and then—counter-intuitively—you step back.

1. The "Two Steps Forward, One Step Back" Rule

When a moment of high intimacy occurs—a deep shared secret, a lingering look, or a passionate kiss—most men make the amateur mistake of "doubling down." They think, *"She liked that, so I should do more of it immediately!"* This is the fastest way to "Ground" the electrical current of tension.

- **The High-Value Move:** After a high-tension moment, you purposefully pull back. You might change the subject to something lighthearted, you might stand up to get a glass of water, or you might even end the date right there.

- **The Result:** You leave her in the "Tension State." You have given her a "Sample" of the intimacy, and now her brain is demanding the "Full Version." Because the loop hasn't been closed, her mind will stay stuck on you for hours or days. This is how you make her want you when you aren't even in the room.

2. Eye Contact: The "Soul-Scan"

We have discussed eye contact as a tool for respect, but for building tension, we use the **"Triangular Gaze."**

- **The Technique:** During a quiet moment in the conversation, look at her left eye, then her right eye, then drop your gaze to her lips for a split second, then back to her eyes. Do this slowly.

- **The Signal:** You are communicating raw sexual intent without saying a word. If she mirrors this or holds the gaze, the tension will skyrocket. If you do this and then immediately look away to talk about something mundane, you have successfully "spiked" the tension and then left it "unresolved." It's a push-pull for the eyes.

Anticipation in the Digital Realm: The "Cliffhanger" Text

Texting is where 90% of modern men kill the tension they worked so hard to build in person. They use the phone as a tool for "checking in" or "chatting," which provides too much **Certainty**. To build anticipation through a screen, you must treat your digital presence like a movie trailer—not the full feature.

1. Don't Close Every Loop

If she asks a question over text that requires a long or interesting story, resist the urge to type out a paragraph.

- **The Response:** *"That's actually a wild story. I'll have to tell you the 'unfiltered' version when I see you on Thursday. You're going to love it (or be slightly horrified)."*

- **The Result:** You have planted a **"Seed of Anticipation."** She is now looking forward to Thursday not just to see you, but to "Close the Loop" on that story. You have made the date "required reading."

2. The "Intermittent Reward" Schedule

Behavioral psychology (pioneered by B.F. Skinner) shows that **"Intermittent Reinforcement"**—where rewards are given unpredictably—is the most addictive form of conditioning.

- **The Application:** Do not be "Perfectly Consistent" in your texting. If you always reply in five minutes, you are a "Linear Reward." If sometimes you reply in two minutes with high-energy humor, and other times you take six hours and provide a brief, masculine update, you become a "Variable Reward."

- **The Goal:** You want her to feel a hit of dopamine when she sees your name on her screen. That only happens if your reply wasn't a foregone conclusion. This keeps her "Checking" for you, which is the digital equivalent of pacing the floor in anticipation.

The "Unfinished Business" Effect

There is a psychological concept known as **Cognitive Dissonance**—the discomfort we feel when things are "incomplete" or "inconsistent." Our brains are wired to "close the circle." By being a man who remains "incomplete" in her mind, you force her to spend her own cognitive energy "finishing" you.

1. Be the Mystery, Not the Open Book

If you tell her your entire life story, your political views, your childhood traumas, and your five-year career plan on the first date, you have "Completed the Task." There is no more work for her brain to do. She has "read" you.

- **The Strategy:** Share your "Scars" (Chapter 5) sparingly. Let her discover your depth in layers. Every time she thinks she has "figured you out," show her a new dimension of your mission or a hobby she didn't know you had. Stay one step ahead of her perception.

2. The "Power of the Exit"

The person who ends the interaction usually holds the "Frame" of the tension. Most men stay on a date until the conversation starts to lag and the energy dips. They wait until the "fire" is out before they leave.

- **The Rule:** Always leave when the energy is at its **Peak**.

- **The Scene:** You are both laughing, the chemistry is high, and the conversation is flowing perfectly. Instead of staying for another hour, you look at your watch and say: *"I'm having a blast, but I've got to get back to [Mission/Project]. Let's pick this up next time."*

- **The Result:** She is left **"Hungry."** You have associated yourself with "Peak Energy." Because you left while the fire was still hot, she will crave the next "Hit" of that energy. She will associate you with the feeling of "more," rather than the feeling of "enough."

Exercises: The Tension Lab

To move from an "Energy Spiller" to a "Master of the Fuse," you must practice these drills until they become part of your natural masculine subcommunication.

1. The "Five-Second Pause" Drill

In your next conversation (with a colleague, a friend, or a barista), wait five full seconds before answering a question.

- **The Goal:** Notice the "Internal Itch" you feel to fill the silence. That itch is tension. Learn to sit in that itch comfortably without smiling or looking away. When you can handle five seconds of silence with a stranger, you can handle the high-stakes silence of a date.

2. The "Tactile Withdrawal" Exercise

During a social interaction, touch her briefly (a hand on the arm to emphasize a point) and then **physically move further away** than you were before.

- **The Goal:** Observe her reaction. Often, she will unconsciously lean forward or move into your space to reclaim the contact. This confirms the **Rubber Band Theory** in real-time and proves that *pulling back* is what creates the *move forward*.

3. The "Visual Anchor" Challenge

During a conversation, look at her lips for one second while she is talking, then immediately look back at her eyes and continue the conversation as if nothing happened.

- **The Goal:** Master the "Intentional Spike." See if her breathing pattern changes or if she loses her train of thought. This is you "playing" the strings of tension like a virtuoso.

Summary: The Master of the Fuse

To build anticipation and tension is to give a woman the greatest gift in dating: **The exquisite feeling of wanting.** Most men try to provide "Satisfaction." They want her to be "happy" and "content" and "sure." But satisfaction is the end of desire. Satisfaction is the "After" photo. Desire lives in the "Before." A High-Value Man provides **Possibility**. He is a man of mystery, a man of depth, and a man who is never fully "possessed" because he is always moving toward his own North Star.

By mastering the rubber band, the pause, and the peak-exit, you transform yourself from a "Commodity" into an **"Experience."** You create a vacuum of unresolved energy that she will naturally want to fill with her attention, her thoughts, and her desire. Stop rushing to the end of the story. Enjoy the stretch. Become the man she can't stop thinking about—not because you did everything right, but because you had the masculine strength to let her wait.

CHAPTER 7

CONCLUSION: BECOMING THE HIGH-VALUE CHOICE

The End of the Chase

We have reached the end of this tactical manual, but we are only at the very beginning of your actual transformation.

When you opened the first page of *Book 4*, you likely did so with a specific, burning question in your mind: *"How do I get her?"* It is the question that has plagued men for centuries, driving them to write sonnets, fight wars, and, in the modern era, send desperate text messages at 2:00 AM.

Over the last six chapters, however, we have systematically dismantled the premise of that question. We have deconstructed the "Nice Guy" conditioning that society—through movies, media, and well-meaning but misguided advice—has instilled in men since boyhood. This conditioning taught you a lie: it told you that if you are just accommodating enough, available enough, self-sacrificing enough, and persistent enough, you will eventually be "rewarded" with desire. It treated affection like a vending machine: insert enough "Nice Coins," and the relationship falls out.

By now, you know that human desire does not work that way. Desire is not a transaction; it is a reaction. It is a biological response to **Value**, **Scarcity**, and **Strength**.

We have replaced that broken, transactional model with the robust architecture of the **High-Value Man**. Let us look at the structure you have built:

1. **The Foundation (Chapter 1 & 2):** You stopped being a leaf in the wind and became the "Unmovable Object." You defined a Mission that is bigger than any relationship, giving you a center of gravity that no woman can shake.

2. **The Walls (Chapter 3):** You learned that "No" is a complete sentence. You erected Healthy Boundaries that command respect, understanding that a man without borders is a man without a country.

3. **The Resources (Chapter 4):** You took control of the clock. By prioritizing your Schedule and creating Scarcity, you turned your time from a cheap commodity into a luxury asset.

4. **The Windows (Chapter 5):** You learned the delicate art of "Integration." You opened the windows of Vulnerability without letting in the draft of Weakness, proving that you are strong enough to show your scars.

5. **The Electricity (Chapter 6):** You mastered the fuse. You learned to build Anticipation and Sexual Tension, understanding that the space between "wanting" and "having" is where obsession lives.

Now, we must synthesize these distinct elements into a singular, cohesive identity. We are moving from "Tactics" (what you do) to "Being" (who you are). This chapter is about the final, irreversible psychological shift: **Becoming the Choice.**

The ultimate goal of this book was never to teach you how to "trick" a woman into wanting you. Tricks expire. Scripts run out. Games fall apart under pressure. The goal was to build a version of yourself that is so undeniably valuable, so grounded in purpose, and so rare in the modern marketplace, that her desire becomes a natural, involuntary reflex. You do not have to "convince" a woman to want a man of high value, any more than you have to convince a person to want water in a desert.

The Copernican Shift: You Are the Sun

For the vast majority of your romantic life, you have likely operated with a **"Ptolemaic"** view of dating.

Claudius Ptolemy was an ancient astronomer who believed that the Earth was the center of the universe and that the Sun revolved around it. In your dating life, this manifests as the belief that the *Woman* is the center of the universe. You acted as the satellite, frantically orbiting her moods, her needs, and her schedule, trying to generate enough centrifugal force to stay in her life. You adjusted your trajectory based on her gravity. If she pulled away, you chased. If she moved left, you moved left.

Becoming the High-Value Choice requires a massive astronomical realignment. It requires a **Copernican Shift**.

Nicolaus Copernicus changed the world by proving that the Sun is the center, and the planets revolve around it. To make her want you, **You must become the Sun.**

1. The Physics of the Solar System

In this new model, your Mission, your Values, and your Life are the gravitational center. You burn brightly regardless of who is watching.

- **The Sun does not chase the planets.** It simply burns. Its gravity is a result of its mass (substance).

- **The Planet (The Woman)** enters your orbit. If the orbit is stable—if she fits your lifestyle, respects your mission, and adds value—she is welcome to stay and enjoy the warmth and light you provide.

- **If she drifts away**, the Sun does not chase her into the dark cold of space. The Sun continues to burn. If she leaves, it is her loss of warmth, not your loss of light.

2. Self-Centrality vs. Narcissism

Critics of this philosophy often mistake it for Narcissism. It is vital that you understand the difference.

- **Narcissism** is the belief that you are *better* than everyone else. It is a fragile ego that requires constant external validation to sustain itself. A narcissist needs the planets to tell him he is bright.

- **Self-Centrality** is the knowledge that you are the **Protagonist** of your own life. It is taking total responsibility for your own orbit. It is the quiet confidence that your path is valid and necessary. A Self-Central man provides warmth to those around him, but he does not derive his identity from them.

When a woman feels that you are the Sun—that you are steady, hot, and dangerous if approached without respect—she feels a primal sense of safety. She knows exactly where the center of the universe is. She can relax, let go of the need to lead, and enjoy the gravity of a man who knows where he is going.

The Paradox of Wanting

The final, and perhaps most difficult, paradox of desire is this: **You cannot make her truly want you until you stop needing her.**

This sounds counter-intuitive. We are taught that "needing" someone is a sign of love. In reality, in the early stages of attraction, **Neediness** is an attraction-killer. It is an energetic vacuum.

1. The Oxygen Mask Theory

Imagine you are on a plane and the oxygen masks drop. Neediness is the man gasping for air, grabbing the woman's mask, and trying to suck the oxygen out of it. He *needs* her validation to breathe. He *needs* her text back to feel calm. He *needs* her approval to feel like a man.

This is repulsive to a woman. It signals that you are an "Energetic Vampire."

A High-Value Man has his own oxygen supply. He derives his self-worth from his internal scorecard—his discipline, his work, his integrity. Because he is breathing his own oxygen, he has surplus energy to *give* to her. He desires her, he enjoys her, but he does not require her for his basic survival.

2. The Leaning Tower

Picture two people standing face to face.

- **The Needy Man** leans forward. He invades her space physically and emotionally. The laws of physics dictate that for her to maintain balance, she *must* lean back. The more he chases, the more she withdraws.

- **The High-Value Man** stands upright. He is grounded. Because he is not leaning on her, she is free to lean toward him.

The Shift in Internal Dialogue:

- **The Needy Man:** *"I hope she likes me. I hope I'm funny enough. I hope I didn't say the wrong thing. Please don't leave."*

- **The High-Value Choice:** *"I wonder if she is kind. I wonder if she is loyal. I wonder if she adds value to my life or if she is just a distraction. I hope she is good enough for my mission."*

This shift changes your pheromones, your body language, and your micro-expressions. You stop looking like a beggar and start looking like a King.

The Practice of Non-Attachment

To cement your status as the High-Value Choice, you must master the spiritual and psychological practice of **Non-Attachment**. This is not about being cold or unfeeling. It is the ability to passionately desire something without being enslaved by the outcome of getting it.

1. The Abundance Mindset: The Buffet vs. The Starving Man

Imagine two men walking into a buffet.

- One man has not eaten in three weeks. He is starving. He looks at the food with desperate, crazy eyes. He shovels it in. He is terrified the food will run out.

- The other man just ate a great meal at home. He is there to taste a specific dish he likes. He is relaxed. He enjoys the food, but he isn't controlled by it.

The Scarcity Mindset is the starving man. It tells you, *"She is the only one. She is 'The One.' If I lose her, I will be alone forever."* This fear makes you act weak. It makes you tolerate disrespect. It makes you compromise your boundaries because you are terrified of the "Empty Plate."

The Abundance Mindset tells you, *"There are 4 billion women on this planet. I am a man of value, fitness, and purpose. If this connection doesn't work, it is simply a data point that we weren't a match. Another connection will come."*

Crucial Note: You cannot fake this. You cannot just "think" abundance. You build it by actually having a life that is full (Chapter 4). When your life is full of high-value friends, passionate hobbies, meaningful work, and potential dating options, losing one prospect is a disappointment, not a tragedy.

2. The "Walk-Away" Power (The Nuclear Option)

In any negotiation—whether it is a billion-dollar merger, a hostage situation, or a relationship—the person with the most power is **always** the person who is most willing to walk away from the deal.

This is the "Nuclear Option" of dating dynamics.

- If she knows, deep down, that you will tolerate bad behavior, flaking, or disrespect because you are afraid to lose her, she loses respect for you. You have become "Safe" in the worst way possible—you are a doormat.

- If she knows that you have a **"Red Line"**—that you have a standard of dignity that you value *more* than you value her presence—she feels a profound respect. She knows that the "Door is Unlocked." You are staying because you *want* to, not because you *have* to.

Your willingness to leave is, ironically, the very thing that makes her want to stay. It signals that you are a man of principle who cannot be coerced.

The Applicant vs. The Selector

To finalize your transformation, you must fundamentally change your internal role in the dating marketplace. You must stop acting like an **Applicant** and start acting like a **Selector**.

Most men treat a first date like a job interview where they are the desperate intern hoping to get hired. They try to say the "right" answers, they hide their flaws, and they try to impress the "boss" (the woman).

A High-Value Man treats the date like *he* is the CEO of a successful company (his Life), and he is interviewing a potential partner to see if she is a good fit for the organization.

The Applicant (Low Value)	The Selector (High Value)
Goal: "Sell" himself to her.	**Goal:** Evaluate if she meets *his* standards.
Strategy: Hides flaws to appear "perfect."	**Strategy:** Owns his scars and filters for compatibility.
Availability: Is available 24/7 to show "interest."	**Availability:** Is available when his Mission allows.
Conflict: Fears conflict; agrees with everything.	**Conflict:** Embraces conflict to establish boundaries.
The Question: *"Does she like me?"*	**The Question:** *"Do I respect her?"*
Reaction to Rejection: Devastation ("I am not good enough").	**Reaction to Rejection:** Clarification ("We are not a fit").

The Biological Reality:

When you operate as the Selector, you naturally generate attraction. Women are biologically wired to seek men who have standards.

- If you accept anyone, your value is zero. You are "Easy."
- If you are selective—if you require kindness, intelligence, and loyalty—your approval becomes a prize. When you finally say, *"I choose you,"* it means something.

The Ecosystem of Desire: How It All Fits

We must understand that the chapters of this book are not isolated tactics to be used one at a time. They are an ecosystem. They rely on each other to survive. You cannot cherry-pick "Tension" while ignoring "Mission." If you do, the structure collapses.

Let's look at the failure modes of incomplete integration:

1. **Mission without Vulnerability = The Cold Tyrant.**

    If you are all mission and boundaries but have no vulnerability, you become a robot. She may respect you, but she won't feel safe with you. She won't fall in love; she will just feel judged.

2. **Vulnerability without Boundaries = The Weak Pleaser.**

    If you share your feelings but have no spine, your vulnerability looks like whining. She will feel pity, not desire.

3. **Scarcity without Tension = The Ghost.**

    If you are never available but when you *are* there, you are boring and create no tension, she will just forget about you. You aren't "mysterious"; you're just absent.

4. **Tension without Mission = The Player.**

    If you are great at creating sexual tension but have no life purpose, she will eventually realize you are "empty calories." You are fun for a night, but not a choice for a life.

The Formula for the High-Value Choice:

We can summarize the entire philosophy of this book into a single equation of value:

$$HighValue = (Mission + Boundaries) \times \frac{Intimacy}{Availability}$$

- **Mission + Boundaries:** This constitutes your "Base Value" (The Man).

- **Intimacy (Vulnerability + Tension):** This is the emotional connection you offer (The Lover).

- **Availability:** This is the denominator. As availability goes down, perceived value goes up (The Prize).

You increase your value by building a massive life (Mission) and strong walls (Boundaries), multiplying that by offering deep emotional and physical experiences (Intimacy), but dividing it by restricted access (Availability).

Final Words: The Work Is Never Done

As we close this book, I must leave you with one final truth: **Becoming a High-Value Man is not a destination; it is a discipline.**

You do not read this book, check a box, and say, "I am finished. I am now High Value." That is not how life works. Entropy is always waiting. The moment you stop rowing, the current pushes you back.

- The moment you stop pursuing your mission, you lose your edge.

- The moment you stop enforcing your boundaries, people will begin to encroach on your territory.

- The moment you stop courting the uncomfortable, you lose your growth.

- The moment you become "Needy," the attraction will fade.

She will test you again. Life will test you again. The "Nice Guy" programming is deep in your neural pathways, and it will try to creep back in when you feel lonely, tired, or insecure. It will whisper, *"Just give in. Just apologize when you didn't do anything wrong. Just skip the gym to see her."*

When that happens, return to the **Unmovable Object**.

Remember that you are the prize.

Remember that a woman does not want a fan; she wants a peer. She wants a partner who challenges her to rise to his level. She wants a man who is whole with or without her.

Go out and build your empire. Build your body. Build your mind. Cultivate your garden so beautifully that butterflies come to you, but be so content with your garden that you are happy even if they don't.

And when you do that—when you truly internalize these seven chapters—you won't have to ask, "How do I make her want me?"

You will realize that the question has changed.

The question is now: **"Is she the woman I want?"**

You are the architect. Build accordingly.

CHAPTER 8

REFLECTION QUESTIONS

If you have read the preceding seven chapters of this book, you now possess more knowledge about masculine psychology, social dynamics, and the mechanics of desire than 95% of the men on this planet. You understand the "Hard" pillars of Mission and Boundaries; you recognize the "Soft" nuances of Vulnerability and Tension; and you have seen the "Copernican Shift" required to become the center of your own universe.

However, knowledge without **Internalization** is merely entertainment.

Passive reading is a low-effort activity. You can read a book on fitness, but your muscles will not grow until you get under the iron. Similarly, you can read a book on attraction, but your value will not increase until you confront the "Nice Guy" shadows within your own mind and surgically remove the limiting beliefs that have kept you in the "Applicant" role.

This final chapter is designed to be your **"Psychological Forge."** It is a comprehensive series of deep-dive reflection questions and field exercises designed to bridge the gap between *knowing* and *being*. To get the full 3500-word depth of value from this section, do not simply skim these questions. Write your answers down. Sit in the discomfort of the truth.

Part 1: The Core Identity (Mission & Frame)

Referencing Chapters 1 & 2

The High-Value Man is defined by his **North Star**. Without a mission, a man is a ship without a rudder—he is at the mercy of the wind and the waves (the whims and moods of others). These questions are designed to help you audit the foundation of your masculine house.

1. The "Ghost" Mission Audit

If a woman were to look at your life through a hidden camera for one week—not listening to what you *say* you value, but watching what you actually *do*—what would she conclude your mission is?

- Is it "Avoiding Conflict"?
- Is it "Gaining Approval"?
- Is it "Numbing Out with Entertainment"?
- **The Reflection:** Be brutally honest. If your current mission is "Keeping her happy," you are building your house on sand. Write down the discrepancy between your *Ideal Mission* and your *Current Daily Reality*.

2. The "Unmovable Object" Stress-Test

Think of the last time a woman (a partner, a date, or even a female family member) became emotional, angry, or critical toward you.

- Did you immediately "mirror" her energy? (Did you get angry back or become defensive?)
- Did you "fold"? (Did you apologize for things you didn't do just to end the tension?)
- **The Reflection:** Why is her emotional state more powerful than your internal peace? What are you afraid will happen if you remain calm and grounded in the face of her storm?

3. The "Deathbed" Perspective

Imagine you are 90 years old, looking back on your life.

- Will you be more proud of the fact that you "never upset anyone" and had a "stable" relationship based on your compliance?

- Or will you be more proud of the risks you took to achieve your mission, even if it meant some people (including women) walked away from you?

- **The Reflection:** Identify one area of your life where you are currently "playing small" to keep a woman comfortable.

Part 2: The Infrastructure (Boundaries & Respect)

Referencing Chapter 3

Respect is the currency of attraction. Without boundaries, respect is impossible. A man without boundaries is essentially telling the world, *"I do not value myself, so you shouldn't either."*

4. The "Red Line" Inventory

Most men have never actually defined their boundaries until they are already being crossed.

- List five specific behaviors that you will no longer tolerate from a romantic partner. These are your "Red Lines." (e.g., flaking, name-calling, passive-aggression, triangulation with exes).

- **The Reflection:** For each red line, ask yourself: *"If she crosses this tomorrow, do I have the courage to walk away, or will I just give her a 'warning' that I don't actually intend to enforce?"*

5. The "Nice Guy" Payoff

We often think being "nice" is a selfless act. In reality, it is often a "Covert Contract"—a form of manipulation where we are "nice" to get a specific result (affection, sex, approval).

- Look at your most recent "Nice Guy" behavior. What were you hoping to "buy" with that niceness?

- **The Reflection:** How did it feel when you didn't get the "payoff" you expected? Did you feel resentful? Resentment is the surest sign that your kindness was not a gift, but a transaction.

6. The O-F-N-A Practice

Review the **O-F-N-A** (Observation, Feeling, Need, Action) framework from Chapter 3.

- Think of a current conflict in your life. Write out a script using this framework.
- **The Reflection:** Notice how much "heavier" and more masculine it feels to say, *"I observe that you are late; I feel my time is being undervalued; I need punctuality; if it happens again, I will leave,"* compared to whining or complaining.

Part 3: The Logistics (Schedule & Scarcity)

Referencing Chapter 4

In the marketplace of desire, **Availability = Low Value**. These questions help you assess whether you are a common commodity or a rare luxury.

7. The "Commodity" Audit

How quickly do you respond to her texts? Do you drop your plans with friends the moment she "might" be free?

- **The Reflection:** If you are always available, you are telling her that your time has no value. Why are you so afraid that if you aren't available *right now*, she will find someone else? (This points to your Scarcity Mindset).

8. The 72-Hour Rule Implementation

High-value interactions require "Lead Time."

- Have you been accepting "last-minute" dates or "Netflix and chill" invites at 9:00 PM?
- **The Reflection:** Write down how you will politely decline the next last-minute request. (e.g., *"I'd love to see you, but I'm focused on [Project] tonight. Let's look at Thursday."*) How does the idea of saying this make you feel? Anxious? Powerful?

9. The "Boredom" Threshold

Do you fill your schedule because you are genuinely pursuing a mission, or are you just trying to "look" busy?

- **The Reflection:** A High-Value Man is comfortable in the silence. If you didn't have a phone or a woman to entertain you for 48 hours, what would you do? The answer to this question reveals your true Mission.

Referencing Chapter 5

Vulnerability is the "Bridge" to intimacy, but only if it is built on the "Pillar" of strength.

10. Scar vs. Wound Analysis

Think of a painful story from your past that you have shared (or want to share) with a woman.

- Is it a **Scar**? (You have processed it, learned from it, and it no longer controls your emotions).

- Or is it a **Bleeding Wound**? (You are still in the middle of it, you feel like a victim, and you want her to tell you it's going to be okay).

- **The Reflection:** If it's a wound, why are you sharing it with her instead of your "Council of Men" or a mentor?

11. The "Shadow" Integration

We all have parts of our personality we try to hide (the Shadow). Perhaps you are afraid people will see you as "selfish," "aggressive," or "failed."

- What is the one thing you are most afraid a woman will find out about you?

- **The Reflection:** Practice "Owning the Narrative." How can you frame that "Shadow" as a part of your humanity and your growth? (e.g., *"I used to be incredibly selfish, and it cost me a lot. It taught me the value of true integrity, which is why I'm so disciplined now."*)

12. The Vocal Depth Check

Pay attention to your voice in your next conversation with a woman.

- Is it "up in your throat"? Is it fast and aimed at entertaining her?

- **The Reflection:** Practice "Dropping the Mask." Can you slow your speech and speak from your chest? Notice how the *energy* of the interaction changes when you stop "performing."

Part 5: The Electricity (Anticipation & Tension)

Referencing Chapter 6

Tension is the "Ache" of desire. Most men try to resolve tension too quickly because they can't handle the pressure.

13. The "Energy Spiller" Identification

When you are on a date, do you feel a compulsive need to keep the conversation going? Do you tell jokes to break "awkward" silences?

- **The Reflection:** This is "Energy Spilling." You are trying to resolve the tension to make *yourself* feel comfortable. What would happen if you just sat in the silence and maintained eye contact?

14. The "Rubber Band" Field Report

Think about a current or past relationship.

- Who was pulling the rubber band? Were you the one constantly moving toward her (making it go slack)?

- **The Reflection:** What was the result of your constant "leaning in"? Did she lean back? Identify one way you can "step back" this week to create the tension of absence.

15. The "Peak Exit" Challenge

Think about your last date or phone call. Did you stay until the energy started to die down?

- **The Reflection:** Next time, plan to leave while you are both still having a great time. How does it feel to "be the one to hang up first"? (This is the ultimate test of non-attachment).

Part 6: The Synthesis (The High-Value Choice)

Referencing Chapter 7

The final shift from "Applicant" to "Selector."

16. The "Sun" Visualization

Close your eyes and visualize your life as a Solar System.

- Is there a woman at the center, and are you a planet?
- Or are YOU the Sun?

- **The Reflection:** If you were the Sun, what would change about your morning routine? What would change about how you handle a "no-reply" text?

17. The "Selector" Interview

Imagine you are hiring someone for the most important role in your company.

- Would you hire someone just because they were "pretty" or because they "liked" you? Or would you have a set of rigorous standards?
- **The Reflection:** List three non-physical traits that a woman *must* have to be worthy of your time. If a woman doesn't have these, are you prepared to "fire" her from your life?

18. The "Abundance" Inventory

List five things in your life that bring you immense joy and purpose that have **nothing** to do with women.

- **The Reflection:** If you lost your current romantic prospect tomorrow, would these five things be enough to keep you focused and fulfilled? If not, you need to work on your "Abundance Infrastructure."

Part 7: The 30-Day High-Value Challenge

To truly integrate the lessons of *Book 4*, you must move from reflection to **Action**. For the next 30 days, commit to the following "High-Value Protocols."

Week 1: The Mission & Frame Protocol

- **Task:** Wake up 1 hour earlier than usual to work on your Mission (the goal you identified in Chapter 2).
- **The Discipline:** During this hour, no phones, no social media, no checking texts from women. This is your "Fortress of Solitude."
- **Goal:** To prove to yourself that your Mission comes before your social validation.

Week 2: The Boundary & Respect Protocol

- **Task:** Identify one boundary that is currently being crossed in your life (at work, with friends, or with a date).

- **The Discipline:** Enforce that boundary using the O-F-N-A framework. Do not apologize for having the boundary.
- **Goal:** To experience the "Respect Spike" that comes from being an Unmovable Object.

Week 3: The Scarcity & Schedule Protocol

- **Task:** Implement the "72-Hour Rule" and the "Lead-Time Protocol."
- **The Discipline:** If someone asks for your time with less than 48 hours' notice, the answer is "No" (or a reschedule). Even if you are technically free, use that time to rest or work on your Mission.
- **Goal:** To recalibrate your value as a luxury asset, not a commodity.

Week 4: The Tension & Non-Attachment Protocol

- **Task:** Practice the "Triangular Gaze" and the "Five-Second Pause" in all interactions.
- **The Discipline:** In your romantic life, be the one to end the conversation/date first, 100% of the time this week.
- **Goal:** To master the "Exit" and become comfortable with unresolved tension.

Part 8: Troubleshooting the Transformation

As you begin this 30-day challenge, you will encounter internal and external resistance. This is the "Nice Guy" program fighting for its survival.

1. The Fear of Loss

- **The Feeling:** *"If I stop being so available, she'll find someone else."*
- **The High-Value Reality:** If her "love" for you is based on you being a 24/7 service provider, it isn't love—it's utility. If she leaves because you have a mission and boundaries, she was never a fit for a High-Value Man. You are clearing space for a woman who respects depth.

2. The Guilt Trip

- **The Feeling:** *"I feel mean for saying no."*
- **The High-Value Reality:** Boundaries are not mean; they are clear. Confusion is mean. Letting someone walk all over you and then becoming resentful is mean. Clarity is a gift to both parties.

3. The "Boredom" Trap

- **The Feeling:** *"Without the 'chase,' I feel bored."*
- **The High-Value Reality:** This is a sign that you have been addicted to the "Dopamine Loop" of external validation. Use this boredom to fuel your Mission. Boredom is the space where creativity and empires are built.

The Final Word: The Integrated Man

The transition from a "Nice Guy" (The Applicant) to a "High-Value Man" (The Choice) is the most significant journey a man can take. It is the journey from **External Validation** to **Internal Authority**.

In *Book 1*, you learned to lead yourself. In *Book 2*, you learned to lead others. In *Book 3*, you learned the nuances of respect. And here, in *Book 4*, you have learned the ultimate art of **Desire**.

Desire is not something you "do" to a woman. It is something you **embody**. When you are a man of mission, a man of boundaries, a man of depth, and a man of mystery, the world responds to you differently. You no longer have to "chase" butterflies; you build a garden so magnificent that the butterflies cannot help but stay.

But remember: The garden is for YOU. You do not build it for the butterflies. You build it because you are a master gardener, and that is what you were born to do.

The shift is now complete. The tactics are in your hands. The transformation is in your heart.

Go out and be the man you were always meant to be.

BOOK FIVE
START A REAL RELATIONSHIP

CHAPTER 1

INTRODUCTION: THE SHIFT FROM DATING TO PARTNERSHIP

The Threshold of Depth: From Pitching a Tent to Building a Cathedral

You have spent the journey of the previous four books mastering the art of the self, the mechanics of respect, the logistics of value, and the electricity of attraction. You have successfully dismantled the "Nice Guy" conditioning that once held you hostage to the whims of others. You have transformed yourself into the **High-Value Choice**. By defining a Mission that serves as your North Star, setting boundaries that command respect, and learning to modulate the "Ache" of desire through scarcity and tension, you have reached a summit.

But as you stand atop this peak, looking out over the landscape of your romantic life, you realize that the climb was merely the beginning. You have reached a new threshold: **The Threshold of Depth.**

In the world of modern dating, many men are "Professional Chasers." They are virtuosos of the first ninety days. They are masters of the "Honeymoon Phase," capable of generating massive amounts of attraction and mystery. They know how to pitch a tent—it's quick, it's exciting, and it serves the immediate purpose of shelter. But when the wind starts to howl and the seasons change, the tent collapses. These men are beginners at the actual, gritty, rewarding work of building a cathedral—a structure designed to stand for a century, capable of weathering any storm, and built upon a foundation that goes deep into the earth.

There is a specific phenomenon known as **"Post-Chase Depression"** that strikes high-value men. It happens the moment the "target" is secured. Once the uncertainty of the chase is replaced by the certainty of commitment, the ego, which thrived on the challenge, suddenly feels starved. The adrenaline fades. The man realizes he has no idea how to lead a partnership once the "game" is over. He either loses interest and sabotages the connection, or he commits a more subtle error: he stops doing the very things that made him attractive in the first place.

Book 5 is about the evolution of the man. It is about moving from the **"Thrill of the Hunt"** to the **"Mastery of the Harvest."** If the previous books were about how to *get* the woman, this book is about how to *keep* the woman while simultaneously building a life that matters. We are shifting from being a "candidate" to being an **Emotional Architect.**

The Psychology of the Shift: Dopamine vs. Oxytocin

To lead a partnership effectively, you must understand the internal chemistry of this transition. Most relationships fail because men try to run a long-term marathon using short-term "sprint fuel."

1. The Dopamine Phase: The Engine of Dating

Dating is fueled almost entirely by **Dopamine.** In the brain, dopamine is not the chemical of "pleasure," but the chemical of **anticipation, novelty, and pursuit.** It is the "Search and Rescue" neurotransmitter. When you are wondering if she'll text back, when you are planning a surprise date, or when you are navigating the sexual tension of those early nights, your brain is bathed in dopamine. It is high-energy, high-voltage, and highly addictive.

However, dopamine has a "Half-Life." By biological design, it cannot be sustained at peak levels forever. The human brain eventually habituates to the stimulus. This is the physiological reason why relationships feel like they "lose their spark" after six to twelve months. The novelty has worn off. The "unresolved energy" you learned to build in Book 4 has been resolved into a routine. If you rely solely on dopamine to keep your relationship alive, you will inevitably find yourself looking for a new partner the moment the current one becomes "predictable."

2. The Oxytocin Phase: The Engine of Partnership

A real relationship is powered by a different engine: **Oxytocin** and **Vasopressin**. Often called the "bonding" or "cuddle" chemicals, these are the neurotransmitters of **stability, trust, safety, and deep connection.** The shift from Dating to Partnership is essentially the shift from **Intensity to Intimacy.**

- **Intensity** is the spike—the thrill of the unknown, the high-stakes risk of the chase.
- **Intimacy** (literally "In-to-me-see") is the slow, psychological melding of two lives toward a common goal. It is the ability to be truly known by another person without losing your masculine edge.

The High-Value Man does not mourn the loss of the dopamine spike. He understands that while dopamine is fun for a season, oxytocin is what allows him to build an empire. You cannot build a legacy with someone you don't trust, and you cannot build trust while playing games of scarcity. In this phase, we learn to transition from "The Prize" to "The Partner" without losing our status as "The Leader."

The Three Pillars of the Shift

Transitioning into a partnership is not merely "dating the same person for a long time." It is a fundamental rewriting of the social and emotional contract. It requires a shift in three specific pillars of your identity.

I. From "Individual Mission" to "Shared Vision"

In the early books, we focused on your **Individual Mission.** You were the "Unmovable Object." Your life had its own gravity, and she was merely a planet orbiting your sun. This was necessary to establish your value.

In a partnership, your Mission does not change—a man without a mission is still a man without a soul—but the **Vessel** you use to achieve that mission evolves.

- **In Dating:** She is a passenger on your ship. She enjoys the view, but she has no say in the navigation.

- **In Partnership:** She becomes the **First Mate.** You are still the Captain (The Frame-Setter), but you now have a co-investor in the journey. Her strengths must complement your weaknesses. You are no longer just asking, "Does she like me?" You are asking, "Can we build together? Do her values amplify mine, or do they create friction that will eventually sink the ship?"

II. From "Self-Protection" to "Radical Integration"

During the dating phase, your primary goal was self-protection. You used boundaries, scarcity, and emotional distance to ensure you weren't taken advantage of and to maintain your mystery. You kept your "scars" hidden until they were earned.

In a partnership, you move toward **Radical Integration.** This is the most dangerous part of the transition for most men. Integration does *not* mean you become a "bleeding wound" or a "Nice Guy" who complains about his problems. It means you allow her into the **Internal Sanctum** of your life.

- You share your long-term strategies.

- You share your fears—not as a victim, but as a general discussing potential risks with his most trusted advisor.

- You invite her to witness your process. You aren't asking her to fix you; you are inviting her to **witness and support** your ascent. This creates a level of loyalty that "dating" can never touch.

III. From "Interest" to "Investment"

Dating is a low-stakes game. If it doesn't work out, you walk away with your dignity intact. This is the "Non-Attachment" we discussed in Book 4. Partnership, however, involves **Investment.** It involves "Sunk Costs"—time, emotional energy, financial integration, and the intertwining of families and reputations.

The shift requires moving from "seeing how it goes" to "making it work." This demands a level of **Active Leadership.** In dating, you can be passive and let the "tension" do the work. In a partnership, you must be the architect of the culture within the relationship. You set the tone for how you handle stress, how you celebrate wins, and how you resolve the inevitable frictions of life.

The "Trap of the Comfortable": Why Men Lose Their Edge

The primary reason high-value relationships fail is a phenomenon I call **"The Softening."**

Once a man secures a partnership, he often falls into the trap of **Complacency.** He subconsciously thinks, *"I've won. The chase is over. I can finally stop all this 'High-Value' work and just relax."*

- He stops going to the gym with the same intensity.
- He becomes "accessible" 24/7, losing the scarcity that once made his time precious.
- He stops enforcing his boundaries because "we're comfortable now," leading to "Boundary Creep" where the woman slowly begins to lead the relationship.
- He becomes a **Fixed Asset** rather than a **Variable Reward.**

The Paradox of the Partnership: To keep a woman in a long-term partnership, you must remain the man who could, at any moment, survive—and thrive—without her.

If you lose your "Walk-Away Power," you lose the respect of the woman. In the feminine psyche, respect is the prerequisite for desire. The moment she feels she "owns" you completely—the moment you become predictable, unchallenging, and emotionally dependent—her attraction will begin to wither.

Many men interpret "Partnership" as a license to be lazy, unmotivated, and emotionally "leaky." In Book 5, we will teach you how to be **Comfortable but not Complacent.** You will learn how to provide her with the safety of commitment (Oxytocin) while maintaining the "Edge" of the man she first fell for (Dopamine).

The Framework: The "Partnership Architecture"

As we move through Book 5, we will follow a specific roadmap for building this structure. We aren't just "staying together"; we are building a legacy.

1. **Clarity (Chapter 2):** We will tackle "The Talk." You will learn how to move from "hanging out" to a "Defined Relationship" (DTR) with authority and without neediness.

2. **Alignment (Chapter 3):** We will go deep into the "Big Four": Finance, Family, Faith, and Lifestyle. You will learn how to audit your partner to ensure your futures are synergistic.

3. **Consistency (Chapter 4):** This is the death of the "Nice Guy" act. You will learn the power of being a **Reliable Man**—someone whose word is iron.

4. **Conflict Resolution (Chapter 5):** You will learn that conflict is not a sign of failure, but an opportunity for "Re-Calibration." You will learn to fight for the relationship, not against the person.

5. **Romance Maintenance (Chapter 6):** We will explore how to keep the "Spark" alive. You will learn to treat your long-term partner with the same intentionality you used when you were first trying to "Make Her Want You."

6. **Legacy (Chapter 7):** Finally, we look at the big picture. How do two high-value people build a life that serves the world and leaves a mark?

The Internal Audit: Are You Ready for a Partnership?

Before you proceed to Chapter 2, you must undergo a "Stress-Test" of your current state. A partnership is a **Multiplier.** If your life is currently a "0" or a negative number, a relationship will only multiply that void.

1. Is Your House in Order?

Look at your finances, your physical health, and your living space. If you are looking for a woman to "organize" your life or provide you with emotional stability you don't already have, you are looking for a mother, not a partner. You must be a "Whole 1" before you can become a "Powerful 2."

- *Diagnostic Question:* If she left tomorrow, would your life still be functioning at 90% capacity?

2. Is Your Mission Large Enough?

Does your life have enough "Gravity" to sustain another person's orbit? If your only goal in life is "Being a good boyfriend," you will become a satellite to her sun. You will become needy. Your mission must be so large that her presence is a **magnificent addition** to a great life, not the **sole source** of it.

- *Diagnostic Question:* Do you have goals that keep you up at night that have nothing to do with her?

3. Are You Willing to be the Architect?

A relationship is not a 50/50 split of effort; it is a **100/100 split of responsibility.** As the man, you are the **Frame-Setter.** You determine the emotional temperature of the home. If the relationship becomes toxic, stagnant, or boring, you must take the lead in fixing it.

- *Diagnostic Question:* Are you ready to take 100% responsibility for the "vibe" of your relationship, even when she is having a bad day?

Summary: The Voyage Begins

Dating was the rehearsal; Partnership is the performance.

In the dating phase, you were proving your value to the world and to her. In the partnership phase, you are **Deploying** that value to build something permanent. You are no longer just looking for a "win" or a "yes." You are looking for a **Legacy.** You are shifting from a man who is "wanted" to a man who is **followed.**

The chapters ahead will give you the blueprints to navigate the deep waters of commitment without losing your identity. We are moving from the "Ache" of wanting to the "Power" of having. It is time to stop playing the game and start building the empire.

CHAPTER 2

DEFINE THE RELATIONSHIP WITH CLARITY

The "Limbo" Problem: Navigating the Grey Zone

In the journey of modern romance, there is a treacherous, fog-shrouded stretch of water known as the **"Grey Zone."** It is that ambiguous period after the first few months of dating where the "Ache" of attraction has solidified into something substantial, but the rules of engagement remain unwritten. In contemporary culture, this is the birthplace of the **"Situationship"**—a state of emotional intimacy and sexual consistency that lacks the structural integrity of a formal commitment.

For the low-value man, the Grey Zone is a place of quiet desperation and high-frequency anxiety. He stays there because he is operating from a **Scarcity Mindset**. He treats the relationship like a fragile glass sculpture that might shatter if he speaks too loudly. He is terrified that if he asks for clarity or expresses a desire for exclusivity, he will "scare her off" or appear "needy." He waits, often for months, for the woman to bring up "the talk," essentially acting as a passive observer in his own life. By doing this, he abdicates his role as the leader and allows the relationship to drift.

For the High-Value Man, the Grey Zone is not a sanctuary of "playing it cool"; it is a systemic **inefficiency** that must be resolved. You are the architect of your life, and as we established in Chapter 1, you are building a cathedral, not a temporary tent. You cannot leave the foundation unfinished and expect the structure to weather the storms of life.

Defining the Relationship (DTR) is not an act of "asking for permission" to be someone's boyfriend. It is an act of **declaring the frame** of the world you are inviting her to inhabit. It is the moment you move from exploring a prospect to allocating your most precious, non-renewable resources—your time, your focus, and your protection—to a single person.

This chapter is about leading that transition with such clarity, strength, and masculine poise that she feels a sense of profound relief rather than pressure. We will explore the timing, the biological imperatives, and the exact psychological scripts required to move into partnership without ever sacrificing the "Edge" that made her want you in the first place.

The DTR Paradox: Why Most Men Fail

The reason the "talk" is so widely feared is that most men approach it from a position of profound psychological **weakness**. They treat commitment as a "confession" rather than a "decision."

The Low-Value Approach (The Applicant)

The low-value man waits until his internal anxiety reaches a breaking point. He sees other men in her social media comments or feels her pulling away, and he panics. He approaches the DTR like a plea:

> *"I really like you and I'm worried you're seeing other people. Can we please be official? I don't want to lose you."*

The Result: This triggers a "flight" response in high-value women. Why? Because it smells like insecurity. It feels like he is trying to "trap" her to soothe his own internal tremors. He isn't offering a partnership; he is asking for a guarantee so he can stop feeling anxious.

The High-Value Approach (The Selector)

The High-Value Man waits until he has vetted the woman and decided she is worthy of his exclusivity. He approaches the conversation as a gift of clarity:

> *"I've reached a point where I value what we have enough to focus on it exclusively. I'm moving in that direction. I want to know if you're ready to build that with me."*

The Result: This is a leadership move. It is an invitation into a higher-value, more secure space. It demonstrates that *you* have evaluated the situation and decided she is worth your exclusive resources. You aren't asking her to save you from your anxiety; you are offering her a seat at the table of your mission.

The Commitment Formula: The Science of "Staying"

To lead a partnership, you must understand that commitment is not a random emotional event; it is a calculated psychological state. Caryl Rusbult's **Investment Model of Commitment** provides the mathematical framework for why people decide to lock down.

The formula is expressed as:

$$Commitment = (Satisfaction + Investment) - Quality\ of\ Alternatives$$

As the leader of the relationship, you must manage these variables:

1. **Satisfaction:** This is the "Dopamine" side. Does she feel good when she is with you? Is the sex great? Is there playfulness and growth?

2. **Investment:** This is the "Oxytocin" side. How much has she "put into" the relationship? This includes time, emotional vulnerability, shared secrets, and shared plans. People value what they work for. If you do everything for her, she has no investment, and thus, no commitment.

3. **Quality of Alternatives:** This is the "Selector" side. Does she believe that you are the best possible man she can attain? When you maintain your mission, your fitness, and your boundaries, you ensure that even if she "looks" at other options, they pale in comparison to the world you have built.

When $Satisfaction$ and $Investment$ are high, and the $Quality\ of\ Alternatives$ is perceived as low, the DTR talk is simply a formal acknowledgement of a reality that already exists.

Timing: The "Goldilocks Zone" of Exclusivity

Timing is the difference between a leader and a "Love Bomber."

1. Too Early (The Week 1-3 Trap)

If you move for exclusivity in the first three weeks, you reveal that you have no vetting process. You are saying, "I have decided you are the one for me based solely on your looks and the fact that you're here." This suggests you have no other options and a low standard for your own life.

2. Too Late (The Month 4+ Danger Zone)

If you are still "just hanging out" after four or five months, you communicate a fear of intimacy or a lack of direction. A woman of value will not wait in the Grey Zone forever. Eventually, her "Attraction Battery" runs dry because she begins to feel that you are using her for temporary companionship rather than building a legacy.

The Goldilocks Zone (8 to 12 Weeks)

For most high-value relationships, the "sweet spot" is between two and three months. This provides enough time for the "Masks" to slip.

- By Week 8, you've seen how she handles a bad day.
- You've seen if she respects your time.
- You've seen her "Consistency" (which we will cover in Chapter 4).

The Rule of Thumb: You move for exclusivity when the **Cost of Non-Exclusivity** (the risk of losing a high-value partner or the inability to build deeper oxytocin-based intimacy) outweighs the **Benefit of Freedom** (the ability to date others).

The Vetting Period: The Selector's Checklist

Before you initiate "The Talk," you must conduct a cold-eyed audit. Do not let your hormones make a decision that your legacy will have to pay for. Ask yourself:

- **Boundary Response:** When I said "no" to her, did she respect it, or did she use manipulation (tears, anger, guilt) to get her way?

- **Mission Alignment:** Does she see my mission as an obstacle to her happiness, or does she see herself as the "First Mate" who helps me achieve it?

- **The "Peace" Test:** When I leave her presence, do I feel energized and focused, or do I feel drained and anxious?

- **Conflict Style:** In our early disagreements, did she try to "win," or did she try to "understand"?

If she fails these tests, the Grey Zone isn't a problem to be solved; it is an exit ramp you should take.

Leading "The Talk" Without Looking Needy

The goal of the DTR talk is to establish the **Monogamy Frame**. This is not a negotiation; it is a declaration of a new reality.

1. The Pre-Talk Audit: The Walk-Away Power

You cannot lead a DTR talk if you are not prepared to walk away if she says "no." If your happiness is 100% dependent on her saying "yes," she will smell the desperation. You must be at peace with the idea that if your values don't align, you are better off alone.

2. The "State of the Union" Setting

Do not do this over text. Do not do this while you are lying in bed after sex (where oxytocin is high and judgment is low). Do this in a neutral, relaxed environment—perhaps while walking or during a quiet dinner.

- **The Opening:** *"I wanted to share where my head is at regarding us."* This is a "Leader" opening. It signals that you have been thinking, evaluating, and have come to a conclusion.

3. The High-Value Script

"I've really enjoyed the last few months getting to know you. I've reached a point where I'm not interested in seeing anyone else, and I'd like to focus my energy on seeing where this goes with you exclusively. I wanted to see if we're on the same page about that."

Why this works:

- **Ownership:** You start with "I." You aren't asking her how *she* feels first. You are leading with your own reality.

- **Resource Focus:** You use the word "energy." This reminds her that your attention is a limited, high-value resource.

- **The Invitation:** You ask if you are on the "same page." This isn't a demand; it's an invitation for her to join your frame.

The "Monogamy Frame": A Choice, Not a Cage

A common mistake men make once they are "official" is treating the relationship like a prison sentence. They stop the "Selector" behavior and start the "Caregiver" behavior. This is where "The Softening" begins.

To maintain attraction, you must frame exclusivity as a **Privilege**, not an obligation. You are choosing to give her your most precious resources, and she is choosing to give you her loyalty.

Feature	The "Cage" (Low Value)	The "Frame" (High Value)
View of Loyalty	"You *have* to be loyal because we're official."	"We are loyal because we value what we're building together."
Communication	Constant check-ins driven by insecurity.	High trust, but high observation of actions.
Growth	"The chase is over, so I can stop trying."	"The chase is over, so I can build faster."
Boundaries	Blurred; the woman now "runs" the schedule.	Defined; the Mission remains the center of the solar system.

Scenario A: She Says Yes

If she agrees, do not over-celebrate. Do not act like you just won the lottery. A simple, *"I'm glad we're on the same page,"* followed by a kiss is perfect. Then, immediately lead. *"Good. Now that that's settled, let's go get some dessert."* This shows that the relationship is the **floor**, not the **ceiling**.

Scenario B: The "I'm Not Ready" Response

This is your "Moment of Truth." If she says she wants to keep things casual or isn't ready for a label:

- **The Weak Response:** *"It's okay, I understand. We can just keep things as they are. I'll wait."* You have just effectively told her that your standards are negotiable and that she can have all the benefits of your value with none of the "cost" of loyalty.

- **The High-Value Response:** *"I respect that. However, I'm at a stage where I'm looking to build a partnership, and I don't stay in the 'grey zone' for long. It sounds like we want different things right now. Let's take some space and see if that changes for either of us."*

The Power of the Walk-Away: In many cases, your willingness to leave when your standards aren't met is the exact "Jolt" she needs to realize your true value. If she lets you walk, she was a "Tourist" in your life, not a "First Mate."

The "Relationship Escalator" vs. Intentional Design

Society teaches us the **"Relationship Escalator."** You date, you become exclusive, you move in, you get married, you have kids—not because you chose those steps, but because that's the "next floor" on the elevator.

The High-Value Man avoids the escalator. Instead, he uses **Intentional Design**.

Defining the Relationship is the first step in that design. It is the moment you decide *how* you will relate to one another. You aren't just "dating exclusively"; you are establishing the **"Rules of the House."** You are deciding that your time is now invested in her growth and yours as a unit.

Summary: The Leader Defines the Terms

Confusion is the enemy of depth. By Defining the Relationship with clarity, you remove the "Dopamine Anxiety" of the chase and replace it with the **"Oxytocin Security"** of the partnership.

You are not "asking her to be yours." You are **declaring a new reality** where you are the Captain and she is the First Mate. You are providing the structure in which love and desire can safely grow. When a woman knows exactly where she stands with a man of value, she can finally stop "performing" and start "investing."

CHAPTER 3

ALIGN YOUR CORE VALUES FOR LONG -TERM SUCCESS

The Mirage of Chemistry: Why "Liking" Each Other Isn't Enough

You have successfully navigated the "Grey Zone." You have defined the relationship, established a frame of exclusivity, and transitioned from the high-voltage dopamine of the chase to the steady-state oxytocin of a partnership. To the outside observer, you are a success story. You have the girl, the status, and the momentum.

But now comes the most dangerous phase of the building process: **The Infrastructure Phase.**

Most relationships do not fail because of a lack of love or a lack of attraction. They fail because of a **Value Mismatch**. Chemistry is the spark that starts the fire, but Core Values are the logs that keep it burning. You can have world-class chemistry—explosive sex, effortless conversation, and shared hobbies—and still be completely incompatible for a long-term legacy.

Imagine two people building a house. One wants to build a beach bungalow made of bamboo and glass, intended for leisure and sun. The other wants to build a mountain fortress made of stone and iron, intended for defense and legacy. They are both hardworking, they both love the "idea" of a house, and they are both attracted to each other. But because their blueprints are fundamentally different, every brick they lay creates more friction. Eventually, the structure collapses under the weight of its own internal contradictions.

In this chapter, we are going to perform a "Value Audit." We are moving past the surface-level interests (the gym, travel, sushi) and diving into the **"Big Four" Pillars** of long-term success. As the High-Value Man, it is your responsibility to lead this audit. You are no longer just looking for a "partner"; you are looking for a **Synergistic Ally.**

Section 1: Interests vs. Values—The Crucial Distinction

Before we dive into the audit, we must define our terms. Most men confuse **Interests** with **Values**, and this is a fatal error in the vetting process.

- **Interests (Surface Level):** These are things you *do*. Examples: You both like hiking, you both enjoy Marvel movies, you both like Italian food, or you both go to the same gym. Interests are great for the first 90 days of dating. They provide the "Dating Glue" that makes spending time together easy.

- **Values (Core Level):** These are the principles that dictate how you *live* and how you *decide*. Examples: How you handle debt, how you view gender roles, how you prioritize career vs. family, and your fundamental philosophy on truth and loyalty.

You can have a successful relationship with someone who has zero shared interests (you like football, she likes ballet), as long as your values are aligned. However, you **cannot** have a successful relationship with someone who shares all your interests but has opposing values (you both love hiking, but you value financial frugality while she values hedonistic spending).

As a High-Value Man, you are looking for **Value Compatibility**. Interests can be developed and shared over time; values are largely fixed by the time someone reaches adulthood.

Section 2: The "Big Four" Pillars of Alignment

To build a legacy, you must ensure alignment in four specific areas. These are the "Load-Bearing Walls" of your cathedral. If any one of these is out of alignment, the whole structure is under threat.

I. Finance: The Strategy of Resources

Money is rarely the *reason* for a breakup; it is the *symptom* of a value mismatch. In a partnership, you are merging (to some degree) your economic futures. You must understand her "Money Script."

- **Risk vs. Security:** Are you an entrepreneur who values high-risk/high-reward investments, while she values the safety of a 9-to-5 and a savings account?

- **Consumption vs. Capital:** Does she view money as a tool to *buy things* (consumption), or as a tool to *build things* (capital)?

- **The Debt Philosophy:** How does she view credit? A man building an empire cannot be anchored to a partner who views debt as "free money."

II. Family: The Blueprint of Generations

This is often where the most "Nice Guy" compromises are made, leading to decades of resentment. You must be clear on:

- **The Children Question:** Do you want them? If so, how many? And more importantly: **How will they be raised?** What are your views on discipline, education, and gender roles within the home?

- **The In-Law Dynamic:** How much influence do your respective families have? A High-Value Man protects the "Internal Frame" of his relationship from outside interference. If she is emotionally enmeshed with a toxic family, she may never be able to fully commit to *your* vision.

III. Faith and Philosophy: The Definition of Truth

Even if you are not religious, you have a **Functional Religion**—a set of beliefs about what is "good," "true," and "just."

- **The Moral Compass:** What is the ultimate authority in your lives? Is it "following your heart" (Subjective), or is it a set of objective principles (Religious or Philosophical)?
- **The Purpose of Life:** Is life about the pursuit of happiness (Hedonism), or the pursuit of meaning and duty (Stoicism/Eudaemonia)? If you are building a life based on duty and she is building a life based on "feeling good," you will eventually view her as shallow, and she will view you as a tyrant.

IV. Lifestyle and Ambition: The Velocity of Growth

This is the "Daily Grind" alignment.

- **Ambition Levels:** A "High-Performance" man needs a partner who either shares that ambition or deeply respects and supports the sacrifice it requires. If you want to work 70 hours a week to build a company and she wants a "work-life balance" where you are home by 5:00 PM every day to watch Netflix, the friction will be constant.
- **Social Circle:** Who do you surround yourselves with? Do your friends elevate you, or are they "Energy Vampires"? If your social values collide, your weekends will become a source of stress rather than recovery.

Section 3: The Synergy Formula

In a high-value partnership, the goal is not "addition" (1 + 1 = 2); the goal is **Synergy** ($1 + 1 = 3+$). When values are aligned, your partner becomes a "Force Multiplier." When they are misaligned, they become a "Coefficient of Friction."

We can represent this mathematically as the **Relationship Synergy Coefficient (S):**

$$S = \frac{A \cdot (V_m \cap V_f)}{D}$$

Where:

- A = Attraction/Chemistry (The starting energy).
- $V_m \cap V_f$ = The intersection (alignment) of Masculine and Feminine Values.
- D = Discordance (The frequency of value-based conflict).

If your values do not intersect, the numerator stays small, and the discordance in the denominator grows, eventually driving the Synergy Coefficient to zero.

Section 4: The Value Audit—How to Vet Without Interrogating

You might be thinking, *"Do I just sit her down with a clipboard and ask these questions?"* No. A High-Value Man leads through observation and "Future Pacing." You don't ask, "What are your views on debt?" You observe how she handles her paycheck. You don't ask, "Are you ambitious?" You watch what she does with her free time.

1. The "Third-Party" Vetting Technique

Talk about a hypothetical situation or a friend's relationship to see her reaction.

- *Example:* "My buddy is dealing with a situation where his wife wants to move closer to her parents, but it would kill his career. What do you think about that?"

- *The Goal:* Her response will reveal her "Internal Blueprint" without her feeling like she's on trial.

2. Future Pacing

Paint a picture of the life you are building and see if she tries to "step into" the frame.

- *Example:* "In five years, I want to have the business automated so we can spend three months a year traveling while the kids are young. I see that requiring a lot of lean years now."

- *The Goal:* Does she say "That sounds amazing, how can I help?" or does she say "Five years is a long time to wait for a vacation"?

3. The Stress-Test

Values are truly revealed only under pressure. Pay attention to how she treats people when she is tired, hungry, or stressed. If her "value" is kindness but she screams at a waiter when her order is wrong, her value is actually **Convenience**, not Kindness.

Section 5: Identifying Deal-Breakers vs. Preferences

A common mistake for "recovering" Nice Guys is becoming a **"Value Perfectionist."** They look for a woman who is a 100% clone of their own beliefs. This is impossible and boring. You must distinguish between a "Preference" and a "Non-Negotiable Deal-Breaker."

- **Preferences (The "Flex" Zone):** She likes a different style of home decor. She prefers a different workout. She has a slightly different political leaning. These are areas where a leader can incorporate her input or agree to disagree.

- **Non-Negotiables (The "Red Line" Zone):** She doesn't want children (and you do). She has a history of financial infidelity. She views your Mission as a "hobby" that gets in the way of her needs.

The High-Value Mandate: You never, under any circumstances, compromise on a **Non-Negotiable**. To do so is to commit "Identity Suicide." You might stay together, but the man you were—the man she was attracted to—will die.

Section 6: The "Softening" of the Frame during Value Conflicts

When a value conflict arises—and it will—the "Nice Guy" either folds or explodes. The High-Value Man remains the **Unmovable Object**.

If she challenges a core value (e.g., she wants to spend the emergency fund on a luxury vacation), you do not get angry. You remain grounded.

> *"I understand you want that experience, and I'd love to give it to you. However, our security and the growth of our capital is a non-negotiable for me. We will go on that trip when the business hits [X] Milestone, and not a day before."*

By holding the line on your values, you actually **increase** her attraction. You are proving that you are a man of your word, a man with a plan, and a man who cannot be manipulated. You are providing the "Calculated Certainty" that her feminine essence craves.

Alignment is not about finding someone who is "perfect." It is about finding someone who is **heading in the same direction.**

If you are a man of high ambition, you need a partner who values growth. If you are a man of deep faith, you need a partner who respects that authority. If you are a man of financial discipline, you need a partner who understands that a dollar is a soldier in your army.

By aligning your core values now, in the early stages of partnership, you ensure that the energy you spend in the relationship goes toward **building up**, rather than **fixing leaks.** You are transitioning from being a "couple" to being a **Dynasty.**

CHAPTER 4

MAINTAIN CONSISTENCY IN YOUR ACTIONS

The Integrity Gap: Where Attraction Goes to Die

In the world of high-stakes performance, there is a saying: *"Amateurs practice until they get it right; professionals practice until they can't get it wrong."*

By the time you reach this stage of your journey, you have already "gotten it right." You have done the heavy lifting of self-transformation. You have navigated the nuances of attraction, set your boundaries, and aligned your values. You have successfully convinced a high-value woman that you are the **"Leader"** she has been searching for. You have marketed yourself as a man of substance, mission, and discipline.

But now, you face the most subtle and pervasive enemy of the masculine spirit: **Familiarity.**

Familiarity breeds a psychological "leak" in many men. Because the "prize" is secured, the urgency to maintain the standard begins to dwindle. This is where the **Integrity Gap** opens. The Integrity Gap is the distance between the man you *presented* yourself to be during the dating phase and the man you *actually are* on a rainy Tuesday morning six months into a partnership.

If the dating phase was the **"Marketing Campaign,"** the partnership is the **"Product Experience."** In business, if the marketing promises a high-performance, sleek, reliable piece of technology, but the product experience is glitchy, slow, and fragile, the customer feels cheated. The brand collapses. In a relationship, if the marketing promised a high-performance, disciplined, mission-driven leader, but the product experience is a complacent, inconsistent, and emotionally reactive "Nice Guy," her respect—and subsequently her desire—will evaporate.

In this chapter, we will master the art of **Masculine Consistency.** We will explore why "The Softening" happens at a neurobiological level and provide the tactical blueprint to ensure your actions remain congruent with your identity, forever maintaining the respect and desire of your partner. Consistency is not about being a robot; it is about being a **Constant.**

Section 1: The Physics of Consistency

Consistency is the ultimate **"Trust Signal"** to the feminine psyche. Because women are biologically tuned to seek Security and Protection, they are hypersensitive to fluctuations in a man's character. They are subconscious experts at detecting "drift."

If you are a lion on Monday—decisive, focused, and physically imposing—but a housecat on Friday—lazy, complaining, and seeking reassurance—she cannot trust your leadership. To her, a man who is inconsistent is a man who is **unpredictable**, and an unpredictable man is a dangerous foundation for a family or a future. If she cannot trust your leadership to remain steady, she will feel a biological imperative to take the lead herself to ensure her own safety. This is the death of the polarity you worked so hard to build.

The "Consistency Coefficient"

Your influence in a relationship is determined by your **Consistency Coefficient (C_c):**

$$C_c = \frac{Actions}{Words}$$

- **Relational Debt:** If your **Words** exceed your **Actions**, you create debt. You said you'd finish that project; you didn't. You said you'd stay in shape; you're gaining weight. This leads to **"The Nagging Cycle."** She isn't nagging because she's "mean"; she's nagging because she's trying to close the Integrity Gap you created.

- **Relational Equity:** If your **Actions** meet or exceed your **Words**, you create equity. This leads to **"Deep Submission."** When a woman sees that you consistently do what you say, her nervous system relaxes. She feels safe to follow your lead because you have proven you are an **Unmovable Object.**

Section 2: Preventing "The Softening"

"The Softening" is the slow, almost invisible degradation of masculine standards that occurs when a man enters a "safe" relationship. It happens in three distinct stages. To maintain consistency, you must identify which stage you are in and "Course Correct" immediately.

Stage 1: The Routine Creep

This starts when you begin to value **Comfort over Challenge.** In the early days, you would never miss a workout because you wanted to look your best for her. Now, you've "got" her.

- **The Sign:** You stop going to the gym at 6:00 AM because "staying in bed with her" feels better. You rationalize it as "bonding," but your body begins to lose its edge. You start choosing the easy path in small ways—ordering takeout instead of meal prepping, or scrolling social media instead of reading.

- **The High-Value Fix:** Maintain a **"Sanctified Routine."** There must be parts of your day that are non-negotiable and independent of her presence. Your mission doesn't take a day off just because you have a partner. In fact, your mission requires *more* discipline now because the stakes are higher.

Stage 2: The Approval Hunger

As the oxytocin grows, you become addicted to her "Good Mood." You start making small, microscopic concessions to avoid friction because you don't want to "ruin the vibe."

- **The Sign:** She suggests a movie you hate or an event that interferes with your work, and you say "Fine," even though you have a project to finish. You think you're being "nice" or "supportive," but you are actually training her that your time, preferences, and mission are malleable.

- **The High-Value Fix:** Re-read Chapter 3 of Book 4. Enforce **"Micro-Boundaries."** If you say "No" to the small things that interfere with your integrity, you never have to have a "Big Blowout" over the large ones. Consistency in your boundaries makes you more attractive, not less.

Stage 3: The Identity Blur

This is the final stage where "I" becomes "We" in a way that erases your individuality. You stop seeing your friends, you stop your hobbies, and you become a "Couple Unit."

- **The Sign:** When people ask what you've been up to, you only talk about things "we" did. You no longer have a "world" of your own; you are merely a inhabitant of the relationship world.

- **The High-Value Fix:** The **80/20 Rule of Presence.** Spend 80% of your focus on the partnership and shared life, but keep 20% of your energy for your **"Masculine Fortress"**—hobbies, brotherhood, and mission that have nothing to do with her. This 20% is what keeps the "Mystery" and "Tension" alive.

Section 3: The Three Pillars of Masculine Consistency

To remain the "High-Value Choice" over the long term, you must be consistent in three specific arenas.

I. Consistency of Mission (The Direction)

Your Mission is the "Frame" of the relationship. If your mission wavers, the relationship loses its sense of purpose. A woman wants to be on a ship that is going somewhere. If the Captain stops looking at the horizon and starts staring at the First Mate all day, the ship will eventually hit an iceberg.

- **The Audit:** Are you still pursuing the same goals you were when you met her? Or have you "parked" your ambitions because the relationship is "enough"?

- **The Practice:** Review your goals with her once a month. Not for her permission, but for her **Awareness.** Let her see that the fire is still burning. When a woman sees a man who is obsessed with his work/mission, her attraction is sustained by the **"Variable Reward"** of his attention.

II. Consistency of Character (The Frame)

This is about emotional regulation. If you were stoic, grounded, and unshakeable during the first three months, you cannot become whiny, reactive, and insecure in the sixth month.

- **The "Lead Pipe" Test:** When life hits you—a job loss, a family crisis, or a financial setback—how do you respond? Do you fold? Do you lash out? Or do you stand like a lead pipe—heavy, solid, and cold?

- **The Practice:** Never use your partner as your primary "Emotional Dump." Use your **Council of Men** (Book 2) for the raw processing, and present the **Strategy** to your partner. This maintains the "Protector" frame. Consistency of character means she knows that no matter how much the world shakes, you will not.

III. Consistency of Desire (The Spark)

Many men think that "consistency" means "routine." Routine is the killer of desire. Consistency in desire means you consistently **Lead the Romance.**

- **The Sign of Failure:** Falling into the "What do you want to do for dinner?" trap.

- **The Practice:** The **"Date Night Protocol."** You lead the planning, you lead the decision, and you lead the seduction. Do not ask for her input on the logistics of romance; lead her into an experience. Say, *"Get dressed, we're leaving at 7:00."* This consistent leadership prevents her from having to "work" for the romance, allowing her to stay in her feminine energy.

No man is perfectly consistent 100% of the time. You will have days where you are lazy, reactive, or inconsistent. The difference between a High-Value Man and a "Nice Guy" is how they handle the slip-up.

- **The Nice Guy:** He feels guilty. He apologizes profusely. He tries to "make it up" by being extra submissive or "buying" his way back into her good graces. This confirms his weakness and highlights the inconsistency.

- **The High-Value Man:** He performs a **Micro-Reset.** He acknowledges the slip-up internally, adjusts his behavior immediately, and returns to the standard without a "Beta-Apology."

The Reset Script:

If you've been "soft" or inconsistent for a week, don't have a heavy, emotional talk about it. Simply say:

> *"I've realized I've let my focus slip lately. I'm getting back on my schedule starting tomorrow."*

Then **DO IT.** Action is the only apology a High-Value Man needs to give for a lack of discipline.

Section 5: Consistency as a "Pre-Emptive Strike" Against Conflict

Most relationship conflicts are not actually about the "dishes" or the "trash." They are **Subconscious Tests of Consistency.** When a woman starts a "pointless" argument or becomes "difficult," she is often checking the "Integrity" of the relationship floor. She is asking: *"Is the floor still solid? Is he still the man I thought he was, or has he softened?"*

If you are consistent in your boundaries and your mission, these "tests" happen less frequently because she already knows the answer. She feels your **"Weight."** When you are inconsistent, she feels "Weightless," which makes her anxious. This anxiety causes her to "Poke the Bear" to see if the bear is still there. Consistency is the most effective form of de-escalation because it prevents the escalation from ever needing to happen.

Section 6: The "Maintenance Audit" Checklist

Every 90 days, you should perform a "Consistency Audit" on yourself. Be ruthlessly honest. If you lie to yourself, you are only building your cathedral on sand. Rate yourself 1-10 on the following:

1. **Physical Edge:** Am I in as good (or better) shape as the day we met?
2. **Mission Velocity:** Am I moving toward my goals with the same hunger and intensity?
3. **Boundary Integrity:** Have I let any of my "Red Lines" slide just to keep the peace?
4. **Romance Leadership:** Am I still "dating" her with intentionality, or am I just "cohabitating"?
5. **Emotional Grounding:** Have I been reactive to her moods or the world's chaos lately?

If any score is below an 8, you have an Integrity Leak. You must perform a Micro-Reset immediately.

Summary: The Weight of the Crown

Consistency is the **"Invisible Force"** that keeps a relationship together. It is not glamorous. It doesn't have the "High" of a first kiss or the "Adrenaline" of an early-stage chase. It is the steady, rhythmic heartbeat of a man who knows exactly who he is and where he is going.

When you are consistent, you become a **Constant** in a chaotic world. You become the lighthouse she looks to when her own emotions are a storm. You are no longer "performing" to get her; you are **Existing** to lead her.

Remember: A woman's desire is a reflection of her respect. Her respect is a reflection of your consistency. If you want her to want you forever, you must be the same man on day 1,000 that you were on day 1—only stronger, wiser, more disciplined, and more focused.

RESOLVE EARLY CONFLICTS CONSTRUCTIVELY

The Baptism of Fire: Why the First Fight Matters

Every building, no matter how magnificent the blueprints, must eventually face its first storm. You can hire the best architects, pour the strongest concrete, and use the finest steel, but until the wind howls and the rain lashes against the windows, you do not truly know if the structure will hold.

In the architecture of a high-value partnership, that storm is the **First Major Conflict.**

Up until this point, your relationship has been protected by what behavioral psychologists call the **"Honeymoon Shield."** During the first 90 to 180 days, your brains are flooded with a potent cocktail of dopamine, phenylethylamine (PEA), and norepinephrine. This chemical bath acts as a lubricant, reducing friction and making alignment feel effortless. You overlook her quirks; she ignores your bad habits. You are both operating on your absolute best behavior, presenting the "Avatar" of your ideal selves.

But eventually, the chemistry settles. The "Honeymoon Shield" dissipates, and reality sets in. The **"Integrated Scars"** we discussed in Chapter 1—the defensive mechanisms, the childhood wounds, and the learned behaviors from past relationships—begin to rub against one another. A boundary is pushed. A core value is questioned. A deep-seated need goes unmet.

Suddenly, the "Perfect Girl" is yelling at you because you didn't text back fast enough, or you are feeling a surge of cold resentment because she questioned your judgment in front of friends.

This moment is the fork in the road.

For the **Low-Value Man**, this moment is a disaster. Operating from a place of scarcity and insecurity, he views conflict as a symptom of failure. He thinks, *"If we were soulmates, we wouldn't be fighting."* He interprets her anger as a rejection of his worth or a sign that he is "losing" her. Terrified of the loss, he defaults to one of two ruinous strategies:

1. **The Nice Guy Withdrawal:** He retreats into passive-aggressive silence, sulking to punish her while secretly hoping she will come comfort him.

2. **The Insecure Tyrant:** He explodes into reactive anger, trying to shout her into submission to regain a sense of control.

Both responses destroy the **"Security Frame"** you have worked so hard to build. They prove to her that you are not a safe harbor; you are just another paper boat getting tossed around by the waves.

For the **High-Value Man**, conflict is not a bug; it is a **feature**. It is the necessary **"Stress-Test"** that reveals where the foundation needs reinforcing. It is an opportunity to prove your consistency (Chapter 4) and your emotional leadership.

If handled correctly, the first major fight doesn't tear the relationship apart—it actually **increases** her respect for you and deepens her attraction. Why? Because a woman cannot fully trust a man until she has seen him angry. She needs to know that when things get messy, when the emotions are high and the logic is low, you are the man who can navigate the chaos without losing his cool. She needs to see that you are dangerous enough to defend yourself, but disciplined enough not to hurt her.

In this chapter, we will master the art of **Masculine De-escalation.** We will explore the "Conflict Loop," the biological differences in how men and women process stress, and the specific "High-Value Resolution Protocol" that ensures you lead the relationship back to peace, stronger than it was before.

Section 1: The Biology of the Blowup

You cannot fix a machine if you do not understand the mechanics. To resolve conflict effectively, you must stop viewing it as a "logical debate" and start viewing it as a "physiological event."

When a fight starts, you are no longer dealing with the woman you love; you are dealing with a nervous system in survival mode.

1. Diffuse Physiological Arousal (DPA)

Renowned relationship researcher Dr. John Gottman calls this state **Diffuse Physiological Arousal (DPA)**, more commonly known as "The Flood." When a conflict triggers a threat response, the body dumps cortisol and adrenaline into the bloodstream.

- Heart rate climbs above 100 BPM.
- Peripheral vision narrows (tunnel vision).
- The **Pre-Frontal Cortex** (the center of logic, empathy, and complex planning) begins to shut down.
- The **Amygdala** (the lizard brain responsible for fight-or-flight) takes the wheel.

Once DPA sets in, **logical communication is biologically impossible.** You cannot reason with an Amygdala. You cannot use a spreadsheet to argue with adrenaline.

2. The Gender Divergence in Stress Response

While both sexes experience DPA, they process it differently due to evolutionary conditioning.

- **The Male Response (The Stone Wall):** Men tend to hit DPA faster and stay there longer. This is an evolutionary hangover;

men were the "perimeter defenders," designed to react instantly to physical threats. In a modern relationship, when emotional intensity spikes, the male brain reads it as a physical threat. To protect himself from "boiling over" (and potentially doing physical harm), a man's instinct is to **Shut Down.** He stops talking, his face goes blank, and he looks away.

> o *How she interprets this*: She sees this as coldness, abandonment, and a lack of care. It triggers her panic.

- **The Female Response (The Pursuit):** Evolutionary psychology suggests that for women, survival was dependent on the social cohesion of the tribe. Therefore, a break in emotional connection is perceived as a life-threatening danger. When she feels the connection severing (because you are Stonewalling), her anxiety spikes. To solve the threat, she enters **Pursuit Mode.** She increases her verbal output, raises her volume, and intensifies the emotional charge to force a reaction that re-establishes connection.

> o *How you interpret this:* You see this as an attack, nagging, or "craziness."

The High-Value Mandate: As the leader, you must be the one to recognize when DPA is happening. You cannot lead a woman who is in a "biological hijack" by using logic. You must first **de-escalate the physiology** before you can address the problem.

Section 2: The "Conflict Loop" and the "Nice Guy" Trap

Most couples get stuck in the **Reactive Conflict Loop.** This is a downward spiral where the man's response to the woman's emotion actually pours gasoline on the fire he is trying to extinguish.

The Anatomy of the Loop

1. **The Trigger:** She expresses a grievance, often with high emotional "charge" and hyperbole (e.g., *"You never spend time with me!"*).

2. **The Nice Guy Mistake:** He takes the emotion literally and the hyperbole personally. He tries to "logic" her out of her feelings (*"That's not true, we went to dinner yesterday"*) or gets defensive because he feels "under-appreciated" (*"After everything I do for you?"*).

3. **The Escalation:** Because he is arguing logic against her emotion, she feels **unheard**. To make herself heard, she increases the intensity. Because she is increasing intensity, he feels **attacked**. To defend himself, he withdraws or shouts back.

4. **The Fallout:** The "Frame" is broken. Respect is lost. The fight ends in exhaustion, not resolution.

Why Logic Fails

The Nice Guy tries to fix her *feelings* because **he** is uncomfortable. Her unhappiness makes him anxious, so he tries to "solve" her unhappiness with facts so that *he* can stop feeling anxious. This is a covert contract. It is selfish.

The High-Value Frame: The "Emotional Container"

The High-Value Man breaks the loop by becoming the **Container.**

Imagine her emotions as a violent storm and yourself as a massive mountain. The storm screams at the mountain. It rains, it thunders, it throws lightning. Does the mountain scream back? Does the mountain try to "argue" with the wind? Does the mountain crumble because the rain is "unfair"?

No. The mountain remains solid. It allows the storm to rage, knowing that eventually, the storm will run out of energy. And when the clouds clear, the mountain is still there—unmoved, unhurt, and majestic.

When you act as the Container, you are sending a powerful sub-communication: *"Your chaos cannot destroy me. I am strong enough to handle your worst emotions without crumbling and without attacking you."* This creates safety.

Section 3: The High-Value Resolution Protocol

When the first fight hits, do not wing it. Fall back on your training. Follow this four-step roadmap to maintain your leadership and lead the relationship out of the DPA zone.

Step 1: The "Tactical Pause"

The moment you feel your own heart rate rising (the "Red Zone") or you see her becoming "unregulated" (screaming, crying uncontrollably, circular logic), you must call a pause. This is not a request; it is a command decision for the safety of the relationship.

- **The Script:** *"I can see we're both getting heated, and I want to make sure I'm actually hearing you. Right now, I'm not processing well. Let's take 20 minutes to cool down, and then we'll sit down and figure this out."*

- **The Critical Detail:** You **must** give a specific time when you will return (e.g., 20 minutes). If you just walk away, that is abandonment. If you set a time, that is **Active Leadership.**

- **Why it works:** You are protecting the relationship from the permanent damage of things said in the heat of the moment. You are overriding the Amygdala.

Step 2: "Validate the Emotion, Don't Negotiate the Logic"

Once you return, your goal is not to "win"; it is to **lower her defenses.** Women often speak in "Emotional Hyperbole."

- *She says:* "You never listen to me!"

- *She means:* "I feel disconnected from you right now."

The Low-Value Man argues the word "never." The High-Value Man validates the feeling of "disconnection."

- **The High-Value Move:** Validate the *feeling* without necessarily agreeing with the *fact*. You are acknowledging her reality, which creates immediate intimacy.

- **The Script:** *"I hear that you're feeling ignored right now, and I understand why that would be frustrating for you. I don't want you to feel that way."*

- **The Result:** Watch her body language. Her shoulders will drop. Her breathing will slow. Once she feels "witnessed," her nervous system de-escalates. She no longer needs to fight to be heard.

Step 3: State the "Frame" and the Boundary

Validation does not mean being a doormat. Once the temperature is down, you must address the **behavior** of the conflict. A High-Value Man does not tolerate disrespect, name-calling, or character assassination, even during a fight.

- **The Script:** *"I'm happy to work through this with you, and I want to hear your perspective. But I won't engage when there is shouting or name-calling. We speak to each other with respect, even when we're angry. Are we ready to do that?"*

- **Why it works:** You are re-establishing the "Rules of the House" (Chapter 2). You are showing that your boundaries are consistent (Chapter 4). You are teaching her how to treat you.

Step 4: The "Solution-Oriented" Pivot

A fight should always end with an actionable "Next Step." Venting without solution is just complaining. You must pivot from the *Past* (what happened) to the *Future* (what we will do).

- **The Script:** *"Okay, I understand the issue. Moving forward, how can we handle [X] differently so we both feel supported? What does 'good' look like to you?"*

- **The Result:** You move from being "Adversaries" back to being "First Mate and Captain" (Chapter 1). You are now problem-solving as a unit.

Section 4: The Art of the "Man-Apology"

There is a misconception in the "Red Pill" space that an Alpha never apologizes. This is false. A weak man never apologizes because his ego is too fragile to admit a mistake. A High-Value Man apologizes effortlessly because his worth is internal, not external.

However, the *style* of the apology matters.

The Nice Guy Apology (Submission)

"I'm so sorry, please don't be mad at me. I'm an idiot. I'll do whatever you want. Just tell me what to do."

- **Sub-communication:** "I am afraid of your anger. I am submitting to you to buy peace. I have no frame."

The High-Value Apology (Ownership)

"I've looked at my part in this, and I realize I dropped the ball on [X]. I said I would handle it, and I didn't. That's on me. That won't happen again. I'm sorry for the frustration it caused."

- **Sub-communication:** "I hold myself to a high standard. I failed that standard. I own it. I am correcting it. I am not afraid of the truth."

An apology of ownership actually **strengthens** your frame. It shows you have the **"Internal Audit"** (Chapter 1) necessary to lead yourself. It signals that you are objective enough to see your own flaws, which makes her trust your judgment of *her* flaws even more.

Section 5: Conflict as a "Polishing" Tool

In the Japanese art of *Kintsugi*, broken pottery is repaired with gold lacquer. The result is a piece that is more beautiful and valuable than the original because of its history.

This is what constructive conflict does for a partnership. Each fight should result in a **"Calibration."** It is data.

- **The "Dishes" Fight:** It's rarely about the dishes. It might be a conflict about **Contribution Values.** Calibration: "We need a clearer system for domestic duties."
- **The "Late for Dinner" Fight:** It's rarely about the food. It might be a conflict about **Respect for Time.** Calibration: "We need a protocol for communication when schedules change."

The Post-Game Analysis:

After the fight is over and the "Oxytocin" has returned (often through "Make-up" intimacy), perform a brief post-game analysis.

> *"I'm glad we got through that. I think we learned that we have different definitions of 'on time.' Let's align on that so we don't have to do this again."*

This turns the conflict into a brick in your Cathedral, rather than a crack in the foundation.

Section 6: When Conflict is a "Red Flag"

While conflict is necessary, not all conflict is constructive. As the Selector, you must distinguish between **"Relational Friction"** (growing pains) and **"Character Toxicity"** (deal-breakers).

Healthy Conflict	Toxic Conflict
Focus: Specific behavior (*"You were late."*)	**Focus:** Character assassination (*"You are selfish/lazy."*)
Response: De-escalates when heard/validated.	**Response:** Escalates regardless of validation (Moving the goalposts).

Healthy Conflict	Toxic Conflict
Outcome: Ends in a solution or compromise.	**Outcome:** Ends in "The Silent Treatment," punishment, or circular arguments.
Accountability: Both parties own their part.	**Accountability:** Blame shifting (*"I wouldn't yell if you weren't so stupid."*)
Boundary: Respects the "Walk-Away" boundary.	**Boundary:** Uses your fear of losing her as a weapon (Break-up threats).

The Danger Zone:

If you execute the High-Value Protocol—you pause, you validate, you own your part—and she *continues* to scream, belittle, or attack, you are no longer dealing with a "passionate woman." You are dealing with a woman who lacks emotional maturity or has high-conflict personality traits.

In this scenario, refer back to the **"Walk-Away Power"** in Chapter 2. A High-Value Man does not stay in a burning building just because he likes the wallpaper. Your peace is the priority. If she cannot respect the rules of engagement, she cannot remain on the ship.

Summary: The Anchor in the Storm

The "First Fight" is a rite of passage. It is the moment she realizes that her "Storm" cannot blow you over.

When a woman tests you with conflict, she is subconsciously asking: *"Is he strong enough to handle me?"*

If you crumble, she feels unsafe.

If you attack, she feels unsafe.

But if you stand firm—validating her emotions while maintaining your boundaries—she feels a profound sense of relief. She realizes that you are the **Anchor**.

By mastering de-escalation, you ensure that the partnership remains a place of **"Recovery"** rather than a place of "War." You prove that the relationship is resilient. You are the Emotional Architect, and every resolved conflict is a brick laid with permanent mortar, building a structure that can weather any season.

CHAPTER 6

KEEP THE ROMANCE ALIVE AS INTIMACY GROWS

The Entropy of Love: Why Passion Decays

There is a fundamental law in physics known as the Second Law of Thermodynamics. It states that in any isolated system, **Entropy** (disorder and decay) always increases over time unless energy is actively injected into the system. If you leave a house alone, it gathers dust. If you leave a garden alone, weeds take over. If you leave a fire alone, it turns to ash.

Relationships operate under this same physical law.

Most men believe that "Love" is a self-sustaining fusion reactor—that once it is lit, it burns forever. This is a fairy tale. The truth is that **Romance is a Campfire.** In the beginning (the dating phase), the fire roars because you are constantly throwing logs on it: the uncertainty, the chase, the first touches, the late-night conversations.

But once the "Grey Zone" is navigated and the "Commitment" is secured (Chapter 2), most men stop gathering wood. They get comfortable. They trade the "Hunter" archetype for the "Settler" archetype. They assume that because they have "won" the woman, the game is over.

This is the **Comfort Coma.**

It is the silent killer of high-value relationships. It is not a dramatic explosion like the conflicts in Chapter 5; it is a slow, suffocating drift into mediocrity. You wake up two years later, and you are not lovers; you are roommates who share a Netflix account and occasionally have "maintenance sex" to relieve tension.

For the High-Value Man, this is unacceptable. You are building a Cathedral, not a dorm room. To keep the structure magnificent, you must master the art of **Romance Maintenance.**

In this chapter, we will solve the **"Passion Paradox"**—the biological conflict between Security (Oxytocin) and Desire (Dopamine). We will provide the tactical blueprint for keeping the "Ache" of attraction alive, ensuring that even after ten years, she still looks at you with the same hunger she did on the first date.

Section 1: The Neuroscience of "The Spark"

To solve the problem of boredom, we must first look at the chemical equation of desire.

The Dopamine-Oxytocin Conflict

Human bonding relies on two primary neurotransmitters that, unfortunately, work in opposition to one another.

1. **Dopamine (The Chase):** This is the chemical of **Wanting.** It is triggered by novelty, uncertainty, risk, and anticipation. It is the fuel of the "Honeymoon Phase." Dopamine screams, *"I must have that!"*

2. **Oxytocin (The Bond):** This is the chemical of **Having.** It is triggered by touch, safety, predictability, and cuddling. It is the fuel of "Long-Term Attachment." Oxytocin whispers, *"I am safe here."*

The Paradox:

- To build a stable relationship (Commitment), you need **High Oxytocin.** You need safety, trust, and routine.

- To maintain sexual desire (Romance), you need **High Dopamine.** You need mystery, novelty, and a touch of danger.

The "Nice Guy" floods the relationship with Oxytocin. He becomes entirely predictable, safe, and "always there." He suffocates the Dopamine. The result is a woman who "loves" him like a brother but is no longer sexually ignited by him.

The "Player" floods the relationship with Dopamine. He is exciting but unsafe. The result is high passion but zero trust, which eventually burns out.

The High-Value Solution: The "Hybrid" Model

Your goal is to build a heavy, stable foundation of Oxytocin (the Cathedral) but to systematically inject spikes of Dopamine (Lightning) into the system. You must be the **Safe Harbor** *and* the **Storm.**

We can express this relationship dynamically:

$$Desire(t) = \frac{Novelty + Distance}{Predictability}$$

If Predictability becomes absolute (100%), Desire approaches zero. You must artificially manipulate the variables of **Novelty** and **Distance** to keep the equation balanced.

Section 2: The Enemy is "Domestic Blindness"

Before we discuss what to *do*, we must discuss what to *stop doing*. The fastest way to kill romance is **Demystification.**

In the early days, you presented your best self. You groomed, you dressed well, you planned. Now, the "Roommate Syndrome" sets in. This manifests as **Domestic Blindness**—the state where you become part of the furniture.

The "Open Bathroom Door" Policy

There is a dangerous modern belief that "true intimacy" means having zero boundaries. This is false. True intimacy requires respect.

- **The Error:** Using the bathroom with the door open, grooming (clipping toenails, etc.) in the living room, or walking around in stained sweatpants for the entire weekend.

- **The Effect:** This kills the "Erotic Imagination." It is impossible to view a man as a conquering King when you have watched him flossing his teeth for ten minutes.
- **The Fix:** Maintain a "Veil of Mystery." Keep your grooming rituals private. Dress well even inside the house. Do not let yourself become "gross" just because you are comfortable.

The Routine Trap

- **The Error:** Every Tuesday is tacos. Every Friday is pizza and a movie. Every Sunday is laundry.
- **The Effect:** The brain stops recording new memories because nothing new is happening. The relationship feels like it is moving in "fast forward" because months blur into one homogeneous blob of routine.
- **The Fix:** You must become an **Agent of Chaos** (benevolent chaos). You must be the one to break the pattern.

Section 3: The Three Pillars of Romance Maintenance

To inject Dopamine back into the Oxytocin container, you must operationalize three specific strategies.

Pillar I: Controlled Distance (The "Rubber Band" Theory)

Desire requires space. You cannot desire something you already have. As relationship expert Esther Perel notes, *"Love rests on two pillars: surrender and autonomy. Our need for togetherness exists alongside our need for separateness."*

If you are constantly texting her, constantly touching her, and constantly in her presence, the "Rubber Band" of desire goes slack. There is no tension.

The Strategy:

1. **The "Blackout" Periods:** Do not be available 24/7. When you are deep in work or at the gym, do not answer texts immediately. Create a window of time where she *wonders* what you are doing. That wonder is the seed of desire.
2. **Social Independence:** Encourage her to go out with her friends *without you.* Go out with your men *without her.* When you reunite, you have new information to share. You are two separate entities colliding, rather than one blob merged together.

3. **The "Return" Ritual:** When you come home from work, do not just walk in and grunt. That is the "Roommate Entry." Instead, pause. Reset your state. Walk in with energy. Kiss her like you haven't seen her in a month. Re-establish the polarity immediately.

Pillar II: Novelty and Adrenaline

The brain releases Dopamine when it encounters something **New.** If you only interact in the living room and the kitchen, your relationship is anchored to those domestic spaces.

The Strategy:

1. **New Environments:** Taking a walk in a new part of the city releases more dopamine than a fancy dinner at the same restaurant you always go to.

2. **Adrenaline Bonding:** Fear and excitement mimic the physiological symptoms of sexual arousal (elevated heart rate, flushed skin). Do things that spike adrenaline: a difficult hike, a boxing class, a rollercoaster, a spontaneous road trip. When her heart races *with* you, her brain associates the excitement *with* you.

3. **Variable Reward Schedule:** Do not bring flowers every Friday. If you do, it becomes an obligation (Routine). Bring flowers on a random Tuesday. Book a hotel room in your own city for no reason. Unpredictability amplifies the emotional impact of the gesture by 400%.

Pillar III: The "Captain" Dynamic (Leading the Experience)

Decision fatigue is a libido killer for women. Modern women are often making high-stress decisions all day at work. The last thing they want to do is come home and manage the "Project Management" of the relationship.

When you ask, *"What do you want to do for dinner?"* you think you are being nice.

She hears: *"I am putting the mental load on you. Please tell me how to lead."*

The Strategy:

Be the **Architect of the Experience.**

- **Bad:** "Do you want to go out tonight?"
- **Good:** "Be ready at 7:00 PM. Wear that black dress. I'm taking you somewhere."

This relieves her of the burden of choice and allows her to relax into her feminine energy. She can simply "be," because she trusts that you have handled the "doing."

Section 4: The Date Night Protocol

"Date Night" is a cliché, but only because most men execute it poorly. A high-value date is not about spending money; it is about **Intentionality.**

You must adhere to the **2/2/1 Rule** of Relationship Rhythm:

- **Every 2 Weeks:** A high-quality Date Night (No phones, intentional connection).
- **Every 2 Months:** A Weekend Getaway (Change of environment, removal of domestic triggers).
- **Every 1 Year:** A Week-Long Adventure (Deep disconnection from the matrix).

The Anatomy of a High-Value Date

1. **The Invite:** Sent in advance. Shows foresight. *"I've cleared the schedule for Friday night."*
2. **The Preparation:** You dress up. You groom. You show her that she is worth the effort. If you show up in the same clothes you wore to clean the garage, you insult the occasion.
3. **The Environment:** Choose a place with "High Atmosphere." Lighting matters. Noise levels matter. You want an environment that encourages intimacy, not distraction.
4. **The Conversation:** DO NOT talk about logistics.
   - *Forbidden Topics:* The mortgage, the kids' school schedule, the leaky faucet, work stress.
   - *Required Topics:* Dreams, philosophy, memories, future vision, "What if" scenarios.
   - *The Goal:* To speak to the *Woman*, not the *Business Partner.*

Ultimately, romance leads to the bedroom. But just like the rest of the relationship, the bedroom can fall victim to "Sameness."

The death of sex in long-term relationships usually stems from a **Loss of Polarity.** The man becomes too soft, seeking reassurance during sex, or the sex becomes "Transactionary" (rubbing her back expecting a reward).

1. Rejection of "Maintenance Sex"

Do not settle for "duty sex." It breeds resentment in her and weakness in you. If the energy isn't there, do not beg for it. Instead, build the tension until the energy *is* there.

- **The Mindset:** You are not a beggar asking for a coin. You are a King offering an experience.

2. Non-Sexual Touch (The Simmer)

Most men only touch their partner when they want sex. This creates a "Pavlovian Defense." When he puts his hand on her leg, she tenses up, thinking, *"Oh god, he wants it, and I'm tired."*

To fix this, you must engage in **Non-Transactional Touch.**

- Hug her from behind while she's cooking, kiss her neck, and then *walk away.*

- Hold her hand in the car with firm pressure, then let go.

- **The Message:** "I desire you, but I don't *need* anything from you right now." This builds safety and anticipation.

3. The "Lover" Archetype

In the bedroom, you must shed the "Provider" and "Protector" roles. The Provider is safe; the Lover is dangerous (in a good way).

- **Variety:** Change the location. Change the time of day. Change the dynamic.

- **Verbal Dominance:** Use your voice. Tell her what you want. Tell her what you are going to do to her. The masculine voice is a powerful aphrodisiac that cuts through her mental chatter.

Section 6: The Art of the Specific Compliment

In the beginning, you told her she was beautiful constantly. Now, you assume she knows. She doesn't. Or rather, she stops believing it because the data is old.

However, generic compliments ("You look nice") are low-value. They feel like autopilot.

The High-Value Compliment:

It must be **Specific** and **Novel.**

- *Generic:* "You look beautiful."
- *High-Value:* "That color green looks incredible on you; it makes your eyes look dangerous tonight."
- *Generic:* "Thanks for dinner."
- *High-Value:* "I really appreciate how much effort you put into making our home feel peaceful. It doesn't go unnoticed."

When you give a specific compliment, it proves you are **Paying Attention.** Attention is the currency of love.

Section 7: The "Check-In" Ritual

Romance requires calibration. You cannot drive a car for 100,000 miles without checking the oil.

Every Sunday evening, institute a 10-minute **"State of the Union"** (brief and positive).

- *Question 1:* "What was your favorite moment with us this week?" (Reinforces positive memory).
- *Question 2:* "How is your 'Love Tank' feeling? High, low, or empty?" (Provides data).
- *Question 3:* "What can I do this week to make you feel more supported/desired?" (Actionable feedback).

This is not a "feelings dump." It is a CEO-level audit of the relationship's emotional health. It catches the "Entropy" before it becomes rot.

Summary: Love is a Discipline

The Disney narrative taught us that "Happily Ever After" is a destination. You arrive there, the credits roll, and the work is done.

The Reality is that "Happily Ever After" is a daily construction project.

Keeping the romance alive as intimacy grows is the ultimate test of the High-Value Man. It is easy to be romantic when the hormones are raging and the stakes are low. It is a feat of strength to be romantic when the mortgage is due, the kids are crying, and you are exhausted.

But this is the work. You are the Fire-Keeper. If you let the fire go out, the room goes cold. If you tend to the fire—with the logs of novelty, the oxygen of space, and the spark of polarity—it will burn warm and bright enough to last a lifetime.

You have built the Cathedral (Foundation). You have protected it from storms (Conflict). Now, you have ensured that it is warm and lit from within (Romance).

CHAPTER 7

CONCLUSION: BUILDING A LEGACY TOGETHER

The Transition: From Partnership to Dynasty

We have traveled a long road together.

In **Book 1**, you mastered the "Internal Audit," stripping away the "Nice Guy" conditioning to find the core of your masculine identity. In **Book 2**, you built your "Fortress," surrounding yourself with a Council of Men and a mission that transcended any individual woman. In **Book 3**, you learned the "Laws of Attraction," understanding the biological triggers that turn interest into desire. In **Book 4**, you navigated the "Selection Process," vetting for quality over quantity. And here, in **Book 5**, you have learned to build the infrastructure of a real, thriving relationship.

You have the foundation. You have the walls. You have the fire in the hearth.

But a house, no matter how well-built, is just a building. A **Legacy** is what happens when that building becomes the headquarters for something greater than the sum of its parts.

Most men view a relationship as the "Finish Line." They think, *"I've found the girl, I've secured the commitment, now I can finally relax."* This is the mindset of the consumer. The High-Value Man views the relationship as the **"Launchpad."** A real relationship is not a destination where you go to hide from the world; it is a strategic alliance designed to help you conquer the world. This final chapter is about the transition from a "Couple" to a **Dynasty**. It is about the "Third Stage" of masculine evolution: moving from *Success* to *Significance*.

Section 1: The Concept of the "Shared Mission"

In the early stages of dating, your missions were separate. You were a man on a path, and she was a woman on a path. You were vetting her to see if she could fit into your "Frame."

In a long-term partnership, a new entity is born: **The Shared Mission.**

This does not mean you abandon your individual purpose. It means you create a "Secondary Objective" that requires both of you to be in total lockstep. A Shared Mission is the ultimate insurance policy against the "Entropy" we discussed in Chapter 6. When two people are looking only at each other, they eventually get bored. When two people are looking at a common goal on the horizon, they become an unstoppable force.

The Synergy Graph

In a low-value relationship, the dynamic is often $1 + 1 < 2$. The drama, the inconsistency, and the lack of alignment drain the energy of both partners. You are both less effective than you would be single.

In a High-Value Dynasty, the dynamic is $1 + 1 = 11$.

What constitutes a Shared Mission?

- **The Creation of a Family:** Not just "having kids," but the intentional engineering of the next generation of high-value humans.
- **Economic Empire Building:** Merging your talents to create wealth that provides freedom for your descendants.

- **Philanthropy and Impact:** Using your combined status to change a community or an industry.
- **The Masterpiece Home:** Creating a physical environment that acts as a sanctuary for your tribe.

Section 2: The "Multi-Generational" Mindset

A "Nice Guy" thinks in terms of weeks and months (how to keep her happy today). A High-Value Man thinks in terms of **Decades and Centuries.**

Building a legacy requires you to view your relationship through the lens of **Time-Horizon Expansion.** You are not just building a life for *you* and *her*; you are building a "Culture" that will be inherited by people you will never meet.

The Family Constitution

Every great institution has a charter. Your relationship should be no different. As you move into the "Dynasty Phase," you and your partner must define the **Non-Negotiable Traditions and Values** of your house.

- *How do we handle conflict? (Refer to Chapter 5)*
- *How do we manage our resources? (Refer to Chapter 3)*
- *What is the standard of excellence for our children?*
- *How do we treat our elders and our community?*

When you have a "Family Constitution," you are no longer making decisions based on "how you feel" in the moment. You are making decisions based on the **Legacy Standard.** This removes 90% of the petty bickering that destroys average relationships.

Section 3: The Woman as the "Force Multiplier"

In the "Selection" phase (Book 4), we looked for a woman who was a "First Mate." In the "Legacy" phase, we see her true value: she is the **Chief Operating Officer (COO)** of the Dynasty.

While you are the "CEO"—the visionary, the provider of the frame, the one facing the external world—she is the one who manages the internal "Vibe" and the "Micro-Culture" of the family.

The High-Value Feminine Contribution

A woman who is truly aligned with a High-Value Man doesn't just "support" him; she **amplifies** him.

- **The Intuition Filter:** She sees the "Red Flags" in people that your logical, mission-focused brain might miss.

- **The Emotional Battery:** She provides the recovery and "Soft Landing" that allows you to go out and face the "War" of the marketplace the next day.

- **The Social Connector:** She builds the "Soft Power" networks—the friendships, the community ties—that sustain a family's status over generations.

If you have led her well (Chapters 1-6), she will *want* to pour her energy into your shared vision. She will view your success as her success, because you have made her an equal stakeholder in the "Corporation of Us."

Section 4: Protecting the Dynasty from the "Modern Rot"

The world is designed to pull families apart. Modern culture celebrates hyper-individualism, temporary "situationships," and the "disposability" of partners. To build a legacy, you must be a **Relational Contrarian.**

1. Guarding the Information Borders

Do not let "The Matrix" (social media, toxic "reality" TV, or bitter friends) dictate the standards of your home. You must be the "Gatekeeper" of the information that enters your partner's mind.

- If she is surrounding herself with women who hate men, your legacy is at risk.

- If you are surrounding yourself with men who cheat and lie, your legacy is at risk.

2. The Sanctity of the Internal Frame

A Dynasty is a "Private Club." The details of your internal struggles, your finances, and your intimacy should never leave the "Fortress." When you vent about your partner to outsiders, you are poking holes in your own ship. You resolve issues **internally** (Chapter 5) so that you can present a **Unified Front** to the world.

Section 5: The Passing of the Torch

The ultimate proof of a High-Value Relationship is not found in the couple themselves, but in their **Progeny.**

Whether you have biological children, adopted children, or mentees, your legacy is defined by the quality of the people you produce.

- **Leading by Example:** Your children will not do what you *say*; they will do what you *do*. If they see a father who is consistent, disciplined, and respectful to their mother, they will seek that for themselves.

- **The Architecture of Character:** Use the "Value Alignment" (Chapter 3) you built with your partner to engineer the environment for your children. You are not just raising "kids"; you are raising the future leaders of your dynasty.

Section 6: The Final Synthesis—The High-Value Man's Peace

At the end of your life, you will not look back at the cars you drove or the individual conquests you made. You will look at the **Web of Impact** you created.

You will see a woman who grew more beautiful in her soul because she spent decades under the protection of a man who loved her with "Calculated Certainty." You will see children who are grounded and capable. You will see an empire (large or small) that stands as a testament to your discipline.

This is the **High-Value Man's Peace.** It is the knowledge that you did not just "exist"; you **ordered** a small part of the universe. You took the chaos of the "Nice Guy" and turned it into the order of the King.

Summary: The Beginning of the Rest of Your Life

This series of books was never just about "getting a girlfriend." It was about **reclaiming your birthright as a leader.**

You have the tools. You have the mindset. You have the blueprint.

1. **Be the Mountain:** Unshakeable, grounded, and focused on the mission.

2. **Be the Selector:** Valuing your time and energy as the ultimate currency.

3. **Be the Leader:** Guiding the relationship with empathy, strength, and consistency.

4. **Be the Builder:** Creating a legacy that outlasts your physical presence.

Go forth and build your Cathedral. The world has enough "Nice Guys." It is waiting for a Man.

CHAPTER 8

REFLECTION QUESTIONS

The Mirror of Mastery

You have reached the end of the text, but you are at the beginning of the application. Information without integration is merely entertainment. To transition from a man who "knows" these principles to a man who "lives" them, you must be willing to engage in a radical internal audit.

This final chapter is your **Diagnostic Tool.** It is designed to expose the "Integrity Gaps" in your current mindset and relationship dynamics. There are no right or wrong answers—only honest ones. Use these questions to calibrate your compass as you move forward into the "Dynasty" phase of your life.

Before you can lead a partner, you must be certain of the man you are when no one is watching.

1. **The "Lighthouse" Question:** If your partner's emotions were a Category 5 hurricane tonight, are you truly the "Unmovable Object," or would you be swept into the storm with her? What was the last specific instance where you lost your "frame," and what was the internal trigger?

2. **The Mission Gap:** If the relationship ended tomorrow, would your life's mission still have its trajectory, or have you "parked" your purpose in the garage of domestic comfort?

3. **The Council Check:** Who are the three men in your life who have the authority to tell you that you are "going soft"? If you don't have them, what is the first step you will take this week to find your Council?

Section 2: The Infrastructure of Value (Alignment & Boundaries)

A relationship is only as strong as the "Terms and Conditions" established at the beginning.

4. **The Value Audit:** Look at your top three core values (e.g., Freedom, Legacy, Fitness). Can you point to a specific action your partner took in the last 30 days that proves she is aligned with those values?

5. **The "Red Line" Review:** What is one boundary you have let "slide" recently to avoid a difficult conversation? What is the "Long-Term Debt" you are accruing by not enforcing that boundary today?

6. **The Financial Philosophy:** Do you and your partner have a "Wealth Language" (Capital-focused) or a "Consumption Language" (Spending-focused)? If they are different, have you established the "Executive Veto" to protect the family's future?

Section 3: The Dynamics of Attraction (Consistency & Romance)

Desire is a biological response to leadership and polarity. It must be maintained.

7. **The Consistency Coefficient (C_c):** On a scale of 1–10, how closely do your daily actions match the "Marketing Campaign" you ran during the first three months of dating? Where is the "Product Experience" failing?

8. **The Decision Fatigue Audit:** In the last seven days, how many times did you ask "What do you want to do?" versus stating "This is what we are doing"?

9. **The Polarization Test:** When was the last time you created "Distance" to allow the "Rubber Band" of desire to stretch? Are you suffocating the spark with too much "Oxytocin-heavy" togetherness?

Section 4: The Conflict & De-escalation Audit

How you fight determines whether the relationship is a "Recovery Zone" or a "War Zone."

10. **The DPA Recognition:** Can you identify the physical sensation in your body (increased heart rate, heat in the face) that signals you are entering "The Flood"? What is your pre-planned "Tactical Pause" script for the next time it happens?

11. **The Ownership Audit:** Think of the last argument you had. Without mentioning her faults, what was the "Ball" that you specifically dropped? Have you made a "Man-Apology" of ownership, or are you still holding onto "Nice Guy" resentment?

Section 5: The Legacy Blueprint

This is the move from "Me" to "We" to "Dynasty."

12. **The "11" Factor:** In what specific way is your life significantly *more* impactful because she is in it? If you cannot name a way she is a "Force Multiplier," are you in a partnership or a distraction?

13. **The Family Constitution:** If you had to write down the "Three Commandments" of your household that must be followed even 100 years from now, what would they be?

14. The End-of-Life Vision: Imagine you are 90 years old, sitting on a porch with this woman. What is the one thing you want her to say about the way you led the family? Are your actions *today* making that statement a reality?

Moving Forward: Your Action Plan

Knowledge is only power when it is applied. Choose **three** questions from the list above that made you the most uncomfortable. Those are your "Integrity Leaks."

Your Task:

1. **Week 1:** Address the Internal Audit (Fix yourself).
2. **Week 2:** Address the Attraction/Consistency (Fix the dynamic).
3. **Week 3:** Address the Legacy/Values (Fix the future).

Final Word

You are now equipped with the psychology, the biology, and the tactics of the High-Value Man. The world needs your leadership. Your partner needs your strength. Your future children need your legacy.

The "Nice Guy" dies here. The King begins his reign.

OVERALL CONCLUSION
YOUR ROADMAP TO A FULFILLING LOVE LIFE

You now stand at the summit of a journey that began with a simple premise: that attraction is not a mysterious accident, but a biological and psychological result of **Masculine Excellence.**

Over the course of these five books, you have deconstructed the "Nice Guy" social conditioning that kept you reactive, anxious, and stuck in a cycle of seeking external validation. You have replaced it with a **High-Value Framework** that prioritizes mission, boundaries, and emotional self-mastery.

But as you close this final chapter, remember that this is not a static destination. A "Fulfilling Love Life" is a living organism—it requires constant oxygen, movement, and defense. To ensure the blueprints you've studied become the reality you live, you must internalize the three final movements of the High-Value Roadmap.

1. The Shift from Consumption to Creation

The low-value man views a relationship as a **Consumer.** He asks, *"What is she giving me? Is she making me happy? Is she providing the validation I lack?"* Because he is a consumer, he is always at the mercy of the "market." If her mood dips or her attraction wavers, his entire world collapses.

The High-Value Man views a relationship as a **Creator.** You are the architect of the "Frame." You do not enter a relationship to *find* happiness; you enter it to *share* the abundance of the life you have already built.

- You create the safety.
- You create the direction.
- You create the spark.

When you operate from a place of creation, you possess **True Agency.** You are no longer reacting to her; she is reacting to the world you have built.

2. The Maintenance of the "Attractive Tension"

The greatest trap you will face moving forward is the **Gravity of the Average.** Society, your peers, and even your own comfort-seeking brain will encourage you to "settle in." They will tell you that it's okay to let the gym slide, to stop dating your wife, or to become "one of the guys" who complains about his partner at the bar.

Reject the Average.

The roadmap to fulfillment requires you to maintain the **Polarity** you've learned.

- **Maintain your Edge:** Keep your Council of Men. Keep your hobbies. Keep your mission.

- **Maintain the Lead:** Do not abdicate your role as the decision-maker in exchange for a "quiet life." A quiet life is often a dead relationship.

- **Maintain the Standards:** Hold her to the high standard you vetted for, and hold yourself to the even higher standard you promised.

3. The Legacy of the Selected Life

Finally, understand that your love life is the primary variable in your overall success. The woman you choose to have by your side will either be the **Wind in your Sails** or the **Anchor around your neck.**

By following the Selection Process (Book 4) and building a Real Relationship (Book 5), you are not just seeking pleasure—you are building **Legacy.** You are creating a stable environment where your genius can flourish, where your children can grow into formidable leaders, and where you can experience the profound peace of being truly respected by a woman of high character.

Your Final Directive

The roadmap is now in your hands. You know how to audit your soul, build your fortress, trigger attraction, select your partner, and maintain your empire.

The "Nice Guy" is a ghost of your past. The **High-Value Man** is the reality of your present. Do not look back. Do not apologize for your standards. Do not shrink to make others comfortable.

Walk your path with "Calculated Certainty." Lead with "Ruthless Compassion." And never forget: **The world does not give a man what he wants; it gives a man what he is.**

Go forth and be the man she was designed to follow.

PRINT AND KEEP CHECKLIST
THE ATTRACTION BLUEPRINT

This checklist serves as the tactical condensation of the entire five-book series. Keep it in your digital notes, print it for your journal, or post it on your mirror. It is your **Operating System** for masculine excellence and relational leadership.

I. The Foundation (Book 1 & 2: Internal Mastery)

- **Daily Mission Audit:** Is my primary focus today on my purpose or on seeking female attention?

- **The Frame Test:** Am I reacting to her moods, or is she adjusting to my grounded energy?

- **Vulnerability Management:** Am I processing my raw emotions with my **Council of Men** rather than "dumping" them on my partner?

- **Physical Edge:** Have I moved my body and tested my limits today? (A King never lets his "Warrior" go soft).

- **Abundance Mindset:** Do I act from a place of *needing* her, or from a place of *choosing* her?

II. The Attraction Engine (Book 3: Triggers & Polarity)

- **The 80/20 Rule of Presence:** Am I maintaining enough space and mystery to allow the "Rubber Band" of desire to stretch?

- **Non-Transactional Touch:** Am I touching her to provide affection and dominance without expecting an immediate sexual reward?

- **Leading the Experience:** Have I made the "Executive Decisions" for our time together, or am I burdening her with choice?

- **Calculated Certainty:** Do I speak and act with conviction, or am I using "Beta-Speak" (e.g., "I guess," "If you want")?

III. The Selection Protocol (Book 4: Vetting & Boundaries)

- **Red Flag Vigilance:** Am I ignoring a character flaw because I am blinded by her physical "Marketing"?
- **Value Alignment:** Does she demonstrate the "Three Pillars" (Respect, Loyalty, Growth) in her actions, not just her words?
- **Boundary Enforcement:** Did I address the "Micro-Disrespect" immediately, or did I let it slide to "keep the peace"?
- **Walk-Away Power:** Do I still have the internal strength to leave if the standards of the relationship are no longer met?

IV. The Long-Term Infrastructure (Book 5: Partnership)

- **The Consistency Coefficient (C_c):** Are my actions today congruent with the man I presented myself to be on Day 1?
- **The Tactical Pause:** When conflict arises, do I stop the "Biological Hijack" (DPA) before it spirals?
- **Validation over Logic:** Am I hearing her *feeling* before I attempt to solve her *fact*?
- **The Legacy Standard:** Are we building toward a "Shared Mission" (Dynasty), or are we just killing time together?

V. Weekly Maintenance Rituals

- **The Date Night Protocol:** One night every two weeks where I lead the adventure. No logistics talk.
- **The State of the Union:** A 10-minute check-in. Is the "Love Tank" full? Are the boundaries intact?
- **Social Independence:** Have I spent time this week with high-value men, independent of my partner?

The Golden Rule of the Blueprint

"You do not attract what you want; you attract what you are."

If the attraction is dying, check your **Consistency.**

If the respect is dying, check your **Boundaries.**

If the spark is dying, check your **Polarity.**

If your peace is dying, check your **Selection.**

HERE'S ANOTHER BOOK BY SEBASTIAN NOCTURNE THAT YOU MIGHT LIKE

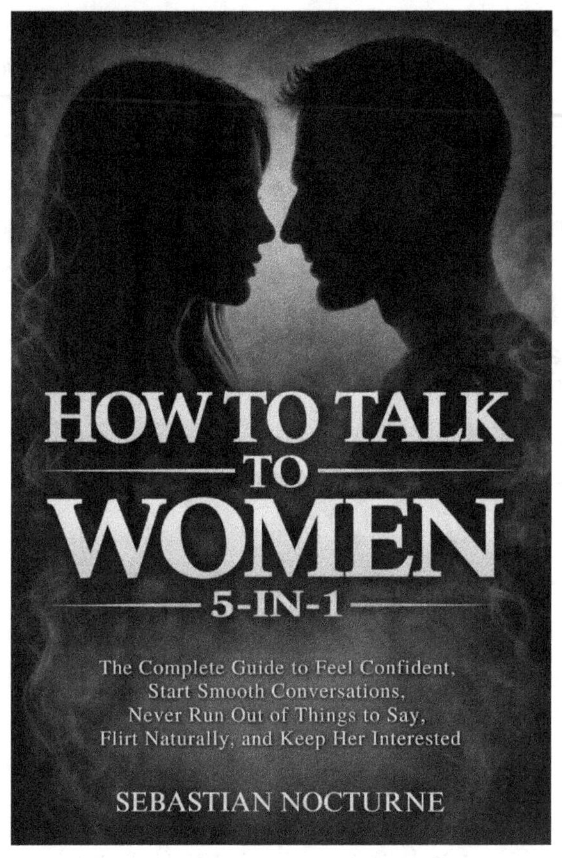

RESOURCE LIST

Introduction

Books:

- Buss, D. M. (2016). *The Evolution of Desire: Strategies of Human Mating*. Basic Books.

- Miller, G. (2000). *The Mating Mind: How Sexual Choice Shaped the Evolution of Human Nature.*

- Anchor. Ridley, M. (1993). *The Red Queen: Sex and the Evolution of Human Nature*. Harper Perennial.

- Pease, A., & Pease, B. (2004). *The Definitive Book of Body Language*. Bantam.

- Cialdini, R. B. (2006). *Influence: The Psychology of Persuasion*. Harper Business.

- Gottman, J. M., & Silver, N. (2015). *The Seven Principles for Making Marriage Work*. Harmony.

- Carnegie, D. (1936). *How to Win Friends and Influence People*. Simon & Schuster.

Online Resources:

- https://www.apa.org/topics/love/attraction
- https://www.psychologytoday.com/us/basics/mating
- https://labs.la.utexas.edu/buss/publications/
- https://www.paulekman.com/micro-expressions/

Book 1

Introduction

Books:

- Ambady, N., & Skowronski, J. J. (2008). *First Impressions*. Guilford Press.

- Buss, D. M. (2019). *Evolutionary Psychology: The New Science of the Mind*. Routledge. Navarro, J. (2008). *What Every Body is Saying*. HarperCollins.

- Trivers, R. (1972). *Parental Investment and Sexual Selection*. Aldine.
- Gladwell, M. (2005). *Blink: The Power of Thinking Without Thinking*. Little, Brown and Company.
- Mehrabian, A. (1971). *Silent Messages*. Wadsworth.

Online Resources:

- https://www.psychologicalscience.org/observer/the-psychological-study-of-first-impressions
- https://www.nature.com/articles/s41598-017-17714-0
- https://www.sciencedaily.com/releases/2007/11/071113091139.htm
- https://www.apa.org/monitor/2012/03/first-impressions

Chapter 1

Books:

- **Buss, D. M. (2016).** *The Evolution of Desire: Strategies of Human Mating*. Basic Books.
- **Gladwell, M. (2005).** *Blink: The Power of Thinking Without Thinking*. Little, Brown and Company.
- **Navarro, J. (2008).** *What Every Body is Saying*. HarperCollins.
- **Todorov, A. (2017).** *Face Value: The Irresistible Influence of First Impressions*. Princeton University Press.

Online Resources:

- https://journals.sagepub.com/doi/abs/10.1111/j.1467-9280.2006.01750.x
- https://scholar.harvard.edu/files/ambady/files/1993.pdf
- https://faculty.haas.berkeley.edu/dana_carney/power.poses.PS.2010.pdf
- https://hbr.org/2013/05/the-surprising-science-of-first-impressions
- https://www.nature.com/articles/s41598-017-17714-0
- https://www.psychologytoday.com/us/blog/the-human-beast/201212/why-women-choose-high-status-men
- https://www.apa.org/monitor/2012/03/first-impressions

Chapter 2

Books:

- **Roetzel, B. (2009).** *Gentleman: A Timeless Guide to Fashion.* h.f.ullmann.
- **Tan, F. (2019).** *Naturally Tan.* St. Martin's Press.
- **Cialdini, R. (2006).** *Influence: The Psychology of Persuasion.* Harper Business.
- **Molley, J. (1975).** *Dress for Success.*

Online Resources:

- https://www.sciencedirect.com/science/article/pii/S002210311200041X
- https://www.nytimes.com/2012/04/03/science/clothes-and-self-perception.html
- https://www.psychologytoday.com/us/blog/the-psychology-dress/201204/enclothed-cognition
- https://www.gq.com/story/style-basics-every-man-should-own
- https://www.wsj.com/articles/the-science-behind-why-dressing-up-matters-11603126040

Chapter 3

Books:

- **Navarro, J. (2008).** *What Every Body is Saying.* HarperCollins.
- **Cuddy, A. (2015).** *Presence: Bringing Your Boldest Self to Your Biggest Challenges.* Little, Brown and Company.
- **Lowen, A. (1975).** *Bioenergetics.* (The link between physical posture and psychological health).
- **Pease, A. & B. (2004).** *The Definitive Book of Body Language.* Bantam.
- **Coates, J. (2012).** *The Hour Between Dog and Wolf: Risk-taking, Gut Feelings and the Biology of Boom and Bust.* Random House.
- **Hall, E. T. (1966).** *The Hidden Dimension.* (Foundational text on Proxemics).

Online Resources:

- https://www.health.harvard.edu/staying-healthy/why-good-posture-matters
- https://www.ted.com/talks/amy_cuddy_your_body_language_may_shape_who_you_are
- https://www.mayoclinic.org/healthy-lifestyle/adult-health/in-depth/posture-align-yourself-for-good-health/art-20044707
- https://www.ncbi.nlm.nih.gov/pmc/articles/PMC4449331/
- https://www.psychologytoday.com/us/blog/the-power-pretense/201206/the-winner-effect
- https://www.scientificamerican.com/article/smile-it-could-make-you-happier/

Chapter 4

Books:

- **Cialdini, R. (2006).** *Influence: The Psychology of Persuasion.* Harper Business.
- **Buss, D. M. (2016).** *The Evolution of Desire: Strategies of Human Mating.* Basic Books.
- **Ferrazzi, K. (2005).** *Never Eat Alone.* Currency.
- **Carnegie, D. (1936).** *How to Win Friends and Influence People.* Simon & Schuster.

Online Resources:

- https://www.sciencedirect.com/science/article/pii/S109051380700085X
- https://www.psychologytoday.com/us/blog/head-games/201309/the-science-social-proof
- https://hbr.org/2001/10/harnessing-the-science-of-persuasion
- https://www.nature.com/articles/s41598-017-17714-0
- https://www.sciencedaily.com/releases/2007/11/071113091139.htm
- https://www.apa.org/monitor/2012/03/first-impressions

Chapter 5

Books:

- **Cialdini, R. (2006).** *Influence: The Psychology of Persuasion.* Harper Business.
- **Buss, D. M. (2016).** *The Evolution of Desire: Strategies of Human Mating.* Basic Books.
- **Ferrazzi, K. (2005).** *Never Eat Alone.* Currency.
- **Gladwell, M. (2000).** *The Tipping Point.* Little, Brown and Company.
- **Dunbar, R. (2010).** *How Many Friends Does One Person Need?* Faber & Faber.

Online Resources:

- https://www.sciencedirect.com/science/article/pii/S109051380700085X
- https://www.psychologytoday.com/us/blog/head-games/201309/the-science-social-proof https://hbr.org/2001/10/harnessing-the-science-of-persuasion
- https://www.nature.com/articles/s41598-017-17714-0
- https://www.sciencedaily.com/releases/2007/11/071113091139.htm
- https://www.socialproof.com/the-psychology-of-social-proof-in-dating/

Chapter 6

Books:

- **Pressfield, S. (2002).** *The War of Art.* (Crucial for understanding the "Resistance" we feel before taking action).
- **Jeffers, S. (1987).** *Feel the Fear and Do It Anyway.* Harlequin.
- **Navarro, J. (2008).** *What Every Body is Saying.* HarperCollins. (Context on "Freeze, Flight, or Fight" responses).
- **Greene, R. (2003).** *The Art of Seduction.* (Sections on "The Bold Strategy").
- **Cialdini, R. (2016).** *Pre-Suasion: A Revolutionary Way to Influence and Persuade.* Simon & Schuster.

Online Resources:

- https://www.psychologytoday.com/us/blog/the-modern-brain/201910/the-neuroscience-the-3-second-rule https://www.sciencedirect.com/science/article/pii/S019188691400155X

- https://hbr.org/2015/01/how-to-overcome-your-fear-of-approaching-strangers

- https://www.ted.com/talks/amy_cuddy_your_body_language_may_shape_who_you_are

- https://www.ncbi.nlm.nih.gov/pmc/articles/PMC4449331/

- https://www.scientificamerican.com/article/the-neurobiology-of-fear/

Chapter 7

Books:

- **Dweck, C. S. (2006).** *Mindset: The New Psychology of Success.* Random House. (Essential for understanding the Growth Mindset vs. Fixed Mindset—why you can change your "personality").

- **Maxwell, J. C. (1993).** *Developing the Leader Within You.* Thomas Nelson. (On the foundational principles of leadership and influence, applicable to social dynamics).

- **Marcus Aurelius.** *Meditations.* (The Stoic philosophy of maintaining internal groundedness regardless of external results).

- **Clear, J. (2018).** *Atomic Habits.* Avery. (On how small changes in style/posture lead to massive shifts in identity).

- **Maltz, M. (1960).** *Psycho-Cybernetics.* (A classic text on self-image and how our internal view of ourselves dictates our external results).

Online Resources:

- https://www.psychologytoday.com/us/blog/the-power-self-sacrifice/202110/the-neuroscience-authenticity https://www.nature.com/articles/s41598-020-79934-x

- https://www.apa.org/news/press/releases/2010/08/power-poses

- https://www.scientificamerican.com/article/the-neurobiology-of-self-confidence/
- https://hbr.org/2012/06/the-new-science-of-building-great-teams
- https://fs.blog/mental-models/

Chapter 8

Books:

- **Clear, J. (2018).** *Atomic Habits: An Easy & Proven Way to Build Good Habits & Break Bad Ones.* Avery.
- **Ericsson, A., & Pool, R. (2016).** *Peak: Secrets from the New Science of Expertise.* Houghton Mifflin Harcourt.
- **Branden, N. (1995).** *The Six Pillars of Self-Esteem.* Bantam.
- **Holiday, R. (2014).** *The Obstacle Is the Way.* Portfolio.
- **Syed, M. (2015).** *Black Box Thinking: Why Most People Never Learn from Their Mistakes.* Portfolio.

Online Resources:

- https://www.sciencedirect.com/topics/psychology/generation-effect
- https://www.simplypsychology.org/cognitive-dissonance.html
- https://hbr.org/2005/07/learning-in-the-thick-of-it
- https://www.nngroup.com/articles/peak-end-rule/
- https://jamesclear.com/deliberate-practice-theory

Book 2

Chapter 1

Books:

- **Goleman, D. (1995).** *Emotional Intelligence: Why It Can Matter More Than IQ.* Bantam Books.
- **Fisher, H. (2004).** *Why We Love: The Nature and Chemistry of Romantic Love.* Henry Holt and Co.
- **Voss, C. (2016).** *Never Split the Difference.* HarperBusiness.
- **Deida, D. (1997).** *The Way of the Superior Man.* Plexus.
- **Sinek, S. (2009).** *Start with Why.* Portfolio.

Online Resources:

- https://www.health.harvard.edu/blog/love-and-the-brain-201511198647
- https://www.psychologytoday.com/us/blog/thoughts-thinking/201708/the-battle-between-thoughts-and-emotions
- https://www.sciencedirect.com/topics/psychology/proxemics
- https://www.ncbi.nlm.nih.gov/pmc/articles/PMC4013311/
- https://www.forbes.com/sites/forbescoachescouncil/2018/02/14/the-power-of-presence-how-to-command-the-room/

Chapter 2

Books:

- **Navarro, J. (2008).** *What Every Body is Saying: An FBI Agent's Guide to Speed-Reading People.* HarperCollins.
- **Lowndes, L. (2003).** *How to Talk to Anyone: 92 Little Tricks for Big Success in Relationships.* McGraw-Hill.
- **Double, S. (2014).** *The Elements of Wit: Mastering the Art of Being Interesting.* Perigee.
- **Cialdini, R. B. (2006).** *Influence: The Psychology of Persuasion.* Harper Business.
- **Alberts, J. K. (1992).** *An Analysis of Couplets and Cohesion in Flirting.* Journal of Social and Personal Relationships.

Online Resources:

- https://www.psychologytoday.com/us/blog/look-it-way/200906/cold-reading-the-secret-the-psychics
- https://www.ncbi.nlm.nih.gov/pmc/articles/PMC4649788/
- https://www.socialanxietyinstitute.org/social-anxiety-and-the-fear-of-entrapment
- https://www.scientificamerican.com/article/the-mirror-neuron-revolution-explaining-what-makes-us-human/
- https://www.apa.org/news/press/releases/2018/06/first-impressions
- https://www.nature.com/articles/nrn3700

Chapter 3

Books:

- **Voss, C. (2016).** *Never Split the Difference: Negotiating As If Your Life Depended On It.* HarperBusiness.
- **Porges, S. W. (2011).** *The Polyvagal Theory: Neurophysiological Foundations of Emotions, Attachment, Communication, and Self-regulation.* W. W. Norton & Company.
- **Nichols, M. P. (2009).** *The Lost Art of Listening: How Learning to Listen Can Improve Relationships.* Guilford Press.
- **Coyle, D. (2018).** *The Culture Code: The Secrets of Highly Successful Groups.* Bantam.
- **Goleman, D. (1995).** *Emotional Intelligence: Why It Can Matter More Than IQ.* Bantam Books.

Online Sources:

- https://www.pnas.org/doi/10.1073/pnas.1202129109
- https://www.health.harvard.edu/mind-and-mood/oxytocin-the-love-hormone
- https://www.psychologytoday.com/us/blog/smashing-the-glass-ceiling/202108/the-power-silence-in-conversations
- https://www.simplypsychology.org/active-listening.html
- https://www.scientificamerican.com/article/the-mirror-neuron-revolution-explaining-what-makes-us-human/
- https://hbr.org/2017/01/the-neuroscience-of-trust

Chapter 4

Books:

- **Gottschall, J. (2012).** *The Storytelling Animal: How Stories Make Us Human.* Houghton Mifflin Harcourt. .
- **Cron, L. (2012).** *Wired for Story: The Writer's Guide to Using Brain Science to Hook Readers from the Very First Sentence.* Ten Speed Press.
- **McKee, R. (1997).** *Story: Substance, Structure, Style and the Principles of Screenwriting.* ReganBooks.

- **Storr, W. (2020).** *The Science of Storytelling: Why Stories Make Us Human and How to Tell Them Better.* Abrams Press.
- **Brown, B. (2015).** *Rising Strong: How the Ability to Reset Transforms the Way We Live, Love, Parent, and Lead.* Random House.

Online Sources:

- https://hbr.org/2014/10/the-strategic-storyteller
- https://www.scientificamerican.com/article/the-science-of-storytelling/
- https://www.psychologytoday.com/us/blog/the-story-your-life/201704/the-heros-journey-in-real-life
- https://themoth.org/share-your-story/storytelling-tips
- https://greatergood.berkeley.edu/article/item/how_stories_change_the_brain

Chapter 5

Books:

- **Linklater, K. (2006).** *Freeing the Natural Voice: Imagery and Art in the Practice of Voice and Language.* Drama Publishers.
- **Rodenburg, P. (1992).** *The Right to Speak: Working with the Voice.* Methuen Drama.
- **Love, R. (1999).** *Roger Love's Vocal Power: Harness Your Inner Voice to Conquer Every Audience.* Little, Brown and Company.
- **Cuddy, A. (2015).** *Presence: Bringing Your Boldest Self to Your Biggest Challenges.* Little, Brown and Company.
- **Navarro, J. (2018).** *The Dictionary of Body Language: A Field Guide to Human Behavior.* HarperCollins.

Online Sources:

- https://www.physicsclassroom.com/class/sound/Lesson-2/Pitch-and-Frequency
- https://www.nature.com/articles/srep20370
- https://www.ncbi.nlm.nih.gov/pmc/articles/PMC3350186/
- https://my.clevelandclinic.org/health/articles/9445-diaphragmatic-breathing

- https://www.sciencedirect.com/topics/psychology/prosody
- https://journals.plos.org/plosone/article?id=10.1371/journal.pone.0097506
- https://www.psychologytoday.com/us/blog/the-human-beast/201711/why-low-voices-are-sexy

Chapter 6

Books:

- **Skinner, B. F. (1953).** *Science and Human Behavior.* Macmillan.
- **Greene, R. (2001).** *The Art of Seduction.* Viking.
- **Deida, D. (1997).** *The Way of the Superior Man.* Plexus.
- **Cialdini, R. B. (2006).** *Influence: The Psychology of Persuasion.* Harper Business.
- **Gottman, J. M. (1999).** *The Seven Principles for Making Marriage Work.* Crown.

Online Sources:

- https://www.nature.com/articles/nrn1366
- https://www.psychologytoday.com/us/blog/the-human-beast/201611/the-power-intermittent-reinforcement
- https://scopeblog.stanford.edu/2011/02/10/robert-sapolsky-on-the-science-of-pleasure/
- https://www.tonyrobbins.com/wealth-lifestyle/polarity-in-relationships/
- https://www.sciencedirect.com/topics/psychology/dominance-hierarchies

Chapter 7

Books:

- **Kahneman, D. (2011).** *Thinking, Fast and Slow.* Farrar, Straus and Giroux.
- **Cialdini, R. B. (2006).** *Influence: The Psychology of Persuasion.* Harper Business. **Voss, C. (2016).** *Never Split the Difference.* HarperBusiness.
- **Halpern, J. (2001).** *From Detachment to Empathy: A Clinical Approach.* Oxford University Press.

- **Baumeister, R. F., & Bushman, B. J. (2010).** *Social Psychology and Human Nature.* Cengage Learning.

Online Sources:

- https://www.nngroup.com/articles/peak-end-rule/
- https://www.psychologytoday.com/us/blog/healthier-say/202111/the-zeigarnik-effect-the-power-unfinished-business
- https://www.scienceofpeople.com/how-to-be-more-selective/
- https://www.healthline.com/health/mental-health/the-psychology-of-texting
- https://www.attachmentproject.com/blog/first-date-anxiety/

Book 3

Chapter 1

Books:

- **Darwin, C. (1872).** *The Expression of the Emotions in Man and Animals.*
- **Pease, A., & Pease, B. (2004).** *The Definitive Book of Body Language.* Bantam.
- **Navarro, J. (2008).** *What Every BODY is Saying: An Ex-FBI Agent's Guide to Speed-Reading People.* HarperCollins.
- **Buss, D. M. (2019).** *Evolutionary Psychology: The New Science of the Mind.* Routledge.
- **Ekman, P. (2003).** *Emotions Revealed: Recognizing Faces and Feelings to Improve Communication and Emotional Life.* Henry Holt and Co.

Online Sources:

- https://www.apa.org/monitor/2014/03/body-language
- https://www.sciencedirect.com/topics/neuroscience/limbic-system
- https://www.nature.com/articles/nrdp20172
- https://www.psychologicalscience.org/news/releases/pupillary-responses-reflect-the-attractiveness-of-faces.html

- https://www.paulekman.com/resources/micro-expressions/

Chapter 2

Books:

- **Ekman, P. (2003).** *Emotions Revealed: Recognizing Faces and Feelings to Improve Communication and Emotional Life.* Henry Holt and Co.
- **Navarro, J. (2008).** *What Every BODY is Saying.*
- **Hess, E. H. (1975).** *The Tell-Tale Eye: How Your Eyes Reveal Your Secret Thoughts and Emotions.* Van Nostrand Reinhold.
- **Givens, D. B. (2005).** *Love Signals: A Practical Field Guide to the Body Language of Courtship.* St. Martin's Press.

Online Sources:

- https://www.paulekman.com/
- https://www.scientificamerican.com/article/eye-opener-the-secrets-of-the-pupil/
- https://www.psychologicalscience.org/observer/the-science-of-smiles

Chapter 3

Books:

- **Hall, E. T. (1966).** *The Hidden Dimension.* Doubleday.
- **Montagu, A. (1971).** *Touching: The Human Significance of the Skin.* Columbia University Press.
- **Navarro, J. (2008).** *What Every BODY is Saying.*
- **Morris, D. (1971).** *Intimate Behaviour.* Jonathan Cape.

Online Sources:

- https://www.ncbi.nlm.nih.gov/pmc/articles/PMC4045501/
- https://www.psychologytoday.com/us/blog/the-power-touch
- https://www.scienceofpeople.com/body-language-feet/
- https://www.nature.com/articles/s41598-020-71513-z

Chapter 4

Books:

- **Tannen, D. (1990).** *You Just Don't Understand: Women and Men in Conversation.* (Classic text on gender communication).
- **Pennebaker, J. W. (2011).** *The Secret Life of Pronouns.*
- **Cialdini, R. (1984).** *Influence.*
- **Givens, D. (2005).** *Love Signals.*

Online Sources:

- https://royalsocietypublishing.org/doi/10.1098/rsbl.2013.0929
- https://www.princeton.edu/news/2010/07/26/speaker-and-listener-brains-sync-during-communication
- https://www.nature.com/articles/s41598-017-04111-2

Chapter 5

Books:

- **Goleman, D. (2006).** *Social Intelligence: The New Science of Human Relationships.*
- **Greene, R. (2018).** *The Laws of Human Nature.*
- **Navarro, J. (2008).** *What Every BODY is Saying.*
- **Miller, G. (2000).** *The Mating Mind.*

Online Sources:

- https://www.healthline.com/health/duchenne-smile
- https://www.psychologytoday.com/us/blog/the-mating-game/201306/the-truth-about-the-friend-zone
- https://web.stanford.edu/~jurafsky/pubs/speeddating.pdf

Chapter 6

Books:

- **Navarro, J. (2008).** *What Every BODY is Saying: An Ex-FBI Agent's Guide to Speed-Reading People.* William Morrow.
- **Pease, A., & Pease, B. (2004).** *The Definitive Book of Body Language.* Bantam.
- **Glass, L. (2002).** *The Body Language of Liars.* Career Press.

- **Ekman, P. (2003).** *Emotions Revealed: Recognizing Faces and Feelings to Improve Communication and Emotional Life.* Times Books.
- **Givens, D. (2005).** *Love Signals: A Practical Field Guide to the Body Language of Courtship.* St. Martin's Press.

Online Sources:

- https://www.psychologytoday.com/us/blog/the-power-of-connection/201712/the-impact-of-phubbing-on-relationships
- https://www.scienceofpeople.com/body-language-feet/
- https://www.health.harvard.edu/staying-healthy/understanding-the-stress-response
- https://www.jnforensics.com/post/the-belly-has-it
- https://link.springer.com/referenceworkentry/10.1007/978-3-319-16999-6_3441-1

Chapter 7

Books:

- **Boyd, J. (1986).** *A Discourse on Winning and Losing.*
- **Gladwell, M. (2005).** *Blink: The Power of Thinking Without Thinking.* Little, Brown.
- **Greene, R. (2001).** *The Art of Seduction.* Viking.
- **Cialdini, R. (2016).** *Pre-Suasion: A Revolutionary Way to Influence and Persuade.* Simon & Schuster.

Online Sources:

- https://hbr.org/2013/09/decision-making-lessons-from-the-cockpit
- https://www.nature.com/articles/nrn3248
- https://www.psychologytoday.com/us/blog/the-brain-and-emotional-intelligence/201112/overcoming-analysis-paralysis
- https://www.frontiersin.org/articles/10.3389/fnhum.2018.00191/full

Chapter 8

Books:

- **Navarro, J. (2008).** *What Every BODY is Saying: An Ex-FBI Agent's Guide to Speed-Reading People.* William Morrow.
- **Ekman, P. (2003).** *Emotions Revealed: Recognizing Faces and Feelings to Improve Communication and Emotional Life.* Times Books.
- **Goleman, D. (2006).** *Social Intelligence: The New Science of Human Relationships.* Bantam.
- **Greene, R. (2018).** *The Laws of Human Nature.* Viking.
- **Boyd, J. (1986).** *A Discourse on Winning and Losing.* Air University Press.
- **Gladwell, M. (2005).** *Blink: The Power of Thinking Without Thinking.* Little, Brown.
- **Pease, A., & Pease, B. (2004).** *The Definitive Book of Body Language.* Bantam.

Online Sources:

- https://www.psychologytoday.com/us/basics/confirmation-bias
- https://www.healthline.com/health/emotional-contagion
- https://www.psychologytoday.com/us/blog/the-brain-and-emotional-intelligence/201112/overcoming-analysis-paralysis
- https://www.jnforensics.com/post/the-belly-has-it
- https://hbr.org/2013/09/decision-making-lessons-from-the-cockpit

Book 4

Chapter 1

- **Books:**
- **Cialdini, R. (1984).** *Influence: The Psychology of Persuasion.*
- **Sapolsky, R. (2017).** *Behave: The Biology of Humans at Our Best and Worst.*
- **Fisher, H. (2004).** *Why We Love: The Nature and Chemistry of Romantic Love.* **Buss, D. (1994).** *The Evolution of Desire.*

Online Sources:

- https://www.psychologytoday.com/us/blog/brain-wise/201311/the-science-the-chase
- https://hbswk.hbs.edu/item/the-ikea-effect-when-labor-leads-to-love
- https://www.nature.com/articles/nrn3239
- https://royalsocietypublishing.org/doi/10.1098/rstb.2016.0245

Chapter 2

Books:

- **Csikszentmihalyi, M. (1990).** *Flow: The Psychology of Optimal Experience.*
- **Deida, D. (1997).** *The Way of the Superior Man.*
- **Maslow, A. (1943).** *A Theory of Human Motivation.*
- **Newport, C. (2016).** *Deep Work: Rules for Focused Success in a Distracted World.*
- **Robertson, I. (2012).** *The Winner Effect: The Neuroscience of Success and Failure.*

Online Sources:

- https://www.nature.com/articles/nn.2508
- https://www.psychologytoday.com/us/blog/head-games/201309/how-relationships-expand-the-self
- https://psycnet.apa.org/record/2010-09043-001
- https://www.verywellmind.com/what-is-the-halo-effect-2795906

Chapter 3

Books:

- **Cloud, H., & Townsend, J. (1992).** *Boundaries: When to Say Yes, How to Say No to Take Control of Your Life.* Zondervan.
- **Glover, R. (2003).** *No More Mr. Nice Guy.*
- **Millman, D. (1980).** *Way of the Peaceful Warrior.*
- **Patterson, K., et al. (2002).** *Crucial Conversations: Tools for Talking When Stakes Are High.* McGraw-Hill.

Online Sources:

- https://www.gottman.com/blog/the-importance-of-respect-in-relationships/
- https://www.psychologytoday.com/us/blog/the-attraction-doctor/201602/why-women-test-men-and-how-pass
- https://www.mayoclinic.org/healthy-lifestyle/stress-management/in-depth/assertiveness/art-20044644
- https://academic.oup.com/jcr/article/39/6/1230/1792671

Chapter 4

Books:

- **Cialdini, R. (1984).** *Influence: The Psychology of Persuasion.*
- **Newport, C. (2016).** *Deep Work: Rules for Focused Success in a Distracted World.*
- **Ferriss, T. (2007).** *The 4-Hour Workweek.*
- **McKeown, G. (2014).** *Essentialism: The Disciplined Pursuit of Less.*

Online Sources:

- https://www.psychologytoday.com/us/blog/magnetic-attraction/201111/the-zeigarnik-effect-and-romantic-attraction
- https://greatergood.berkeley.edu/article/item/how_to_break_your_addiction_to_digital_notifications
- https://hbr.org/2016/12/the-new-status-symbol-is-being-overworked
- https://www.aeaweb.org/articles?id=10.1257/jep.27.3.115

Chapter 5

Books:

- **Brown, B. (2012).** *Daring Greatly: How the Courage to Be Vulnerable Transforms the Way We Live, Love, Parent, and Lead.*
- **Jung, C.G. (1959).** *Aion: Researches into the Phenomenology of the Self.*
- **Bly, R. (1990).** *Iron John: A Book About Men.*
- **Real, T. (1997).** *I Don't Want to Talk About It: Overcoming the Secret Legacy of Male Depression.*

Online Sources:

- https://changingminds.org/explanations/theories/pratfall_effect.htm
- https://www.theschooloflife.com/article/the-importance-of-vulnerability/
- https://greatergood.berkeley.edu/article/item/how_to_build_closeness_through_disclosure
- https://www.sciencedirect.com/journal/journal-of-experimental-social-psychology

Chapter 6

Books:

- **Greene, R. (2001).** *The Art of Seduction.*
- **Perel, E. (2006).** *Mating in Captivity: Unlocking Erotic Intelligence.*
- **Cialdini, R. (1984).** *Influence: The Psychology of Persuasion.*
- **Skinner, B.F. (1938).** *The Behavior of Organisms.*
- **Online Sources:**
- https://www.psychologytoday.com/us/blog/magnetic-attraction/201111/the-zeigarnik-effect
- https://www.jsm.jsexmed.org/
- https://www.nature.com/nrn/

Chapter 7

Books:

- **Deida, D. (1997).** *The Way of the Superior Man.*
- **Manson, M. (2011).** *Models: Attract Women Through Honesty.*
- **Branden, N. (1994).** *The Six Pillars of Self-Esteem.*
- **Aurelius, M. (180 AD).** *Meditations.*
- **Fisher, R., & Ury, W. (1981).** *Getting to Yes: Negotiating Agreement Without Giving In.*

Online Sources:

- https://human.libretexts.org/Social_Exchange_Theory
- https://scholar.harvard.edu/sendhil/scarcity
- https://www.psychologytoday.com/us/basics/locus-control

- https://www.apa.org/science/about/psa/2009/04/sci-brief

Chapter 8

Books:

- **Clear, J. (2018).** *Atomic Habits: An Easy & Proven Way to Build Good Habits & Break Bad Ones.*
- **Moore, R., & Gillette, D. (1990).** *King, Warrior, Magician, Lover: Rediscovering the Archetypes of the Mature Masculine.*
- **Frankl, V. E. (1946).** *Man's Search for Meaning.*
- **Dweck, C. S. (2006).** *Mindset: The New Psychology of Success.*
- **Zweig, C., & Abrams, J. (1991).** *Meeting the Shadow: The Hidden Power of the Dark Side of Human Nature.*

Online Sources:

- https://hbr.org/2017/03/why-you-should-make-time-for-self-reflection-even-if-youre-too-busy
- https://www.psychologytools.com/self-help/cognitive-behavioral-therapy-cbt/
- https://www.ncbi.nlm.nih.gov/pmc/articles/PMC5854216/
- https://www.verywellmind.com/zeigarnik-effect-2795903

Book 5

Chapter 1

Books:

- **Fisher, H. (2004).** *Why We Love: The Nature and Chemistry of Romantic Love.*
- **Lieberman, D. Z., & Long, M. E. (2018).** *The Molecule of More: How a Single Chemical in Your Brain Drives Love, Sex, and Creativity—and Will Determine the Fate of the Human Race.*
- **Gottman, J. M., & Silver, N. (1999).** *The Seven Principles for Making Marriage Work.*
- **Perel, E. (2006).** *Mating in Captivity: Unlocking Erotic Intelligence.*
- **Deida, D. (1997).** *The Way of the Superior Man.*

Online Sources:

- https://www.nature.com/articles/nrn1298

- http://www.robertjsternberg.com/love
- https://www.sciencedirect.com/topics/psychology/coolidge-effect
- https://greatergood.berkeley.edu/article/item/can_you_celebrate_the_good_times

Chapter 2

Books:

- **Rusbult, C. E. (1980).** *Investment Model of Commitment.*
- **Gahran, A. (2017).** *Stepping Off the Relationship Escalator: Uncommon Love and Life.*
- **Levine, A., & Heller, R. (2010).** *Attached: The New Science of Adult Attachment and How It Can Help You Find—and Keep—Love.*
- **Voss, C. (2016).** *Never Split the Difference: Negotiating As If Your Life Depended On It.*
- **Glover, R. (2003).** *No More Mr. Nice Guy.*

Online Sources:

- https://psychology.iresearchnet.com/social-psychology/social-relationships/investment-model-of-commitment/
- https://www.psychologytoday.com/us/blog/the-state-our-unions/202208/the-rise-the-situationship
- https://www.britannica.com/topic/social-exchange-theory
- https://journals.sagepub.com/home/spr

Chapter 3

Books:

- **Cloud, H., & Townsend, J. (1992).** *Boundaries: When to Say Yes, How to Say No to Take Control of Your Life.*
- **Keller, T. (2011).** *The Meaning of Marriage: Facing the Complexities of Commitment with the Wisdom of God.*
- **Kiyosaki, R. (1997).** *Rich Dad Poor Dad.*
- **Gottman, J. M. (2011).** *The Science of Trust: Emotional Attunement for Couples.*
- **Peterson, J. B. (2018).** *12 Rules for Life: An Antidote to Chaos.*

Online Sources:

- https://www.sciencedirect.com/journal/journal-of-research-in-personality
- https://www.nefe.org/research/polls/2021/financial-infidelity-poll.aspx
- https://www.pewresearch.org/social-trends/2014/06/12/inter-party-marriage/
- https://positivepsychology.com/values-clarification/

Chapter 4

Books:

- **Willink, J., & Babin, L. (2015).** *Extreme Ownership: How U.S. Navy SEALs Lead and Win.*
- **Clear, J. (2018).** *Atomic Habits: An Easy & Proven Way to Build Good Habits & Break Bad Ones.*
- **Deida, D. (1997).** *The Way of the Superior Man.*
- **Sinek, S. (2009).** *Start with Why: How Great Leaders Inspire Everyone to Take Action.*
- **Gottman, J. M. (2011).** *The Science of Trust: Emotional Attunement for Couples.*

Online Sources:

- https://selfdeterminationtheory.org/theory/
- https://www.psychologytoday.com/us/blog/the-brain-and-emotional-intelligence/201306/the-habituated-mind
- https://www.health.harvard.edu/blog/emotional-agility-4-steps-to-becoming-your-best-self-2016110310574
- https://www.apa.org/pubs/journals/fam

Chapter 5

Books:

- **Gottman, J. M., & Silver, N. (1999).** *The Seven Principles for Making Marriage Work.*
- **Voss, C. (2016).** *Never Split the Difference: Negotiating As If Your Life Depended On It.*
- **Deida, D. (1997).** *The Way of the Superior Man.*

- **Tatkin, S. (2011).** *Wired for Love: How Understanding Your Partner's Brain and Attachment Style Can Help You Defuse Conflict.*
- **Patterson, K., et al. (2002).** *Crucial Conversations: Tools for Talking When Stakes Are High.*

Online Sources:

- https://www.gottman.com/blog/making-sure-emotional-flooding-doesnt-capsize-your-relationship/
- https://www.health.harvard.edu/concept-of-amygdala-hijack
- https://www.couplesinstitute.com/the-pursuer-distancer-dynamic/

Chapter 6

Books:

- **Perel, E. (2006).** *Mating in Captivity: Unlocking Erotic Intelligence.*
- **Fisher, H. (2004).** *Why We Love: The Nature and Chemistry of Romantic Love.*
- **Gottman, J. M., & Silver, N. (2012).** *What Makes Love Last? How to Build Trust and Avoid Betrayal.*
- **Nagoski, E. (2015).** *Come as You Are: The Surprising New Science that Will Transform Your Sex Life.*
- **Carder, D. (2008).** *Close Calls: Managing Risk and Resilience in Marriage.*

Online Sources:

- https://www.nature.com/nrn/
- https://psycnet.apa.org/record/1986-28562-001
- https://academic.oup.com/jcr
- https://www.ted.com/talks/esther_perel_the_secret_to_desire_in_a_long_term_relationship

Chapter 7

Books:

- **Daniell, M. H., & Hamilton, S. (2010).** *Family Legacy and Leadership: Preserving True Family Wealth in Challenging Times.*
- **Gottman, J. M., & Silver, N. (1999).** *The Seven Principles for Making Marriage Work.*

- **Covey, S. R. (1989).** *The 7 Habits of Highly Effective People.*
- **Ward, J. L. (2004).** *Perpetuating the Family Business: 50 Lessons from Long-Lasting Family Enterprise Families.*
- **Perel, E. (2017).** *The State of Affairs: Rethinking Infidelity.*

Online Sources:

- https://greatergood.berkeley.edu/article/item/the_benefits_of_building_a_shared_reality_with_your_partner
- https://www.apa.org/news/press/releases/2025/10/sharing-positive-emotions-partner
- https://www.cleardocs.com/clearlaw/estate-planning/importance-of-family-constitutions.html
- https://www.unwomen.org/en/what-we-do/economic-empowerment/facts-and-figures

Chapter 8

Books:

- **Stanier, M. B. (2016).** *The Coaching Habit: Say Less, Ask More & Change the Way You Lead Forever.*
- **Peterson, J. B. (2018).** *12 Rules for Life: An Antidote to Chaos.*
- **Glover, R. (2003).** *No More Mr. Nice Guy.*
- **Dalio, R. (2017).** *Principles: Life and Work.*
- **Whitmore, J. (1992).** *Coaching for Performance.*

Online Sources:

- https://positivepsychology.com/socratic-questioning/
- https://hbr.org/2017/03/why-self-reflection-is-the-key-to-effective-leadership
- https://www.thebowencenter.org/theory/eight-concepts/multigenerational-transmission-process
- https://www.hubermanlab.com/episode/the-science-of-making-and-breaking-habits